Library of
Davidson College

OSCAR SHAFTEL

An Understanding of the Buddha

SCHOCKEN BOOKS / NEW YORK

Copyright © 1974 by Schocken Books Inc.
Library of Congress Catalog Card No. 72-80041
Manufactured in the United States of America

Permission to make extensive quotations from the following sources is gratefully acknowledged:

From *Buddhist Texts Through the Ages*, edited by Edward Conze, I. B. Horner, D. L. Snellgrove, and Arthur Waley. Bruno Cassirer (Publishers) Ltd., Oxford, England, and Harper & Row, Publishers, Inc., New York.

From Edward Conze, *Thirty Years of Buddhist Studies*, © 1968 by Edward Conze. Reprinted by permission of the University of South Carolina Press and Bruno Cassirer (Publishers) Ltd.

From *Mysticism and Philosophy*, by W. T. Stace. Copyright © 1960 by W. T. Stace. Reprinted by permission of J. B. Lippincott Company.

From *The Central Philosophy of Buddhism*, by T. R. V. Murti. Reprinted by permission of George Allen & Unwin Ltd.

From *The Culture & Civilisation of Ancient India*, by D. D. Kosambi. Reprinted by permission of Routledge & Kegan Paul Ltd. and Pantheon Books, a Division of Random House.

From *The Practice of Zen*, by Garma C. C. Chang. Reprinted by permission of Harper & Row, Publishers, and Rider & Co., London.

From *The Three Jewels*, by Sangharakshita. Reprinted by permission of Rider & Co., London, and Doubleday & Co., Inc.

From *The Tantric Tradition*, by Agehananda Bharati. Reprinted by permission of Rider & Co., London, and Doubleday & Co., Inc.

From *The Vimalakirti Nirdesa Sutra*, translated by Lu K'uan Yu (Charles Luk). Shambhala Publications, Berkeley and London, 1972. Used by permission of the publisher.

From *The Tantric View of Life*, by Herbert V. Guenther. Shambhala Publications, Berkeley and London, 1972. Used by permission of the publisher.

From *Buddhist Philosophy in Theory and Practice*, by Herbert V. Guenther. Penguin Books, Baltimore and London, 1973. Used by permission of the copyright holder, Shambhala Publications, Berkeley and London.

From *Treasures on the Tibetan Middle Way*, by Herbert V. Guenther. Shambhala Publications, Berkeley, 1969, and E. J. Brill, Leiden, Holland. Used by permission of the publisher.

From *Meditation in Action*, by Chögyam Trungpa. Shambhala Publications, Berkeley, 1969. Used by permission of the publisher.

Contents

PREFACE	V
1. The Legend and the Life	1
2. What Can We Know About What the Buddha Really Said?	8
3. What Buddhists Have Believed	21
4. Background: Orthodoxy, Heterodoxy, and Buddhism	47
5. Lamps Unto Themselves	72
6. The Paradoxes of Mahayana	89
7. Tantra and Zen: The Restorers	109
8. What Is Nirvana?	140
9. Toward the Unified World	182
NOTES	199
BIBLIOGRAPHY	236
INDEX	245

To M. B. S.
of the good name

Preface

To many serious western investigators, the Buddha's injunction to conquer worldly attachment seems at first a chilling asceticism, a desensitizing of human response. On closer study of his terms and their contexts, one can follow his intention to a relaxation of urgency in habits and opinions; an increase in sensitivity through reduction of clinging to fixed ways of belief and action. One becomes more alert to how things may be apart from our notions of them, and how quickly they change. The key process is depersonalization, a reversal of the West's obsessive self-assertion. This detached look at the (nonexistent) Ego scorns the external trappings of conceit: status and its symbols, possessiveness, compulsive habits, allegiance to one's dogmas, concern for fashions in ideas and dress, outworn loyalties. In practice, recognition of mutability of both perceiver and perceived allows a salutary adaptation even to disaster—which may be no more than a timely change in a way of life no longer viable. Awareness of ego-clinging helps one distinguish between physical need for subsistence and ego-desire for appropriation. It also prepares the mind for a Buddhist economics which charts parsimonious production for use and distribution according to need, rather than production for plethoric profit, self-assertion, and human decay.

Ashoka said the dharma awakened his conscience to the cruelty of his youthful military exploits. Whether Buddhism actually tempered state military policies when it came to China, Japan, and Tibet is questionable. The voice of the Buddha is heard truly only from man to man. Buddhism has accepted traditional relationships—rich and poor, rulers and ruled—and it hopes for a slow civilizing of all men as the dharma inspires individuals to strive through many incarnations for human perfection as arhants, or for divine perfection as bodhisattvas exuding disinterested love; or, here and now, to seek the guidance of roshis to new awareness. But a commitment to slow change may expose men to sudden, brutal repression on a mass scale, the scale and tempo of the modern junta coup; and self-immolation in Saigon and on the steps of Congress has no impact on the oppressors and short effect on fellow citizens. Projecting aeons for the remaking of human nature is not very different from asserting the useful slogan of privilege, "You can't change human nature" (thus countenancing both individual greed and institutionalized exploitation).

Because the time scale of political change is so short and its path so twisty, and because in politics we become like our enemies, Buddhists rarely seek political leadership. Although they are not apt to lead a society in rapid flux, they are trained to suspect their own dogmas, so their teaching on the vanity of attachment to any one way of life may help some ride with change into new ways. In our anxious time, so like the Buddha's, Buddhist skill-in-means wed to prajna-wisdom is guiding many to humane resistance to dehumanizing forces. Along with other doctrines of righteousness and brotherhood it may help set limits to devious political leadership; compassion and modesty may arouse instinctive dismay at the cynical gamesmanship of Watergate.

Seeking after strange gods and demons is one sign of a dying culture. A victimized populace losing faith in its way of life turns violently upon itself and seeks quick answers from saints and fuehrers. Swamis and gurus coming west for fatter flocks are nothing new, but now their audiences are not only abdicants from established beliefs without mystery but also young people turning away from the corrupt material establishment and its rationalist base.

Buddhism attracts few of these, and not for long. It offers no certainty, no quick trip to bliss; its enlightenment has no prescription or label and requires of its western students drastic intellectual and psychic refashioning no longer expected in the doctrines they have turned from. But there is much we can use in the messages Sakyamuni taught 2500 years ago, and in the several forms they have taken across the centuries to meet the needs of many societies. Some people find refuge in the discipline practiced in one of the Buddhist countries today; others accept a dynamic challenge to adapt the perceptions of the Buddha in a new synthesis with the discoveries of our own time.

This book looks at Buddhism as an ever-developing doctrine and practice. The author confesses benign infection over years of study and teaching, the symptoms being a quizzical view of his ego, a degree of depersonalization; an alertness to spontaneous sensation, to the aesthetic moment; a more relaxed acceptance of vicissitude, the down and up of career; a partial emancipation from the demands of status (teaching his children that "the bigger one gives in"); a recognition of the spiritual and physiological benefits of meditation. On the other hand, such dogmas as reincarnation and absolute ahimsa have been reduced to occasionally useful figures of speech.

The initial objective of this study, to investigate who the Buddha was and what he said, was soon seen to be vain: the legend is more important than the life, and the mechanics of transmitting the word make it conjectural. But the main outlines of his teaching are clear, and a valid objective emerged: to study how the accepted doctrines took on different meanings and led to different practices. We compare the roads to liberation of Theravada and Mahayana, derived from the Buddha's own practices of modifying contemporary beliefs. We see the strait path of the arhant refracted by the strange and jeweled splendors of the bodhisattva; ultimate nirvana reduced to a way station on the way to Buddhahood or to satori, or epistemologized into identity with samsara; we solidify the Void into the intense immediacy of Zen and the complex aesthetic energies of Tantra.

A central theme is that ultimate ground of most eastern and primitive religion, the mystical experience. The unitive trance is seen as the authentication of intuitive cognition, of liberation from time and space, and defined as union with godhead, identity with Brahman, self-knowledge, or yogic bliss—depending on the experient's cultural background. The zero-experience, along with meditation, is analyzed in the context of recent laboratory research on altered states of consciousness, applying brain-wave and biofeedback techniques, and the new thriving discipline of psychic research. A final chapter attempts a synthesis of ancient and modern strivings toward social and psychic unity. It hypothesizes success of the Chinese economic and social experiment as a step toward fuller utilization of man's many-sided capacity for psychic communication. Unless some convincing demonstration of this capacity comes within the next generation, we shall have to wait, alas, until the Buddhahood of Manjusri and Avalokitesvara.

Certain technical decisions have been imposed by inflation. Vowel lengths in Sanskrit and Pali words are ignored, and indicators of consonant pronunciation, such as the two *sh* sounds, the nasal dot, visarga, and the semi-vocalization of *l* and *r,* are omitted. Inconsistencies force their way in: Sakyamuni and Avalokitesvara alongside Ashoka and Ashvaghosha. The author increases his debt to Thomas, Conze, and

Robinson by suggesting reference to their books for orthography. A Gordian knot was cut by the decision not to italicize the names of canonical works—another source of inconsistency. Book titles and page references are included in the text or appended to quotations; notes at the end of the book are limited to substantive content, such as additional citations, and commentary. Sanskrit forms are preferred, but Pali (sutta, dhamma, nibbana) is used in context.

The author acknowledges gratefully the help of those who provided information, havens for work, and corrections of error. Among the last are his editors at Schocken Books, John Thornton and Diana Levine, who fought doughtily for correctness and clarity against heavy odds; K. R. Norman of the Faculty of Oriental Studies at Cambridge University, who asked some significant questions at an early stage; and David Rome, *cari patris filius doctior.* For ideas he thanks Joseph Needham, Master of Gonville and Caius College, Cambridge, P. Lal and P. N. Shastri of the Writers Workshop, Calcutta, Dr. Robert A. McDermott of Baruch College, and his students at Pratt Institute and Queens College; for hospitality, Dr. Robert Brittain and Greta Burkill of Cambridge, Carl and Sonja Krummel of Geneva, Dr. Aristides Poulianos of Athens, and Dr. Anand Krishna and Kalyan Krishna of Banaras Hindu University. Mildred Gaims Shapiro contributed the index.

New York City
April 1974

ONE

The Legend and the Life

The Legend

Little is known of the life of the Buddha; the legend is the foundation of Buddhist understanding and practice.

Queen Maya, long childless, dreamed during the Midsummer festival that a superb white elephant, bearing in his silver trunk a white lotus flower, came to her, struck her side gently with the flower, and disappeared (into her womb, she thought). The king, Suddhodana Gautama, was overjoyed at the dream, and the queen conceived.[1] When her time came, on her way to her family home she stopped at the Lumbini pleasure grove, all aflower and alive with sweet birds. She reached up and grasped a branch of a saltree, and was delivered through her right side.[2]

The babe's body showed the thirty-two Good Omens, including the spot of fine white hairs between the eyebrows, fine black body hair growing upward on the glowing, golden skin, small prints of wheels on the soles of the feet, and long earlobes.[3] It was prophesied by the brahmin Asita that he would become either a universal monarch, a chakravartin[4] (wheel turner), or, if he "left the house," a great spiritual leader. What might make the king's son forsake the world? The brahmin seer told of the "Four Omens"—a man worn with age, a sick man, a corpse, and a "wanderer," one who has put the world behind him.

As the child grew, the father attempted to shield him. All was ordered, luxurious—as it would have been without the prophecy. The young Siddhartha was the perfect prince: he was good at military exercises and sports and at his father's knee showed acumen at the law and helped judge. Once, however, at the annual rite when the king ceremonially ploughed the fields, the child was left under a tree, and there he experienced his first meditative trance.[5]

As a youth he was surrounded by handsome companions and lovely singing and dancing girls.[6] At nineteen he was given or chose a wife, Yasodhara. A garden of delight was under construction, where no touch of mortality would be seen, but on the carefully swept and decorated road one untoward sight, by intent of the gods, escaped the vigil of the king's officers: "a man wasted by age, with decayed teeth and grey hair, bent and broken down in body," in the words of the Jataka book.[7] The prince's charioteer, Channa, explained that to everyone that is born old age must come. Soon the prince rode out again and saw his first diseased man; and again, and saw his first corpse, and was much agitated.

"Once again, when the future Buddha, as he was going to his pleasure ground, saw one who had abandoned the world, of composed mien and simply clad, he asked his charioteer, 'Friend, what kind of man is that?' 'That is a mendicant, a *sannyasi.*' And thus the four omens were fulfilled, and the future Buddha cherished the thought of renouncing the world."

About this time Yasodhara bore a son. Siddhartha (then aged twenty-nine and pondering his future course) said, "An impediment, a fetter (*rahula*) has come into being."[8] So was the son named, Rahula.

The prince entered his palace and the usual dancing and singing began, the performers being richly dressed women, skilled in the arts of entertainment and love, and as beautiful as celestial nymphs. But he was pensive, and he ignored the entertainers, and then fell asleep. They gave up and slept too. "And the future Buddha awoke and perceived these women lying asleep, with their musical instruments scattered about them on the floor, some with their bodies wet with trickling phlegm and spittle, some grinding their teeth and muttering in their sleep, and some with their dress fallen apart to disclose their loathsome nakedness." Surfeited with sensual pleasures, he saw that magnificent apartment as a charnel house full of corpses, and the three modes of existence—the world of passion, the world of form, and the world without form—seemed like houses all afire.

He resolved to accomplish the Great Renunciation that very day. He called to Channa to saddle the horse Kanthaka. Then he went to look at his son. But Yasodhara's hand was hiding the infant's head, and the man feared that if he woke his wife he would lose his resolution.

They left the city, the gods muffling the hoofs of Kanthaka; after riding some way, the prince stopped, gave his ornaments to Channa, and bade him return with the weeping horse to Suddhodana. Then he proceeded on foot to Rajagriha, having first cut off his long hair, sign of the kshatriya leader, and changed his rich robes for those of a huntsman. He went from house to house begging scraps of food, and could eat the mess only by an act of will.[9] Then he sought out a teacher. In turn he studied under two famous yogins, in the caves of the hills south of the city. From Arada Kalama he learned the various stages of meditation, and from Udraka (or Rudraka) Ramaputra the Samkhya or dualistic interpretation of the Vedas.[10]

But neither his spirit nor his mind found there what he was seeking, a message for all mankind. He moved on to the pleasant grove at Uruvela, where he met five ascetic yogins, and philosophized and practiced traditional brahminical austerities (tapasya). For six years he sought liberation by yoga from human physical limitation and the frustration of time. As a climax he fasted unto the edge of death and fell senseless to the ground. But he awoke and decided, "These austerities are not the way to enlightenment." He took some nourishment and later, when Sujata, a respectful young matron, brought a bowl of rich milk-rice, he accepted it, to the scorn of the five companions, who went off to meditate at Benares. But he conceived the wisdom of the Middle Way between self-deceiving indulgence and self-mortifying austerity. He remembered his spontaneous trance experience as a healthy child, his first intimation of freedom from this-worldly consciousness.

And then, bodhi, Enlightenment. He spread a mat of kusa grass (the sacred grass of the Vedic rites) under a pipal tree (*ficus religiosa*) and applied the full powers of a mature man with trained intellect, a body disciplined in yoga and austerity, and rich human experience. He knew social power, indulgence to surfeit in human pleasures, love of wife and child, and the vanity and evanescence of them all. His mind started with the beginning of his quest, his realization of man's sorrow, and worked back to an ultimate cause, which he found to be Ignorance, man's misconceiving of his own being. Once one pierces through to the basic human ignorance in bondage to desire, one can conceive of liberation, a happiness beyond physical sensation, a state beyond the unending cycle of rebirth into mortal frustration.

But as he sat there, the Jataka tale relates, he was beset by Mara the Tempter, the Adversary.[11] "Siddhartha the prince wants to free himself from my dominion. I will not let him get free yet!" As Siddhartha sat there awaiting Mara's onslaught, alone like Everyman, he thought, "My mother and father are not here, nor any other relatives. But I have these Ten Perfections, like old retainers long cherished at my board."

Mara sent wind, and rain, and rocks, and weapons, and live coals, and hot ashes, and sand, and mud, and darkness—ordinary fearsome things. Then he sent his three daughters, Tanha, Arati, and Raga (Craving, Discontent, and Lust) to distract the yogin, who was well on his way to samadhi. They considered, "Various are men's tastes. Some fall in love with virgins, some with young women, some with mature women, some with older women. We shall tempt him in various forms." But he noticed them not at all, or only with understanding and pity. Then Mara challenged his right to the ground where he sat, and the Great Being stretched his hand toward the earth and called the earth to bear witness to all the sacrifices for fellow men he had performed in previous Buddha-existences.

And Mara was defeated before the sun had set. Before the last watch of the night Gautama's intellect fathomed the twelve steps of Dependent Origination, the key to the understanding of man's condition, especially his misapprehension that he has an abiding individual soul.[12] He entered the first dhyana, and then the other three trances dependent on form, then the four trances not dependent on form, and finally on that night Siddhartha Gautama—Sakyamuni, the sage of the Sakyas—entered the state of the Buddha, the Enlightened One, the Tathagata.

How long he remained in the trance of Enlightenment, of Non-duality, is lost in poetry, but afterward he sat in joy, contemplating the fulfillment of his yearnings and his disciplines. Then he had to face the decision that was so fateful for mankind. Should he, like many another Indian mystic, retire from the world with his revelation, his mastery of Oneness, or should he go back among divided, stumbling men and try to teach them the way? Mara, his remnant of mortality, urged him to accept victory and nirvana. If he went back among men, would he not need to dilute or falsify his message, tempering it to their understanding? Should he gain part of the whole world and lose a small part of his own perfection? As son, as husband, as prince he had learned responsibility and compassion, and at thirty-five he was too young to seek the forest out of weariness with the world of men.

He first thought to give his message to his teachers, Arada and Udraka. But his superknowledges, gained in trance, told him that they were recently dead. Then he thought of his five former companion ascetics. He made his way to Issipatana, near Benares, to their hermitage in the deer park. When they saw him at a distance, they resolved to spurn him still. But he was resplendent in his state of conqueror, and "the sense of his love diffused itself through their hearts." They listened to the words of the first sermon, "which set turning the wheel of Dharma." Kondanya understood even as the Master spoke and was enlightened; on the next day the others "attained to the Fruits of the First Path," and also became arhants (perfected ones). And so the fellowship grew. The great Kasyapa became his disciple, and he preached the fire sermon. King Bimbisara, who had honored him when he first arrived at Rajagriha six years before, now revered him and gave him a monastery. There he converted the great mystics Sariputra and Maudgalyayana, who became his chief disciples.

Suddhodana heard of his son's new life and invited him home. The Master led his followers to Kapilavastu, where he was honored by the Sakyas, who came to meet him, all except his wife, who awaited his visit. He received the boy, Rahula, into the order as his birthright and later his wife, Yasodhara, and stepmother, Pajapati. Here, too, the beloved kinsman Ananda entered the faith.

And so for forty-five years he walked through the Ganges valley and preached to all who would listen, lay and religious, kings and subjects, rich and poor, on the level each could understand. The rainy seasons were spent in viharas, monasteries built for the order by wealthy lay adherents. He organized rules for the monks so that they would help each other put aside their false notions of individual soul entities, the major obstacle to Enlightenment. And when he died at eighty, about 480 B.C., he reminded them in his last words that all composite things (including men) are evanescent and that they should be lamps unto themselves and look out for their own spiritual welfare.

The Life

Most of the legends about the Buddha are untrue or without basis. Details in the Nikayas[13] are meager, perhaps because his followers during his lifetime and shortly after had little interest in the man before the Enlightenment. There is no continuous biography in the Pali canon, and the later "lives" such as the *Mahavastu* and the *Lalitavistara*[14] are fanciful.

The Sakyas, who occupied rice, pasture, and forest land on the southern foothills of the Himalayas, had oligarchic rule, in which the kshatriya, called rajan, elected their leaders. So Sakyamuni's father, who is called Suddhodana[15] in the Mahavagga narrative in the Vinaya, was not a king, nor was his son a pampered prince with three palaces, as the legends tell. According to some of the late and conflicting genealogies, the father is supposed to have married the sisters Maya and Pajapati, his first cousins (close intermarriage among the Sakyas suggests a non-Aryan background).

Maya may actually have died shortly after childbirth (about 560 B.C. is one of several suggested dates), thus providing support for the notion that the mother of a Tathagata must not bear another child.[16] The fact that King Ashoka set up a pillar (found in 1895) to mark his pilgrimage to the birthplace at Lumbini (modern Rummindei in Nepal) tells us only that three hundred years after the event a certain site was reputed to be the birthplace. Pajapati is said to have taken over as stepmother; and a Pajapati is mentioned several times in the Vinaya and the Nikayas, especially as a leader of women requesting ordination, but her family relationship with Gautama is not specified.

There is no reference in early texts to the childhood, except that in the Mahasaccaka sutra of the Majjhima Nikaya the Buddha, relating his Enlightenment, tells of his jhanic experience as a child "while his father was working." The stories of the triumphant words at birth,[17] the thirty-two body marks, and the prophecy of Asita are of late origin, as are the father's attempts to protect him from knowledge of the world, the Four Omens, and the details of his marriage. There are several names for his wife in various sources: Bhaddakacca, Gopa, Yasodhara, Bimbasundari; and she may well have been his first cousin. In Mahavagga his son is called Rahula, but the mother is not named. When the Buddha returns to Kapilavastu and converts the Sakyas, the child is ordained. According to some pious versions even Suddhodana was reconciled to the loss of his heir and successor; but the victory of the son in taking away from their secular and military duties the flower of Sakyan youth may have contributed to the historical invasion and destruction of the Sakya tribe in the next generation.

The poetic elaboration of the effect of the Four Omens, the revulsion against luxury, and the Great Renunciation are all absent from the Nikayas. In the Sutta Nipata of the Khuddaka Nikaya, generally accepted as early, there is a conventional comment: "Cramped is this household life, free as the air is going forth." In Majjhima I, 163, the Buddha seeks "what is good, the peerless way of desirable peace." His exact age is stated only in the later legends. Probably the conversion was of the same order as that of the numerous wandering paribbajakas whom we keep meeting in the sutras, arguing and being converted: the inception of a search for spiritual peace of self-conquest not possible amid family responsibilities. Nothing short of a taped psychoanalytic seance would tell us aught of a man's own notion of his motivations. Nothing can provide the actual motivations. We must fall back on broad but still reasonable explanations: "leaving the house" was a traditional and accepted step toward liberation, and the young man's desire to reach spiritual understanding was stronger than the bond of his family; and a compassion for mankind's troubles was an additional motive for seeking a new way of understanding.

He went to the groves that were the contemporary marketplaces of ideas. It is probable that he actually studied with Arada and Udraka but decided that yogic trance led to only temporary release and not to the quiescence of passions, full understanding of man's condition, and lasting freedom from the malaise of attachment to samsara, the wandering from incarnation to incarnation. Then his undergoing austerities is probably authentic, both because tapasya was the traditional way to mastery over the gods, and because his rejection of it is clearly and repeatedly declared in the Vinaya. The imaginative details of the Enlightenment, such as his ritual preparations, the onslaughts of Mara, the first words of the Buddha, the number of days he spent under the tree enjoying the bliss of the new state, and the intervention of Brahma to urge the preaching mission, are all in several late versions. The earlier, matter-of-fact Nikayas are spare of information.

After the early days of preaching, there is no continuous narrative until the last days, related in the Mahaparinibbana (the Great-Decease Book, Digha Nikaya Sutta 16). Whatever the facts of the first days, they contain some symbolically significant events: the conversion of the rich setthi, the father of Yasa, and the favor of King Bimbisara and later of King Pasenadi and his queen, Mallika. Historically the new faith received the support of independent merchants, perhaps because it broke with restrictive traditions of caste and ways of livelihood and encouraged individual decision rather than acquiescence in brahmin control; and rulers approved of a civilizing, nonviolent, and noncompetitive way.

We must not take the claims of rapid growth of the Sangha at face value. It grew and spread to the west, and later to the south, but it never achieved dominance in any region.

TWO

What Can We Know About What the Buddha Really Said?

The Enlightened One, like Confucius, Socrates, and Jesus, did not write his message. He spoke directly to his disciples and to all who would listen, eye to soul. The students of Confucius tried to do right by their revered master in repeating his words, but the Analects contain many he did not say; and Socrates' friends, like Plato and Xenophon, were probably too independent and too literate for full submission to the spoken word. The message of the Buddha was probably in three forms: the rules he set down for the Order, often in response to specific incidents,[1] as indicated in the Vinaya; the fixed homily, such as the first sermon in the deer park; and the *ad hoc* disputation in response to a challenge by a disciple or an opponent. The Vinaya Pitaka (basket, or collection) is the book of disciplines, with some narrative background; the Sutra Pitaka contains sermons and discussions; the Abhidharma Pitaka contains commentary, meditative disciplines, and metaphysical analysis.

By their very nature the Vinaya rules must have developed quickly into fixed formulations; some were repeated aloud, sometimes in unison, in regular ceremonies. Eventually the sutra material fell into patterns too. Because he addressed all who came to listen, kings and commoners, the illiterate as well as the philosophically trained, he probably used the age-old devices of rhythmic repetition, formulaic phrases, and self-question and answer to make the word memorable. The oral style, whether in Homer or the Bible, the Vedas or the sutras, helps fix and make holy what is repeated until such time as it becomes convenient or no longer forbidden to write it down, jot and tittle preserved.[2] The words of the Buddha, repeated and refined for impact and memorability for the forty-five years of his ministry, and absorbed and repeated by men trained to memorize Vedic hymns and rituals, could very well have survived intact for generations until written down centuries later.

Then why does the redoubtable Edward Conze declare, "No sane man can, in fact, say anything conclusive about the doctrine of the Buddha himself"? ("Recent Progress in Buddhist Studies," in *Thirty Years of Buddhist Studies,* p. 10.)

The Buddha as Preacher

The Master's own words, even if memorized and fixed, probably did not travel very far. In his sermons he chose to use the local speech of his hearers ("whatever might have been their sort I made myself of like sort, whatever their language so was my language," Digha Nikaya 2, 109, Sutta 16),[3] some of whom spoke a different Prakrit than his own, which was a form of Magadhi, while others spoke non-Prakrit tongues. He refused, the legend goes, to let his ex-brahmin followers chant his message in pure Sanskrit verse. "This will not conduce, O foolish ones, either to the conversion of the unconverted, or to the increase of the converted. . . . I allow you, O Bhikkhus, to learn the word of the Buddhas each in his own dialect." (Cullavagga 5, 33)[4] Even if his words were put into verse, the ordinary way of making important material memorable, the verses were often translated lamely into related languages.

The Master seems to have been strict in the statement and enforcement of the Pratimoksha (Pali, Patimokkha) and the other rules for the committed monks but not dogmatic about fine points of belief in the Sutra Pitaka, relying on parables, images, and simple explanations. He believed the message was simple and clear and wanted each follower to understand it in his own way without falling back on the Master's authority. He set up no hierarchy except that of strict seniority of membership, and before he died he refused to appoint a successor. A high form of local democracy seems to have prevailed in the Order, especially since groups of monks, who were at first supposed to be homeless wanderers by profession, and who had to depend on limited supplies of donated food, could grow only so large before fission occurred and they moved into new territory—where they were independent. As a result, the spreading Dharma had no center which would keep the groups related to each other. The Rule was reasonably secure, but the sutras, in which the encounters of the Master were told, and his preaching, his death, his birth, and much later, his previous births, were skillfully retold, and in the reordering incident was embroidered and doctrine elaborated.

Recent archaeological and textual developments have made it possible to arrive closer to what the Buddha really said than when the Pali canon was considered to be most of what we knew and all we needed to know. Editions of manuscripts in Sanskrit, Tibetan, or Chinese, found in museums, libraries, private collections, and the sands of Turkestan, now give us better ideas of the canons of the various schools. Future scholarship in these scriptures is likely to prove further that, to quote Conze, "each of them can equally well claim to represent the teaching of Buddha"—or some part of it, at any rate.

Some recently edited sutras and Vinayas are older or more authentic than their Pali counterparts, their editors believe. Conze reports Waldschmidt saying that the Mahaparinirvanasutra (the account of the Buddha's last days) of the Sarvastivadins, who were for a long time the dominant school in India, has in many places "probably preserved the original tradition more faithfully, and it has at least the same value as the Pali text." Hofinger examined eight canonical accounts of the Council of Vaisali, about 380 B.C., where the Mahasanghikas were born, and concluded that the version contained in the Vinaya of these schismatics is the oldest. J. J. Jones, editor and translator of the same sect's *Mahavastu,* states that one "must proceed from the assumption that both the Pali and Sanskrit texts preserve as a fixed core a very primitive tradition."

Before the Schools

When texts of the same material from different schools agree, there is a reasonable presumption that the common version dates to before the split, before the sects began to develop not only their own sequence for reciting the sutras and Vinayas, but their own interpolations and rewritings as well. Conze says, "Where we find passages in which these two texts, the one in Pali and the other [Sarvastivadin] in Sanskrit, agree almost word by word, we can assume that they belong to a time antedating the separation of the two schools, which took place during Asoka's rule. . . . This approach cannot, however, get us beyond 340 B.C. with the Sutra texts, because their Mahasanghika version is lost." Waldschmidt's edition of the Sanskrit Mahaparinirvana has the Pali and versions from a Tibetan and Chinese Vinaya in parallel columns; his analysis shows that three-fourths of the text has a common basis, which goes back to 250 B.C. or earlier. But the Patimokkha, the oldest part of the Pali scriptures, was compared by Pachow in 1955 with nine other versions of the monks' rules, and "all sects agree about most of them, and therefore they must have been formulated within the first century after the Buddha's Nirvana."

A crucial event in the history of the transmission of the Buddhavacana, the word, was the First Council—if it occurred. According to the Pali legend, upon hearing of the death of the Master, Kassapa said to his fellow disciples at Rajagaha:

Come, Sirs, let us chant together the Dhamma and the Vinaya before what is not Dhamma is spread abroad, and what is Dhamma is put aside; before what is not Vinaya is spread abroad, and what is Vinaya is put aside; before those who argue against the Dhamma become powerful; and those who hold to the Dhamma become weak. (Cullavagga 11, 1)

Then Kassapa had Upali, the "Vinaya-dhara," answer his questions "as to the matter, and as to the occasion, and as to the individual concerned" in the rules of the Vinaya; and then Ananda, who had achieved trance and arhantship ("he became free from attachment to the world, and his heart was emancipated from the Asavas") only the night before the session, answered Kassapa's questions "as to the occasion of the Brahmajala . . . and the Samannaphala . . . and in like manner did he question him through the five Nikayas."

It would have been manifestly impossible for the meeting to go as the legend describes: the corpus of the Vinaya occupies three modern volumes, the sutras in the first four Nikayas occupy sixteen volumes of the Pali Text Society translations. On the other hand, what may have existed then of the Vinaya (only the rules, without the accretion of legends and the incidents that are supposed to have given rise to the rules) and the sutras (the bare events and the homilies and parables of the Buddha, without the exhaustive incremental repetitions, so dear to an audience, and appearances of the same incidents and formulations in numerous other sutras, often stated in identical terms or in slight variations) could perhaps have been recited in one or two sessions, although perhaps not by two men. It seems likely that the followers would have held some kind of meeting after the funeral, in order to huddle together forlorn in their Great One's passing, to adjust their relationships, to jockey for positions of leadership (even among vanity-free arhants). Certainly the Pratimoksha ("binding") regulations, which were and are recited at the new-moon and full-moon observations, must have had special significance at that moment.

That both Upali, the former barber, and Ananda, the kinsman and favorite disciple of the Buddha, were Sakyas, and that their recitations would have been in his Magadhi tongue, may add a hint of authenticity to the Council story. Also, even if the Cullavagga mentions the Second Council, which it dates a century after the Parinirvana, and all five[5] Nikayas, this fact need not make us deny the occurrence of the First Council but should make us question the authenticity of its narration, since it was compiled so long after the event.

Some Criteria

To decide what the Buddha is likely to have said out of all that is attributed to him calls upon the same processes of judgment that are applied to deciding who he was. We have seen, in comparing the "acceptable" version of the Enlightenment in Majjhima 1, 240, Sutta 36, the Mahasaccakasutta, with the lush versions in *Lalitavistara* and *Mahavastu,* that we were applying the modern criteria of simplicity and the razor of parsimony in rejecting the miraculous elements (Mara) and unduly elaborated formulations of doctrine in favor of the sparer narration. Similarly, we cut away the miraculous, the mechanically repetitive, the elaborate formulas to get close to what we shall choose to call the true word. These criteria seem reasonable, but we risk committing the historical sin; perhaps the Buddha was not so far ahead of his time as to dispense with the miraculous, or loath to complicate his message with metaphysical formulas—despite his distaste for both pastoral practices, if we believe the sutras we prefer to believe!

Modern scholars seeking the parts of the canon closest to the source prefer simple verses. If the verses do not always scan perfectly in Sanskrit or Pali, all the better: it might mean they were taken directly from a closely allied Magadhi original—not composed by the Buddha himself, of course, but perhaps in his generation—as the normal way to make his words memorable.[6] If prose accompanies the verse, and repeats it, the prose is likely to be a later embellishment.

Apart from literary taste, there are several technical criteria used to mark sections of the canon as early or late, and to distinguish stratifications within a single work. If a work is found without much variation in more than one canon, it is likely to have originated before the divergence of the schools. The Pratimoksha, mentioned above, is the prime

CAN WE KNOW WHAT THE BUDDHA SAID? 13

example. To a lesser degree, the presence of all the sutras of Digha Nikaya in one or another of the Agamas (the term in the Sarvastivada canon corresponding to the Nikayas), translated into Chinese from the original Sanskrit, suggests a certain authority of the Digha. The first of the three Digha books is accepted as the oldest, with an apparent plan relating its twelve suttas.

Another test is the presence of the pat formulas. The Brahmajalasutta, despite the abstraction of its sixty-two speculative theses, is considered to go back to an early base because it does not list the five skandhas, and has only ten items in the Dependent Origination list.[7] Similarly the second Digha sutta, the Samannaphala, presents man as a complex of "kaya" and "vinnana" (body and consciousness) rather than of the skandhas. Between the two views, Pande says, in *Studies in the Origins of Buddhism*,

there is a clear gulf fixed by the difference in the meaning of vinnana. In the former it is "consciousness as individualized through embodiment," in the latter it is "perception regarded as one of the four aspects of empirical consciousness." This reflects not only increased psychological analysis but also a changed epistemological standpoint.[8]

Another test is that of vocabulary. Words change in meaning in different strata, and new technical words come into use. For example, from Pande:

The "doctrine" is Dhamma, because it proclaims the Norm that lies behind things; and since it is through the mind that the abstract norms behind sensible things are apperceived, dhammas are the objective counterpart of "Mano." This second meaning seems to have mediated in the progress of the meanings of dh. from "the Norm behind things" to the "things" themselves. (P. 41)

Asava—In the earliest texts it seems to have a quite general signification; then, for long, it denotes a set of three evils, which is later increased to four. (P. 38)

The proliferation of miracles and of mythological personages, such as devas and local deities transformed into Buddhas and bodhisattvas, and the exaggeration in numbers (aeons, distances, followers) are distinctly Mahayanic and late, and when found in Old Wisdom texts are likely to indicate a patch laid on by a late compiler. For example, sutta 32 of Digha, the Atanatiya, is a protection charm. As Pande states:

It is much more mythological, and much longer than the "Ratana" sutta of the Sn [Sutta Nipata], which has the same purpose. It bows to the seven Buddhas, describes the retinue of the four maharajas and then names the more violent yakkhas, some of whom are Vedic gods and sages! It clearly belongs to a late stratum. (P. 113)

We run the risk, of course, of improperly imposing our rational tastes on an age that believed in magic. The man Gautama performed siddhi like other yogins, and it need not have required centuries to produce a hagiographical Parson Weems. The right mixture of textual criticism and historical tact will eventually guide scholars to a fair judgment of what parts of the Dharma go back to or at least near to the Buddha.

The Frauwallner Thesis

An example of technical scholarship at work provides a useful precaution about most of what has been said in this chapter. What if there were no First Council to give some of the words of the Vinayas and sutras? What if we find that even exact correspondence of the texts of different schools, indicating a common source, were to lead back not to the words of the Buddha, but to an imaginative reconstruction, possibly a prevarication? Such is the thesis of Erich Frauwallner in *The Earliest Vinaya and the Beginnings of Buddhist Literature,* which Conze calls "a remarkable piece of inspired detective work." Following his argument will teach us something of the contents of the scriptures, the spread of the Dharma, and the nature of the early sects.

The Frauwallner thesis starts from the fact of a striking similarity in parts of the Vinayas of six different schools, in whose other scriptures there is wide diversity. The Sarvastivada, Dharmagupta, Mahisasaka, Theravada, Mulasarvastivada, and Mahasanghika Skandhaka sections show "agreement of texts that reaches deep into particulars." The Vinaya Pitaka is divided into two parts, the Sutta-vibhanga, containing the Pratimoksha (the confession formula), 227 regulations and commentary, and the Skandhaka (the exposition of the monastic rules). The first four schools named show complete agreement on all twenty sections of rules. "Such a deep-going agreement leads us to the necessary conclusion that all these texts go back to the same origin" (p. 4).

The dogmatic schools developed within communities already existing, Frauwallner continues, so that monks of various theological interpretations, whether Old Wisdom or schismatic or even Mahayana, would live amicably in the same vihara under the same rules. The period of 250 B.C. under Ashoka has multiple significance for the develop-

CAN WE KNOW WHAT THE BUDDHA SAID? 15

ment of Buddhism. The Third Council, at Pataliputra, was called in recognition of the diversity of belief and the need to achieve some cohesion; the famous mission to Ceylon, led by Ashoka's son, Mahinda, was the origin of the Pali tradition; and, less well known, similar missions brought identical doctrine to eight other places within Ashoka's realm, as well as to "Antiyoga, Tulamaya, and Alikyshadula," Greeks far off (Rock Edict 13).

All the missions carried the same Vinaya rules, as formulated in the region of Vidissa, their starting point. These rules, it is assumed, appeared later in the canons of the various sects. But the same Skandhakas appear in the texts of two schools established long before Ashoka, the Mulasarvastivadins at Mathura and the Mahasanghikas at Vaisali. The former's Vinaya differs widely in other respects: it contains many more fables. Frauwallner concludes that all six schools, the older two and the four that grew in the younger establishments, derived their Skandhaka sections from a common source.

All the canons have an account of the Parinirvana and the First Council, most of them after the twenty parts (ten Skandhakas in the Mahavagga, ten in the Cullavagga) of the rules proper; likewise part of the life of Gautama, then the Enlightenment, and the beginning of the teaching as a proper introduction to the statement of the rules. Usually the full account of the death has been cut loose, as in the Pali, and made a separate sutta, as the Mahaparinibbana, Digha 16. Frauwallner postulates the existence of a unified literary work composed about the time of the Vaisali Council, but before the Mahasanghika movement became an actual schism—say, about one hundred years after Parinirvana.

Frauwallner believes that the First Council was a concoction of this work by an effective literary artist. One reason he gives is the curious incident, after the recitation of the sutras, in which Ananda is humiliated by Kasyapa for various errors, especially in forgetting to ask the Master before his death which minor rules could be revoked and worse, in failing to take a clear hint and "beseech the Blessed One to remain on for a kalpa for the good and happiness of the great multitudes," rather than accept Parinirvana. Also, he had urged admission of women "into the Dhamma and Vinaya proclaimed by the Tathagata." This section of the Mahaparinirvana sutra in its various versions, and the Bhumicala sutra as well, which tells the same story of Ananda's responsibility for the Buddha's passing, is therefore also the composition of the Skandhaka author. Frauwallner says:

It was always agreed that it [the First Council] could not be an historical event. There may have been early attempts to collect the word of the Buddha, but a council in this form immediately after his death is unthinkable. (P. 64)

He believes that the purpose of the writing was to place the holy tradition under a common authority, to which recourse could be made through a list of teachers in the Vedic model; such lists, bringing authority from the First to the Second Council, are retained in the Mulasarvastivada and Mahasanghika versions, as if to follow the model of the Upanishads, which still had intellectual authority among Buddhists of the fourth century (p. 61).

Frauwallner conjectures that this work, so imaginative and well-knit, supplanted earlier versions of the Buddha stories, remnants of which remain in such works as the Pravaranasutra (fourth Skandhaka of the Mahavagga), which gives confession rules and reports rainy-season conversations of the Buddha and his disciples. Also there are hints that sutras were collected in other ways than by recitation at Rajagriha: if someone sends a messenger to bhikkhus in the rainy season, saying, "Might their reverences come and learn this suttanta; otherwise this suttanta will fall into oblivion," they should leave their vihara for up to seven days (Mahavagga 3, 5, 9).

The conclusion of the thesis is that the prevalent biography of the Buddha was composed by the Skandhaka author and became the basis of the famous later biographies. It is not authentic, but a legendary tale.

What we know and are able to know about the person and the life of the Buddha is therefore even less than we have hitherto believed; we must prepare ourselves to relegate in the realm of fable many things which were believed to be trustworthy tradition. (P. 164)

As for the Pali scriptures, Frauwallner believes that the first mission took to Ceylon only a small part of the canon; it was in well-established oral form, but some of the later transmissions may well have been written long before the documentary date of the inscribing of the Pali canon in the reign of Vattagamini about 50 B.C.

Frauwallner's case is persuasive and provides an answer to longstanding questions. Pande notes, for example:

Beal remarks on the close resemblance that exists in the order of representation between the Pali and the Mahasanghika Vinayas where the Mahavagga is concerned. It appears that the diversity of the Vinaya redactions is a later growth based on an originally common stock of rules. (P. 3)

CAN WE KNOW WHAT THE BUDDHA SAID? 17

Further, it has been suggested recently . . . that Cv. XI–XII originally formed part of the Mahaparinibbana sutta. That Cv. XI–XII form a kind of appendix to the Cv. and could not have originally belonged to it, is very probable. Further, Cv. XI begins abruptly unlike any other chapter of the Cv. It commences in the same way as the Mahaparinibbana sutta and is closely allied to it in contents. (P. 9)

But the case also runs contrary to criteria we accepted earlier, that purple passages, mythology and magic, and elaborate repetitions and formulas argue for late development. How late is late? One century after the passing seems early, but Frauwallner's hypothetical author included the following in his Mahaparinibbana (Digha Nikaya, sutta 16):

A. A prominent part for Mara, especially the report of his tempting the newly enlightened Buddha to remain in nirvana rather than walk among men and his return to remind him of his promise to leave the earth when he had imparted his message. When Ananda failed to take the Buddha's hint that an Enlightened One may choose to live out the kalpa, Mara pressed his claim.

B. The repeated meetings with each of the eight assemblies of gods and men, each addressed in its own "varna" and "language" (or voice), in rote formula.

C. Sariputra's reference to abandoning the five Nivaranas and cultivating the four Satipatthanas and the seven Sambojjhangas. And the inclusion of the Four Truths and Eightfold Path formulas.

D. Miraculous earthquakes caused by the Bodhisattva's decision to leave heaven and become a Buddha; also at his birth, Enlightenment, etc.

E. The Buddha's levitation over the Ganges and the fire games with the Jatila Kassapas.

We must ask whether the "author" singlehandedly made up all these items, many of which occur in other parts of the canon as well (Rhys Davids concludes that one third of the sutta thus recurs), or whether an incrustation of later patching is responsible for additions to the original creation. Pande says, "Of the mosaic character of the M. there can hardly be any doubt." Some passages seem early and authentic happenings to a human being: the narrative of the final illness, the grief of Ananda, also a number of simple verses. Others, like the miracles, references to the relics and erection of stupas, and the tendency to apotheosize the Buddha, are palpably late, according to established standards. It appears that Frauwallner has not answered all the questions.

The Divergent Way

Even if continuing scholarship will get us around such diversions from the true path of the Teacher's word, will knowing the word ensure that we know the doctrine? Would it be the Middle Way between the extreme nontheism of modern Theravada and the soteriology of late Mahayana? In all the texts, of whatever school, alongside the pluralism of the skandhas we find the mystery of the Tathagata. We also have a fairly firm statement of the rules of behavior and observance, and a flexible filling out of the basic concepts of the Dharma. Suppose Frauwallner's poet contributed the imagery of Mara's assault to the initiation rite of the Enlightenment and then skillfully brought Mara back at the end (after Ananda's lapse) to remind the Buddha of his vow to pass away; yet he is not likely to have modified the actual rules as the Sangha knew them. In the sutras, the Master's own approach encouraged divergence. The venerable Purana, who was not present at the First Council, refused to submit himself to the text rehearsed there, declaring, "Even in such mannner as it has been received by me from the very mouth of the Blessed One, in that manner will I bear it in my memory" (Cullavagga 1, 11). (Was the "poet" encouraging schism? There are many hints throughout the various canons, and within the Pali canon itself, of manipulation of incident by different versions to further the interests of factions. We can only guess what the lines of encounter were until the open break of the Mahasanghikas at Vaisali.)

Conze points to an interesting discrepancy between two versions of the last words of the Tathagata. The Pali says, "Doomed to extinction are composite things; exert yourself in wakefulness" (Mahaparinibbana 6, 10).[9] The Sarvastivada version has only the ontological statement, no exhortation. Conze comments: "A mere statement about the facts of life, and no word about the need 'for striving,' so dear to the European moralist!" He also explains the reasons for believing that formulaic enumerations—Four Truths, Eightfold Path, etc.—are later than Ashoka, whose inscriptions do not mention them.

It seems probable that at a certain stage in the history of the order, fairly late, meditation was increasingly based on numerical lists, which it was the purpose of the Matrikas to enumerate. The Matrikas in their turn developed among the rationalists into the Abhidharma, among the mystics into the Prajnaparamita. ("Recent Progress," p. 7)

CAN WE KNOW WHAT THE BUDDHA SAID? 19

Whatever the date and the use to which they were put, the legends, the sermons, the enumerations, the standard imagery became the currency of all branches of the faith. In the Mahayana *Lotus of the Good Law*, Sariputra, now newly taught and saved, uses old legend to speak of his earlier anxiety:

> I am excluded from the thirty-two marks,
> Excluded am I from the golden color of the skin . . .
> At first I felt mightily afraid
> When I heard the Leader's words.
> I feared that it might be Mara, intent on harming me,
> Who had conjured up the guise of the Buddha.

The skandhas, a distinctive feature of Theravada pluralism, are turned around:

The Lord: What do you think, Subhuti? Do the five grasping skandhas, after they have trained themselves in the perfection of wisdom, go forth to the knowledge of all modes?

Subhuti: No, Lord. For the own-being of the five grasping skandhas is non-existent. The five skandhas are similar to a dream. The own-being of a dream cannot be apprehended, because it does not exist. In this way the five skandhas cannot be apprehended, because of the non-existence of their own-being.*

Perhaps the final word on what the Buddha really said is that of the Mahayana, as implied in the two last quotations: *it doesn't matter.* According to the principle of "skill in means," in any age the Tathagata will practice wholesome opportunism and tell his hearers what they are able to understand (as even in the Old Wisdom sutra he saved Vaccha from confusion). In *Lotus* the Tathagata becomes all things to all doubting bodhisattvas, like Sariputra, because they need encouragement to continue beyond nirvana toward final Buddhahood. The recently enlightened Sakyamuni and the other tathagatas (first met in late sutras and the birth stories) beginning with Dipankara are all, the Buddha says, "conjured up by me as an emission of the skill in means by which I demonstrate Dharma." The Tathagata "makes a show of entering Nirvana, for the sake of those who have to be educated." He continues:

And whatever the Tathagata says to educate beings, and whatever the Tathagata utters—whether he appears as himself or as another, whether under his own authority or another—all these discourses on dharma are taught as factually

---

*Buddhist Texts Through the Ages, ed. Conze, Horner, Snellgrove, Waley, p. 178. Hereafter referred to as *BT.*

true by the Tathagata, and there is no false speech in them on the part of the Tathagata. For the Tathagata has seen the triple world as it really is: It is not born, it dies not; there is no decease or rebirth, no Samsara or Nirvana; it is not real, or unreal, not existent, or non-existent, not such, or otherwise, not false or not-false. Not in such a way has the Tathagata seen the triple world as the foolish common people see it. The Tathagata is face to face with the reality of dharmas; he can therefore be under no delusion about them. Whatever words the Tathagata may utter with regard to them, they are true, not false, not otherwise. (*BT,* p. 141)

Perhaps even the words that the Tathagata does *not* utter are also true. The history of religion is familiar with the twofold heritage, the *exoteric* doctrine formulated for oral and written dissemination, and the *esoteric,* conveyed orally only to initiates, as in the Greek mysteries, or in opaque texts requiring keys within keys to unlock imagery, as in Tantra and Cabala. Nagarjuna, perhaps whimsically, claimed the Buddha as the source of the Madhyamika doctrine, kept hidden by the Dragons until people were ready for it. But what of the Buddha's declaration, reiterated in his last hours to Ananda, who asked for instructions concerning the Order, that "the Tathagata has no such thing as the closed fist of a teacher, who keeps things back"? And that "I have preached the truth without making any distinction between exoteric and esoteric doctrine"? Well, was it the arhant or the Tathagata who spoke?

Perhaps we should accept the views of most scholars today, "that Buddhism is as much the work of Buddhists as of the Buddha himself," and agree with Conze that "it would be quite uncritical to jump from the existing Scriptures straight back to the Buddha's time . . . to go through the Pali Scriptures, take out the bits which take one's fancy, and call them 'the original gospel' " ("Recent Progress," pp. 3, 7–8).

If so far in this treatment there has been too heavy a reliance on the Pali, too much unqualified predication of "the Buddha said," the reason is simply that for most of the Old Wisdom material only the Theravada is edited and translated, and that it is cumbersome to say, "the text in which the Buddha is represented as saying." Much of what he is quoted as saying sounds more like the "original, human" gospel than much else he is quoted as saying. But perhaps only to a western nonbeliever.

THREE

What Buddhists Have Believed

Between the lamas from Tibet and the bhikkhus of Sri Lanka there are wide differences in belief as to the nature of the Buddha and in devotional practices and social roles. Within two hundred years of the Buddha's passing there were eighteen or more schools diversely interpreting the Dharma, and the process of divergence has continued. But there is a central core of doctrine, psychological rather than religious, that is held in common by Theravadins in Ceylon, who insist that their teacher was a man,[1] Shin Buddhists in Japan, who take refuge in Amida, their guide to Paradise, and Americans and Europeans seeking spiritual reorganization.

Some Basic Ideas

Wherever it has spread, Buddhism has made adjustments to local popular systems of magic and has provided fairly serviceable vehicles for the perilous path of life. But at its highest levels Buddhism is a still-evolving system of practice and metaphysics that can help bring order into the most complex confusions of our dying culture.

The search for the core of common doctrine becomes two questions: Is there agreement on what the Buddha really said? and, if so, How do Buddhists interpret what they agree he said?

What the Buddha Taught

It is possible to reach agreement on a rather limited content of what the Buddha taught his followers, even though there is no text that can be assigned directly to him and little agreement on what parts of the many Buddhist texts derive directly from his teaching. Most Buddhists will agree on this minimum statement about the Buddha's ministry:

that he, like other teachers of his time, formed a fellowship dedicated to a certain way of life, the object of which was to achieve "liberation." For others, this liberation was identified with the psycho-physiological state called variously the trance of yogic "realization," the mystical experience, samadhi, kaivalya, dhyana, union with God, the Absolute, or Brahman, the dissolution of the separate self. This state was the climax of Siddhartha Gautama's own Enlightenment under the pipal tree on the night of the full moon in May 528 B.C., or thereabouts. But what came out of this victory over himself, in which he achieved nirvana while in this life, was a message profoundly different from that of others seeking similar fruition. First, he required more than a samadhic experience of ecstasy or enstasy; he demanded a restructuring of the psyche achieved by a new understanding (*prajna*) of man's own nature and his relation to other phenomena. Second, he stated a remarkable psychology: that there was no Ego or self-identifying personality, permanent or temporary, to be found behind or above the ever-changing emotions, memories, and activities that make up the functioning individual whose actions cause a rebirth or who achieves a permanent refuge in nirvana. Third, he built compassion and social responsibility into his discipline as ways of depersonalization and growth.

In the centuries after the Parinirvana certain traditional formulations of this message grew up and are still repeated by Buddhists whose interpretations of them differ widely. These are the Four Noble Truths, the Eightfold Path, the five skandhas, the dozen or so steps of the law of Dependent Origination, and various other mnemonic enumerations. These formulas are elaborated and repeated in various forms of the scriptures, whether in Pali, Sanskrit, Chinese, or Tibetan. What made for divergence was the Buddha's own distaste for dogma and the potential for development inherent in his ideas and the cultural ground they came from, as well as the varied ground in which they took root. What has unified Buddhism over the centuries is a fairly distinct meditative practice and the unique personality of the Buddha himself.

The Master embodied a variety of ideals: the firm, confident leader committed to a way of life; the gentle teacher who knew the needs of his students; the humorous man of the world who worked around human frailty; the subtly trained mind that knew all the distinctions but still warned against nonessentials; the guru who had magical powers but scorned to use them; the materialist who kept returning to the human body as the medium of all experience; the mystic who transcended sensation and discursive rationalism; the political thinker who told

WHAT BUDDHISTS HAVE BELIEVED

kings their responsibility; the religious innovator who knew that his teaching must be retaught and adapted for each generation.

Divergences in doctrinal detail are attributable to the Teacher's respect for the spirit rather than the letter. His qualities bloom through a bimillennial accretion of homily, poetry, and commentary, and have inspired new ways to meet widely varying needs in new lands. They brought new ways of seeing to Tibet, China, Japan, and Southeast Asia. They may help bring a direly needed inner control to the self-assertive, destructive West—in another new blending, of course.

The Buddha in His Time

Is it not possible that the Buddha's words (repeated and refined by him over forty-five years of preaching and then, presumably, repeated reverently by his disciples, many of whom were trained in the scrupulous memorization of traditional texts) were carried on orally for centuries before being written down?[2] Yes. Some of the rules of the order he founded, especially the Pratimoksha (the semimonthly confession), have come down to us probably as formulated by the Founder and repeated faithfully by the Disciples. But the sutras, the reports of the Master's discourses bearing the doctrine, are agreed to be later and by many hands.

The message of the Buddha is best introduced to a modern audience as it was to his: in the context of then prevailing belief. He had to establish an intellectual position against numerous other leaders in a time of flourishing inquiry: materialists, monists, dualists, skeptics, eternalists, annihilationists, and especially the brahmin priests. These last were beginning to extend their sway from the northwest of India, the old Aryavarta, to the eastern Gangetic plain, the Buddha's country, and they were expanding their function from the exploitation of old Vedic ritual and sacrifice to broader social dominance through establishment of caste orthodoxy. The Buddha accepted from his contemporaries a then comparatively new complex of ideas relating karma, rebirth, and liberation, but developed them uniquely. Against the brahmin notion of karma as the proper observance of ritual laid down in the Vedas and controlled by the priesthood, he proposed a karma of personal restraint and social morality; against a formula of rebirth into a higher or lower caste, he proposed a potential of individual improvement over many existences leading to eventual spiritual perfection; against the crude early brahmin notion of liberation into a heaven inhabited by Vedic gods, or the more refined concept of the Upanishads, in which the liberated Self, the Atman, rejoins the Absolute Brahman, he proposed the undefinable condition of nirvana.

He refused to define nirvana, but an indispensable element must have been the enstatic (Eliade's term) trance state that has always defined liberation in India, whether for atheistic yogins, Buddhists, and Jains, or for theistic Upanishadic rishis, Shaivite saddhus, and modern Vedantist swamis, followers of Ramakrishna. Yet the Buddha, in his great-souled concern for the lot of all mankind, devoted his major attention not to yogic instruction but to daily existence, the sadness of samsara, the wandering from birth to birth. The cause of man's unsatisfactory existence in samsara is his false evaluation of his own nature, his need for a permanent entity that perceives, feels, acts, and strives to maintain itself. It is this craving that keeps man chained to the wheel of rebirth. The Buddha refused to speculate on the nature of rebirth, to describe what was reborn, but instead spoke of man's true nature. All of the early texts agree that his schema for the human organism denied a continuing entity of personality structure. Instead he saw a series of interrelated events, a succession of interactions with the external world that were called perceptions, feelings, actions. After a couple of centuries this description was formalized into the skandha (Pali, khandha), the constantly changing aggregates or "heaps" that make up the empirical individual.

Where Is the Ego?

The five skandhas were: (1) *rupa,* form and matter, the material elements, the sense organs and their corresponding objects in the external world; (2) *vedana,* sensations or feelings, pleasant, painful, or neutral, derived from contact with the external world, including mind-objects (since mind was considered one of the senses or organs, like the eye or ear); (3) *samjna* (Pali, sanna), conceptions, the recognizing or naming faculty; (4) *samskarah* (Pali, samkhara), psychic disposition or compositions, volitional activities involving karma; (5) *vijnana* (Pali, vinnana), acts of consciousness or thought, especially in relation to the six internal faculties and their corresponding external objects. Despite the seemingly exact allocation of organic functions, there is much overlapping of definition and jurisdiction accorded each of the skandhas in texts of different schools, and in interpretation of the terms in modern languages.[3]

When the skandhas are analyzed in relation to Contingent Origination (or Chain of Causation, or Dependent Co-arising), pratityasamutpada (Pali, paticcasamupada), in which they are incorporated in the ineluctable sequence that begins with ignorance and ends with birth, old age, death, and misery over-all, then we seem to be confronted with a determinism, a radical pluralism, in which the individual is nothing but a resultant of innumerable forces and influences, in which a Self cannot be distinguished. David Hume came to a similar conclusion.

When I enter most intimately into what I call *myself*, I always stumble on some particular perception, i.e., some particular mental content or other, of heat or cold, light or shade, love or hatred, pain or pleasure. I never catch *myself* at any time without a perception.[4]

Hume's phrase, "a bundle or collection of different perceptions," brings us close to the Buddhist skandhas. The Buddha's dying words were "All composite things are temporary," and he was referring to man. Hume, or any nontheistic materialist, such as the Buddha seems to have been, would envision only one process at the decease of such a human organism: dissolution and the redistribution of its atoms.

Rebirth and Nirvana

But other parts of the message as they come down to us present the Buddha as no annihilationist. The karma effected by an individual in this generation influences an individual in the next, although in strict terms it is not a transmigration of the same soul entity, as it is in brahminical doctrine. The process of rebirth accepted by early Buddhists is never explained to the satisfaction of a western rationalist,[5] or indeed to the satisfaction of many Buddhists, who through the centuries have fallen back on various "person" theories. But however difficult to accept, the notion of rebirth and karmic influence without a continuing soul was essential to the early Buddhist and perhaps to the Buddha's own view of the human condition and its solution. Therefore, any attempt to understand the machinery of rebirth must, like defining nirvana, be regarded as a useless exercise of the lower faculties of knowledge: sense perception and reason, both of which are limited to this worldly experience. The higher knowledge, an intuitive integration achieved in the trance condition of illumination, was sufficient warranty to early followers that the forking road, to rebirth or to nirvana, was a reality.

Annihilationists and unconditioned materialists ended up, in the Buddha's view (see Chapter 4), as socially irresponsible, offering no guidance to suffering man. "Some ascetics and brahmins accuse me wrongly, basely, falsely, and groundlessly, saying the ascetic Gotama is a nihilist, and preaches the annihilation, destruction, and nonexistence of an existent being. . . . Both previously and now I preach pain and the cessation of pain" (Majjhima Nikaya I, 140).

The Buddha's teaching, even though deterministic on one level, as later formulated in the Dependent Origination, nevertheless opened out into freedom by making the individual, however conditioned, responsible for his own salvation. One chooses one's own actions and can follow the Path to conquer ignorance and achieve release from the necessity of rebirth, either in this existence or after a requisite number of lives. Speculations on rebirth and nirvana—despite the Buddha's warnings that such speculations were vain because nirvana is a permanently transcendent state that cannot be defined or described in the terms of rational discourse—provided two of the grounds of divergence among Buddhists trying to fit them into diverse metaphysical systems.

For example, the matter of the Buddha's own rebirth brought complications into the straightforward message we have posited. His enlightenment and liberation brought to an end his own earthly careers. But if he was a man, he must have had previous existences in which he accumulated virtue and strength, aiming toward this culminating one, in which Gautama the sage of the Sakyas would become the Buddha and go off into nirvana. In the early centuries after the Mahaparinirvana, the Great Passing, he was depicted only by means of footprints marked with the wheel, or an empty throne, or a pipal tree, or an umbrella. Or—since the world was untold ages old—was Gautama one in a series of Buddhas, all of whom had appeared for the same purpose, to show the way of enlightenment to lesser men? Or were all past Buddhas really only manifestations of the same Tathagata, the numinous "one who has come" (or gone) and who adapts himself and his teachings to the limited capacities of the generations of man? In these questions we have moved from what were probably the earliest doctrines of the Disciples to later Theravada to wide-open Mahayana.

We cannot know when the concept of the Tathagata developed as a supernatural being distinct from Gautama the man who became enlightened. It is probable that the Enlightened One, in his confidence and self-assigned leadership, set himself off from other men.[6] How far off, we cannot know. We cannot know whether he applied the term Tathagata to himself, or if he did, what he meant by it. There is a wide distance between the term's use in the Old Wisdom schools (e.g., the Theravada and Sarvastivada) as an appellation of the Teacher, and in the Mahayana as a timeless, pervasive presence. For example, we read in the Digha Nikaya, the first of the five books in the Pali collection of sutras:

Monks, the Tathagata's body remains although he has cut off the conduit for becoming. As long as his body remains, devas and men shall see him; but at the breaking up of his body at the end of his life-time devas and men shall see him not. (Sutta 1, in *BT,* p. 103)

But the Tathagata of the Lotus of the Good Law, one of the most important Mahayana texts, is quite other:

The Lord said: As a result of my sustaining power this world, with its gods, men and Asuras, forms the notion that recently the Lord Sakyamuni, after going forth from his home among the Sakyas, has awoken to full enlightenment, on the terrace of enlightenment, by the town of Gaya.
But one should not see it thus, sons of good family. In fact it is many hundreds of thousands of myriads of Kotis of aeons ago that I have awoken to full enlightenment. . . . Ever since, during all that I have demonstrated Dharma to beings in this Saha world system, and also in hundreds of thousands of Nayutas of Kotis of other world systems. But when I have spoken of other Tathagatas, beginning with the Tathagata Dipankara, and of the Nirvana of these Tathagatas, then that has just been conjured up by me as an emission of the skill in means by which I demonstrate Dharma. (Saddharmapundarika 15, 268–72, in *BT,* pp. 140–41)

The major part of this chapter is given to a sketch of the basic doctrines of Buddhism as they developed from an early formulation in the Old Wisdom schools, primarily an outline of disciplines leading to individual salvation, to a world religion dedicated to the salvation of all. Each runs into metaphysical difficulties, as must any attempt to explain the relation of the phenomenal to the absolute—especially when the basic dogma is the denial of an absolute!

The Hinayana, or Old Wisdom Doctrine

For about a century, until a generation ago, Buddhism meant to the western world the beliefs presented in the Pali canon, the only complete set of scriptures, much of which has appeared in English in the work of the Pali Text Society. In recent years the Pali scriptures, which are the version of the Theravada ("Elders"; Sanskrit, Sthavira) sect, have been shown their proper place beside the Sanskrit, Tibetan, and Chinese versions of other schools, such as the Sarvastivada, which was much more important in India than the Theravada, which held sway in Ceylon.

The "Old Wisdom" school is a term (preferable to Hinayana—"little career"—which still bears the pejorative tone of its original use by a few of the more contentious Mahayanists) applied by Professor Conze[7] to those sects that placed emphasis on prajna, Wisdom, as the highest of the five cardinal virtues: Faith, Vigor, Mindfulness, Concentration, and Wisdom. Wisdom is also the climax of the triple discipline for the training of those aspiring to liberation, or arhantship: *sila*, moral discipline; *samadhi*, concentration or trance; and *prajna*, the recognition of things as they really are, especially the nonexistence of the Ego, demonstrated in the supertrance of enlightenment by the merging or suppression of the consciousness. The rules for self-liberation and the achievement of wisdom and enlightenment are exemplified and preached in Old Wisdom texts (such as the Pali canon) by Sakyamuni. These texts emphasize the skandhas and Dependent Origination as the key to understanding the dharmas, the elements and events that make up the world of experience.

Dependent Origination

Dependent Origination[8] is regarded in some descriptions of the Great Enlightenment as the intellectual achievement that brought Gautama to that goal. The standard versions present twelve steps in the sequence, although there are versions, deemed earlier, with fewer. (It is a generally accepted rule of dating that the more specific and elaborated such enumerations become, the later the date of composition or collation.) The natural progression of the Buddha's rationale of the human condition is to start with the given, the observed condition of duhkha (Pali, dukkha)—a complex word meaning sorrow, malaise, troubled awareness of transience—and then work back step by step to its ultimate cause. This is done in the late Sanskrit *Lalitavistara* (a Mahayanist work but presenting the traditional Sarvastivada Old Wisdom doctrine):

So the Bodhisattva, with his mind concentrated, purified, cleansed, luminous, spotless, with the defilements gone, mild, dexterous, firm and impassible, in the last watch of the night at dawn . . . directed his mind to the passing away of the cause of pain. He thought: wretched is it that this world has come about, namely, is born, grows old, dies, passes away, is reborn. And thus one knows no escape from this whole mass of pain. Alas! no means of ending all this great mass of pain is known, this old age, sickness, death, and so forth. Then, again, the Bodhisattva thought: when what exists do old age and death come to be, and what is the cause of old age and death? He thought: when birth exists, old age and death arise, for old age and death have birth as their cause.[9]

So the second link, the cause of old age, sickness, death, is birth. Birth is caused by Coming into Existence (bhava); behind that is Grasping (upadana); then Craving (trshna); then Sensation (vedana); then Contact (sparsa); then the Six Sense-Organs (sadayatana); then Mind-and-Body (nama-rupa); then Consciousness (vijnana); then the Aggregates, or compositions (samskarah); then the ultimate cause, Ignorance (avidya).[10] Then he reverses the sequence. "When what exists do the Aggregates come to be? . . . When Ignorance exists, the Aggregates come to be. . . . Even so the origin of all this great mass of pain comes to be, the origin! Thus as the Bodhisattva duly reflected repeatedly on these things' unheard before, knowing arose, vision arose, knowledge arose, full knowledge arose, light appeared."

The Four Noble Truths

The inclusion of the skandhas (sensation, perception, body, consciousness, aggregates) in the sequence of twelve indicates the interrelatedness of the formulations, although we cannot know which series achieved final formulation first. Both lists are necessary for an understanding of the first sermon, the Dhammachakkappavattanasutta, the setting in motion of the wheel of doctrine. Addressing the five ascetics, who had spurned him when he left the way of austerity as clouding rather than clearing his perceptions in his quest for truth, the newly Enlightened One first justified that decision:

There are two ends not to be served by a wanderer. What are these two? The pursuit of desires and of pleasure which springs from desire, which is base, common, leading to rebirth, ignoble, and unprofitable; and the pursuit of pain and hardship, which is grievous, ignoble, and unprofitable. The Middle Way of the Tathagata avoids both these ends.

Then he proceeds to the Four Noble Truths, referring indirectly to the skandhas and some of the elements of the Contingent Origination series (sorrow, birth, craving):

And this is the Noble Truth of Sorrow. Birth is sorrow, age is sorrow, disease is sorrow, death is sorrow, contact with the unpleasant is sorrow, separation from the pleasant is sorrow, every wish unfulfilled is sorrow—in short all the five components of individuality are sorrow.

And this is the Noble Truth of the Arising of Sorrow. It arises from craving, which leads to rebirth, which brings delight and passion, and seeks pleasure now here, now there—the craving for sensual pleasure, the craving for continued life, the craving for power.

And this is the Noble Truth of the Stopping of Sorrow. It is the complete stopping of that craving, so that no passion remains, leaving it, being emancipated from it, being released from it, giving no place to it.

And this is the Noble Truth of the Way which Leads to Stopping of Sorrow. It is the Noble Eightfold Path—Right Views, Right Resolve, Right Speech, Right Conduct, Right Livelihood, Right Effort, Right Mindfulness, and Right Concentration.[11]

The Eightfold Path is a practical course of psychological discipline leading to the final state of mind, Wisdom (prajna), which opens into nirvana. It is common practice to distribute the eight steps among the three disciplines: e.g., sila, morality or ethical conduct, includes Right Speech, Right Conduct, and Right Livelihood; samadhi, mental discipline, includes Right Effort, Right Mindfulness, and Right Concentration; prajna includes Right Views and Right Resolve. The objective of the discipline is to break the hold of the sense of Ego, which mistakes the component skandhas for a continuing personality.

It is easy to free oneself of passion for the body, since obviously it decays and dies.

But that which is called mind, intellect, consciousness—here the ignorant, unconverted man is not equal to conceiving aversion, is not equal to divesting himself of passion, is not equal to attaining freedom. . . . Because, O priests, from time immemorial the ignorant, unconverted man has held, cherished, and affected the notion, "This is mine; this am I; this is my Ego." [Even the body has more permanence than the ego.] "But that, O priests, which is called mind, intellect, consciousness, keeps up an incessant round by day and by night of perishing as one thing and springing up as another."[12]

WHAT BUDDHISTS HAVE BELIEVED

The explanation lies in Dependent Origination: "Behold this exists when that exists, this originates from the origination of the other." So the way to wisdom and liberation is to put the skandhas in proper proportion:

> Perceiving this, . . . the learned and noble disciple conceives an aversion for contact, conceives an aversion for sensation, conceives an aversion for perception, . . . for the predispositions, . . . for consciousness. And in conceiving this aversion he becomes divested of passion, and by the absence of passion he becomes free, and when he is free he becomes aware that he is free; and he knows that rebirth is exhausted, that he has lived the holy life, that he has done what it behooved him to do, and that he is no more for this world.(Warren, p. 152)

According to the elaborately formulated procedures found in later Old Wisdom texts, prajna is reached by aspirants to liberation normally only after progress through many grades of self-improvement. After self-development in the moral disciplines, one masters the eight levels of samadhi (the four trances requiring detachment from physical sensations and emotions—the rupa-dhyanas—and the four higher trances or attainments, the formless dhyanas, in which one graduates to a condition of pure contemplation after the cessation of all conceptions). Having progressed through the eight dhyanas (Pali, jhana) Gautama acquired a number of magical capabilities (siddhi, Pali, iddhi) such as levitation and far hearing, and special knowledges (abhijna; Pali, abhinna), i.e., knowledge of his former existences and the knowledge of the passing away and rebirth of individuals. The highest knowledge of all is prajna, in which the aspirant becomes aware of the destruction of the asrava (Pali, asava). This is the decisive event in liberation. The asrava are variously defined as the taints, the misconceptions, the inflows and outflows of karma formations caused by sensual desire (kama), desire for experience (bhava), and ignorance (avidya), especially the false belief in one's ego.

The movement toward nirvana is described in Samyutta Nikaya 22, 53, with, of course, references to escape from the confinement of the skandhas:

> Not to seek for anything, O monks, is to be free; to seek for anything is not to be free. . . . If passion for form is abandoned, then through the abandonment of passion the support is cut off, and there is no resting place for consciousness. If passion for sensation . . . for perception . . . for the predispositions is abandoned, the support is cut off, and there is no resting place for consciousness.

When that consciousness has no resting-place, does not increase, and no longer accumulates karma, it becomes free; and when it is free, it becomes quiet, and when it is quiet, it is blissful; and when it is blissful, it is not agitated; and when it is not agitated, it attains Nirvana in its own person; and it knows that rebirth is exhausted, that it has lived the holy life, that it has done what it behooved it to do, and that it is no more for this world. (Warren, pp. 162–63)

This blissful quietness, the separation from the world of sensation and thought, could be accepted by many mystics as a quality remembered after an experience of ultimate unitive trance. The qualities of Oneness, a merging of all dualities and distinctions, the dissolving of the Self in the All, appear in the writings of Eckhart, Plotinus, Ruysbroeck, St. Teresa, and many others. The Buddhist emphasis on negating the individual personality has for the arhant (who has attained nirvana in his own person) a more convincing basis than mere dogmatic epistemology. It derives directly from the nonduality of the samadhic experience.

Movement Toward Nirvana

Meditation, the first step toward nirvana, is open to all and is indispensable in Buddhist practice for several reasons. First, sitting down to meditate marks a decision to separate oneself, however briefly, from samsaric activity requiring decision, choice, and therefore close involvement in desire and duhkha. Second, the process itself induces calm, a separation that is the first step toward a reorganization of the personality away from self-concern. Third, the specific Buddhist way of meditation, free-flowing awareness leading to insight (by letting every sensation and thought enter and leave consciousness without interest or "clinging") is the polar opposite of yogic concentration and exclusion, but accomplishes the same psycho-physiological objective, the unitive experience that transcends discrimination, differentiation, the assertion of subject–object dualism; it is also a demonstration of Buddhist epistemology, which makes a unity of what the West regards as three separate elements: the perceiving sense, the "object" perceived, and the perception (what the body makes of the transaction). Fourth, the stages of meditation (dhyana) mark progress toward abstraction and depersonalization culminating in nirvana.

A logical consequence of the pluralistic Old Wisdom ontology of the skandhas and Dependent Coarising, the belief in constantly shifting physical, mental, and emotional states that can be stilled only in nirvana, is the concept of Momentariness. "As there is no permanent, unchanging substance, nothing passes from one moment to the next," writes the Theravadin Bhikkhu Rahula.[13] On the wheel of change and desire (desire that causes pain when unsatisfied and even when satisfied may cause someone else pain and then arouse new desire and pain), man is the plaything of Mara the tempter. The individual, anatta (without soul) despite his conviction of Ego, is like the physical world, tossed in continuous flux. How long is a thought?

Strictly speaking, the duration of the life of a living being is exceedingly brief, lasting only while a thought lasts. Just as a chariot wheel in rolling rolls only at one point of the tire, and in resting rests only at one point; in exactly the same way, the life of a living being lasts only for the period of one thought. As soon as that thought has ceased the being is said to have ceased. As it has been said:—

"The being of a past moment of thought has lived, but does not live, nor will it live.

"The being of a future moment of thought will live, but has not lived, nor does it live.

"The being of the present moment of thought does live, but has not lived, nor will it live." (Buddhaghosa, *Visuddhimagga* II, 8, in Warren, p. 150)

How is man to escape from this predicament, so logical, yet so humanly unacceptable? The Buddha's answer is simple: there is no escape from the momentary, the impermanent (anicca; along with anatta, notself, and dukkha, comprising the three marks of human existence) except liberation and nirvana; whence the need for the strenuous disciplines set forth in the Vinaya, the rules of the Order, and the Abhidharma, leading up to attainment of prajna and then nirvana itself. But many men will reject the logic of momentariness and attempt to bring back what is equally logical and more observably true: that there is continuity, rhythm of the sun and the seasons, and, in man, consistent response, memory, feedback that defines moral law, the *rta* of the Vedas, *moira* for the Greeks. Perhaps the Buddha's own phrase, the Middle Way, used in the first sermon to condemn extreme asceticism, can be used to extricate us from momentariness and the extreme pluralism of the skandhas.

The Buddha's own life demonstrated the middle way between the narrow path of the Vinaya and the uncharted, haphazard wandering of struggling humanity. His basic message was bold in its demands on the few who could aspire to liberation in this life, but moderate in its hopes for the many. He preached both prajna for the few and karuna, compassion, for all.

The monastic rules laid down for the disciples can be called a Middle Way between asceticism and self-indulgence only by comparison with the self-mortification practiced in his day (and ours) by many saddhus.[14] These hyper-ascetics sought not only mukti, liberation and union with the Absolute Brahman, but also magical and superhuman powers through tapasya, the practice of austerities that can bend the gods to one's will. The Buddha's followers, as described in Old Wisdom texts, practiced self-restraint, especially in sex and food, for a less self-assertive objective: liberation from craving or thirst for human experience (trshna; Pali, tanha). Spiritual peace through self-conquest, a logically parsimonious ideal of all ages and most societies, was developed in Gautama's India into a technique for achieving mukti while alive and moksha, freedom from rebirth.

The Order: Monks and Laity

The dynamics of the Buddha's teaching and example kept his followers from going off into the forest to concentrate on their own internal affairs, like so many of the recluses whom we meet continually in the sutras as opponents and converts. We have seen how the premise of rebirth led in a too-logical process to a many-times reborn Tathagata motivated to return by boundless compassion. Similarly, given the basics of the Rule and the dependence of the monks on the laity for sustenance and spiritual exercise, Buddhism became a way of life for the many as well as an intense discipline for the few.[15]

The begging bowl, for instance, was an instrument of socialization as well as an enforcement of humility. At the beginning, when disciples were few and they had no permanent home, the rule was to go from house to house before noon and accept whatever scraps were given, whether in respect or in contempt. The repute of all depended on the mildness and dignity of each. Contact with the laity was continual, and unlike the brahmin priests the Buddhist bhikshus performed no sacrifices and demanded no cash. The growth of the Order depended in great part on the response of the householders.

In the rainy seasons at first, and then when permanent viharas were established, day-to-day begging in the nearby village or town was no longer feasible, and permanent logistics had to be devised. Wealthy donors, like Anathapindika, who purchased the Jetavana grove for the Buddha, and Ambapali, the devout courtesan, brought the Order into permanent relations with established laity, until centuries later monasteries in both India and China took on the functions of banks for safekeeping of funds and as sources of capital for investment; they also provided an escape, in T'ang China, from taxes, the corvée, and military service.

The scriptures declare that in response to the interest of the laity the Buddha established wholesome guidelines for family and social relationships. The Sigalasutta (Digha Nikaya 31) is the standard document on the treatment of parents, teachers, wife and children, relatives and neighbors, servants, and religious devotees. The five rules of conduct, borrowed from Jain rules, and modified from the ten rules for monks, were provided for laymen: (1) reverence for life; (2) refusal to take anything not offered; (3) chastity in sexual relations; (4) respect for truth; (5) avoidance of intoxicants and drugs. The category of lay disciples, upasakas, was set up for laymen who wished an honored relation with the Order. To the question whether it was possible for a layman to achieve enlightenment, the Master replied that many hundreds had followed his teachings successfully.

One of the spiritual disciplines or subjects of meditation that the Buddha is supposed to have taken from the cultural ambience of his day was the sequence called the Abodes of Brahma (the Brahmaviharas), or the four Unlimiteds: universal friendliness and good will (maitri; Pali, metta); compassion for all living beings (karuna); sympathetic joy in others' good fortune (mudita); and even-mindedness, equanimity (upeksha).[16] Characteristically, the state that is most completely divorced from emotional response to external events is considered the highest. For the monks the objective of the first three states of emotional involvement was to jolt them loose from any concern with their own falsely conceived personalities. By identification with others' needs and fortunes one can move toward depersonalization, the decisive manifestation that prajna is within reach. Equanimity demonstrates one's victory over circumstance, whether good or ill.

Few attained equanimity. But whatever the doctrinal intention of the series, the outer-directedness of the first three states betokened the Buddha's sympathy for all on the wheel of samsara, even those without many preparatory existences of training for liberation. The movement toward a way of salvation for all, not merely those prepared for the final stage, took impetus, then, from the very disciplines set up for the elect.

Toward the Mahayana

We have seen how the doctrine of rebirth introduced an ambiguity into the nature of the Buddha, or the Tathagata. Although we cannot assign dates to the composition of the various sutras treating this subject, we can set up a reasonable order in the appearance of attitudes toward the nature of the Buddha. Probably earliest is the historical Buddha, the man who after six years of study and psychic experiment broke through to self-integration and a world-view, dramatized by the declaration of an ecstatic night of agony and triumph. At the other extreme is the embodied Tathagata, a transcendent mystery.

> Since a Tathagata, even when actually present, is incomprehensible, it is inept to say of him—of the Uttermost Person, the Supernal Person, the Attainer of the Supernal—that after dying the Tathagata is, or is not, or both is and is not, or neither is nor is not. (Samyutta Nikaya 3, 118 in *BT,* p. 106)

This tetralemma was the formulaic way of indicating that a subject was not amenable to normal rational forms of discourse involving verbal definitions and discursive rather than intuitive ideas.

An indication of late composition, it is agreed, is the appearance in a sutra of a series of former Buddhas, either the previous incarnations of Gautama or other embodiments of the Tathagata (the distinctions become indistinct in the Jataka tales, the narratives of the former appearances). The reappearance of the Buddha raises the question of nirvana. How did Gautama, successor of seven or twenty-four or more Buddhas, emerge from nirvana, the condition of the puffing out, the cooling of mortal existence and desire, in order to move on earth again to teach and exemplify dharma?[17] And there is a further question. If Gautama was the reappearance of Sumedha, who according to the Jataka story was dedicated to future Buddhahood by the realized Buddha Dipankara "four asankheyas and a hundred thousand cycles ago," may he not return again? The Buddha, in a Pali text, graciously promises as part of a playful look into the future, the coming of Metteya (Maitreya in the Mahayana Sanskrit), the friendly Buddha of the future:

> At that period, monks, there will arise in the world an Exalted One named Metteya, Arahat, Fully Awakened, full of wisdom and a perfect guide, himself having trodden the path to the very end; with knowledge of the worlds, unsurpassed as an educator, teacher of gods and men, an Exalted Buddha, just as in the present period I am now.[18]

Although Old Wisdom scriptures included the notion of a multiplicity of Buddhas and a future Buddha, it is clear that their main concern remained the disciplines of liberation leading to the ineffable nirvana—the realm of the complete dissolution of the unwholesome roots of greed, hate, and delusion; where the skandhas are completely dissolved; without foundation, without beginning or end; where there is no coming, no going, no striving, neither ceasing-to-be nor coming-to-be. But the multiplicity of Buddhas caused inevitable divergence of doctrine and threw doubt on the permanence of nirvana. One doctrinal development was the compassionate Buddha or bodhisattva attentive to people's needs and prayers; another was a notion of human liberation that would look more and more like a heaven within the imaginable grasp of ordinary people.

Within the old psychological and disciplinary procedures the germ of religious faith was gestating. Immediately after the Master died a council was called, the legend goes, to set down for the future his authentic rules and discourses. A century later a second council was called at Vaisali to deal with a group of monks who wanted to adapt some of the rules to changed conditions and to question some points of doctrine as interpreted by the Elders, the inheritors of the Disciples. The Elders said No, but the rebels set up a majority caucus called the Mahasanghikas (the great sangha) and went their own way, which was to lead to the Mahayana. In the succeeding century, before Ashoka called the third council, at Pataliputra (Patna), the potential for metaphysical and procedural development had engendered at least eighteen schools differing mostly on doctrinal rather than procedural matters. The speculation about the unknowable that the Master impatiently scorned found much exercise in the numerous viharas, where adherents of different schools spent the rainy seasons amiably debating. Such themes as the bodhisattvas, the Perfections, and the two truths, relative and absolute, the main subjects of early Mahayana sutras, are found in Sarvastivada and Mahasanghika texts, and even in the Pali. And five centuries after the Mahaparinirvana, many Buddhists had a religion as well as a psychic syllabus. As Stcherbatsky said in an oft-quoted passage:

It has never been fully realized what a radical revolution had transformed the Buddhist church when the new spirit, which however was for a long time lurking in it, arrived at full eclosion [sic] in the first centuries A.D. When we see an atheistic, soul-denying philosophic teaching of a path to personal Final Deliverance consisting in an absolute extinction of life, and a simple worship of the memory of its human founder, when we see it superseded by a magnificent High

Church with a Supreme God, surrounded by a numerous pantheon, and a host of Saints, a religion highly devotional, highly ceremonial and clerical, with an ideal of Universal Salvation of all living creatures, a Salvation not in annihilation, but in eternal life, we are fully justified in maintaining that the history of religions has scarcely witnessed such a break between new and old within the pale of what nevertheless continued to claim common descent from the same religious founder.[19]

The Middle Way to Mahayana

The Teacher proclaimed repeatedly that he had come to preach duhkha and the cessation of duhkha. There were certain questions that he refused to answer because they were purely speculative and would require him to characterize the Unconditioned in terms of the empirical realm of discourse, from which definitions must come. The practice of the life directed toward cessation of duhkha does not depend on resolving such matters.

There is still birth, there is old age, there is grief, lamentation, suffering, sorrow and despair, of which I preach the destruction even in this present life. Therefore bear in mind what I have not determined as being undetermined. . . . And why have I not determined them? Because they are not useful, do not belong to the principle of the religious life, and do not tend to revulsion, absence of passion, cessation, tranquility, insight, enlightenment, Nirvana. (Majjhima Nikaya I, 431, Sutta 63, the Cula-Malunkyasutta; also in Warren, p. 122)

Plato figured forth the Absolute Realm of Ideas by myth (the Cave) or projected analogy (the divided line). The Theravadins talk of nirvana mainly in negative terms: the stopping of being, the getting rid of craving. "The steadfast go out [*nibbanti*] like this lamp." The going out of the lamp itself was deliverance of the mind, indicating the unchanging state, where is no-thing, where nought is grasped—the utter extinction of aging and dying (in *BT,* pp. 92–94). There are, of course, poetic passages aimed at suggesting the glories of nirvana, but it is realized that the more urgently evocative they are, the more contradictory they are to the actual unchanging state that must remain incomprehensible—and indescribable—to the temporal mind.

On similar speculative matters the Buddha, always the pastor first, was chary of confusing his people. Vacchagotta the Wanderer asked, "Is there a Self?" If the Teacher had said Yes, he would have been siding with the brahmins and those recluses who were eternalists; and would the reply have accorded with the knowledge that all things are impermanent? If he had said No, he would have been siding with the Annihilationists, and have caused more bewilderment for Vaccha, who would say, "Formerly I had a self, but now no more." To answer such questions would be dogmatic, theoretical.

The Tathagata, O Vaccha, is free from all theories; but this does the Tathagata know,—the nature of form, and how form arises, and how form perishes [and so through the other skandhas, sensation, perception, predispositions, consciousness]. . . .

Therefore say I that the Tathagata has attained deliverance and is free from attachment, inasmuch as all imaginings, or agitations, or false notions oncerning an Ego or anything pertaining to an Ego, have perished, have faded away, have ceased, have been given up and relinquished. (Warren, p. 125)

Theories held for their own sake, or for victory in debate, or in idle conjecture, distract from serious concerns:

To hold that this world is eternal or to hold that it is not, or to agree to any other of the propositions you adduce, Vaccha, is the jungle of theorizing, the wilderness of theorizing, the tangle of theorizing, the bondage and the shackles of theorizing, attended by ill, distress, perturbation and fever; it conduces not to detachment, passionlessness, tranquility, peace, to knowledge and wisdom of Nirvana. This is the danger I perceive in these views which makes me discard them all.[20]

This is certainly a practical answer. Is it only the Teacher's pragmatism that is offered to explain his rejection of speculation, the famous "Silence of the Buddha"? It would seem so from his reply to Malunkyaputta, in a late composition that contains the parable of the arrow, which may go back to the Buddha himself. Malunkyaputta came to him with a list of questions similar to those of Vaccha, questions that came to be known as the Avakata (Pali, Avyakrta), the Undetermined, the Inexpressible, the Unedifying questions. After reminding the man that he had never promised him to elucidate such questions, the Teacher said, "It is as if a man had been wounded by an arrow thickly smeared with poison and the sick man were to say, 'I will not have this arrow taken out until I have learnt whether the man who wounded me belonged to the warrior caste, or to the Brahman caste.'" Then the Buddha points out that the religious life does not depend on any of the dogmas proposed, such as whether the world is finite or infinite, or soul and body are identical, or one exists after death. "There still remain birth, old age, death, sorrow, lamentation, misery, grief, and despair, for the extinction of which in the present life I am prescribing."

The Teacher's pastoral pragmatism did not prevent his Old Wisdom followers (the Avyakrta of Vaccha and Malunkyaputta occur also in the Sarvastivadin Agamas in Chinese, which correspond to the Pali Sutras) from presenting elaborate speculative analyses of questions that were both *necessary* for proper understanding, action, and meditation, and *answerable*. Dependent Genesis, the skandhas, the eightfold path, and techniques of meditation are thoroughly treated.

A second and quickly disposable explanation of the Silence is a lack of finesse in metaphysics. Here we can fairly conjecture that Gautama's six years as a seeker involved intensive debate with all styles of thinkers, including study with Arada and Udraka, who taught him Samkhya and advanced yoga. The two suttas at the beginning of the Digha Nikaya are the Brahmajala (the net of Brahma) and the Samannaphala (the fruits of ascetic-hood). They are a primer of contemporary beliefs, both orthodox brahmanical and, in the second sutta, those of six heterodox schools. The various dogmas are not met head on but are shunted aside for a celebration of the Tathagata's wisdom "beyond the region of logic," a wisdom derived from the trance experience of nirvana.

These, brethren, are those other things, profound, difficult to realize, hard to understand, tranquillizing, sweet, not to be grasped by mere logic, subtle, comprehensible only by the wise, which the Tathagata, having himself realized and seen face to face, had set forth. (Brahmajala 17)

The conclusion of the first sutta is devoted to the stages of the meditative discipline leading to arhantship, a practical subject for seekers of liberation.

All those ascetics and brahmins who construct systems about the past or the future, or both, or hold theories about both, and who make various assertions about the past and future, are all caught in this net of sixty-two subjects. There they are caught in the net, though they plunge and plunge about.

No, it was not ignorance that turned the Master away from speculation but weariness and a brighter light.

The significance of the Silence for the development of metaphysics and the future of Buddhism is indicated by Murti in *The Central Philosophy of Buddhism*:

He characterizes all speculations as ditthi-vada, dogmatism, and consistently refuses to be drawn into the net (jala). He is conscious of the interminable nature of the conflict, and resolves it by rising to the higher standpoint of criticism. Dialectic was born. To Buddha, then, belongs the honour of having discovered the dialectic long before anything approximating to it was formulated in the West. . . . On the opposition of the eternalist and nihilist views (sasvatavada and ucchedavada), Buddha erected another and more fundamental opposition—that between dogmatism (both sasvatavada and ucchedavada are species of dogmatism) and criticism which is the analytic or reflective awareness of them as dogmatic theories. Criticism is deliverance of the human mind from all entanglement and passions. (Pp. 40–41)

Murti's book, subtitled "A Study of the Madhyamika System" is impressive in detail and learning but its basic approach raises and its working out leaves unanswered two questions: (1) How much of the elaboration of rational critique attributed to the Buddha, as in this quotation, can be justly assigned to the early stage of Buddhism as the source of the centuries-later Brahmajala, Samannaphala, Malunkyaputta and Vaccha suttas? (2) Is he correct in attributing the double rejection of eternalism and annihilationism solely to a cerebral critique of dogmatism, rather than to a kind of evidence that was completely acceptable to the followers of the Buddha and to most thinkers of the time: a third state of being, the experience of Otherness that occurs in the mystic's experience?

Logically, the Buddha's own position would reject Eternalism (if there is one idea that one *must* accept as going back to the Founder, it is the insistence on anatta—non-Ego); but, pluralistic and materialistic as it is, it would not reject Annihilationism. The *argument* against ucchedavada is not presented as logic; it is emotional and pragmatic. But that does not make the Buddha and his followers, the realized arhants, opportunistic quibblers. The basis of their conviction was universally accepted as far superior to mere logic and empirical evidence: the state of jnana,[21] the intuitive knowledge of the transcendent and unconditioned, the testimony of the naked psyche exposed to the utmost glare of the Ultimate, the blending of the self in enstatic depersonalization with timeless pure being.

Murti, in his eagerness to establish the Buddha as a metaphysician and Madhyamika as the logical outcome of his dialectic, ignores the dozens of repetitions of the stages of discipline toward Enlightenment and higher knowledge, especially the concluding passages of the first two Digha suttas. The abhinna "omniscience" of former existences would provide a more parsimonious reason for rejecting Nihilism than the assumption that the Buddha founded dialectic.[22]

But the scorn of ditthi (Sanskrit, drsti), however motivated, can still be taken as a first step toward the basic doctrine of Madhyamika thought, Emptiness, sunyata. Kant's *Critique*, which Murti says is nearest to the Madhyamika's concept of philosophy, "shows the futility of all views, of Reason itself to reveal to us the unconditioned; . . . it exposes the pretensions of dogmatic philosophy to give us pure knowledge" (p. 213). Correspondingly, mystical experience also induces a quizzical attitude toward the firmness of empirical conclusions. When one has seen eternity "like a great ring of pure and endless light" (Vaughan), one tends to look beyond sunrise, sunset, and time that passes. When all things merge into the One (Plotinus and Eckhart), and distinction and definitions lose their sharpness, this finite and conditioned flux can be taken seriously only conditionally—only to the extent that one must, with senses that function by trained discernment, which is less than global intuition. So the main content of sunyata, that the phenomenal and Unconditioned are both undiscussable, that there is a relative truth for application in the phenomenal world, and an Absolute truth for Sunday, and that samsara and nirvana are one, is comprehensible whether as the paradox that lies in wait for any attempt to explain the world, or as makeshift verbalization of the merging, oceanic state of things experienced by such mystics as the Enlightened One.

A final way to explain the Buddha's refusal to discuss the Undiscussables like rebirth and nirvana would be that (unlike the Buddhists, who like most people needed rewards and punishments) he did not believe in such hypotheses or, like Laplace, had no need of them. As Oldenberg put it almost a century ago, "through the shirking of the question as to the existence or non-existence of the ego, is heard the answer, to which the premises of the Buddhist teaching tended: The ego is not. Or, what is equivalent: The Nirvana is annihilation."[23] A rigid following of the implications of Impermanence would have put Gautama side by side with the thoroughgoing materialist, Ajita, one of the six unorthodox thinkers presented (not very fairly) in the Samannaphala (see Chapter 4 below). Ajita said, "A man consists of the four elements, and when he dies and is cremated the elements return to their places. Both fools and sages with the dissolution of the body are cut off and destroyed, and after death they are not."

But the Buddha's basic message was the cessation of pain, a state of peace upon "the complete and utter dissolution of the unwholesome roots of greed, hate, and delusion" (or passion, aversion, and confusion). He and the arhants achieved bodhi, or nirvana, the blowing out of ego and desire, *in this life*. Parinirvana was the act of moving off where the body could no longer be seen. Murti says:

> His position was not Nihilism even in an implicit form. Neither Buddha nor any Buddhistic system ever took this to be so. Buddha avers in the most explicit terms the existence of Nirvana as the implication of his doctrine and the spiritual discipline. Numerous are the passages in which Nirvana is spoken of in positive terms as reality beyond all suffering and change, as unfading, still, undecaying, taintless, as peace, blissful. It is an island, the shelter, the refuge and the goal. (Pp. 47–48)

At this point we reunite the Buddha and Buddhists. The intellectual mastery leading to spiritual and physical mastery cannot remain, on their terms, a this-worldly achievement. The supreme state cannot be described in empirical terms, nor can rebirth. Upanishadic atmavada (belief in atman, the soul) had no trouble with rebirth or nirvana. It had the integral atman transmigrate to a new incarnation if it had not achieved moksha, or rejoin Brahman, the Absolute, if it had. But Buddhist dharma was less explicit:

> There is no element which migrates from this world to the other; but there is realization of the fruits of karma, as there is continuity of causes and conditions. It is not as it were that one, dropping out from this world is born into another, but there is continuity of causes and conditions. (Salistamba Sutra, in Murti, p. 33)

The question of how karma operates across generations of the not-yet-liberated should perhaps be spurned as Avyakrta. Both Vaccha in Sutta 72 of the Majjhima Nikaya and Malunkyaputta in Sutta 63 present the four subjects in practically the same form. Murti's formulation (p. 38) of the tetralemmas is:

1. Whether the world is eternal, or not, or both, or neither;
2. Whether the world is finite (in space), or infinite, or both, or neither;
3. Whether the Tathagata exists after death, or does not, or both, or neither;
4. Is the soul identical with the body or different from it?

Tradition fails to give the last question the fourfold form.

The Avyakrta indicate, as Thomas pointed out (p. 128), that "the Buddhists had reached the consciousness of a state of which neither existence nor non-existence could be asserted." The Buddha, who is given credit by Murti for again choosing the Middle Path of refusing to choose between Eternalists and Nihilists, was not merely suspending judgment, like any skeptic. He was elevating discussion to the higher level of criticism; thus he discovered dialectic.

Nor is it ignorance of metaphysics. He was not only conversant with philosophical speculations of the time, but was himself a metaphysician of no mean order. By his penetrative analysis he had reached a position which transcended and annulled the dogmatic procedure of Reason. His rejection of speculative metaphysics was deliberate and sustained. Criticism itself is philosophy for him. (P. 47)

We are now at the third formulation of the Middle Way, which gives the sanction for the broad explorations of the Mahayana, of which the central and most flexible position, acccording to Murti, is the Madhyamika.

Dialectic is engendered by the total opposition between *two* points of view diametrically opposed to each other. And the required opposition could have been provided only by the atma-view of the Brahmanical systems and the anatmavada of earlier Buddhism. The Ratna-Kuta-Sutra . . . makes this explicit:
"That everything is permanent" is one extreme; "that everything is transitory" is another . . . "that atman is" (admeti) is one end; "that the atman is not" is another; but the middle between the *atma* and *nairatmya* views is the Inexpressible. . . . It is the reflective view of things. This is the Middle Path (madhyama pratipad) of the Madhyamika. (Pp. 27–28)

Under the earlier interpretation of Dependent Origination (Pratityasamutpada), as "the causal law regulating the rise and subsidence of the several elements," the middle path was that taken in the answer to Vaccha, the steering clear of both Eternalism and Nihilism. The Madhyamika proposes that interrelatedness refers not to temporal sequence but to "the essential dependence of things on each other; i.e., the unreality of separate elements." Pratityasamutpada "is now equated with Sunyata—the empirical validity of entities and their ultimate unreality. The middle path is the nonacceptance of the two extremes—the affirmative and the negative (the sat and asat) views, of all views." The concept of sunyata, Emptiness, the receptacle, the potential, occupies a position corresponding to the Absolute of the Brahman, but in a much more dynamic relation with appearance and the phenomenal. Along with the bodhisattva ideal, it is the distinguishing characteristic of Mahayana.

Mahayana pointed to the arhant as the highest but still incomplete ideal of Hinayana: by striving to escape from samsara's demands, he was still mired in them; by yearning for nirvana, he clung to Ego; by debating on the dharmas (the basic realities of existence, and what Stcherbatsky called the Central Conception of Buddhism), the Old Wisdom Abhidharma books failed to declare their true emptiness. The Mahayana, once it declared *any* judgment about this world inherently faulty because it was filtered through man's perceptions and reason, and because no dharma had its own-being (every entity and incident being contingent in Pratityasamutpada), was free to propose the double truth: a pragmatic, as-if acquiescence to the physical demands of samsara, and the deep-down conviction that only the Void, sunyata, the infinite potential of the Tao, was Ultimate. As Milarepa sang, "Form, Voidness, and Non-distinction / Are the three real Refuges." The Bodhisattva, applying mystical prajna and practical skill-in-means, or wisdom and compassion, demonstrated that samsara and nirvana were equally unreal, and *sub specie* sunyata, the same. So a subplot of the Mahayana sutras was to make the arhant realize that his yearned-for nirvana was merely a pusillanimous haven-grasping, and make him seek true manhood in aiming to become a bodhisattva and eventually a Buddha.

Nirvana—A Preliminary Discussion

The bodhisattva is Mahayana's successor to the arhant, the ideal of Old Wisdom discipline. In preparation for later discussion of arhant, bodhisattva, and the changing function of nirvana, it would be well to look at the elements that came together in the training of the arhant.

If the origin of duhkha is craving for experience and the assertion of the ego, cessation and liberation come with the putting down of desire; and wisdom, the chief of the perfections, is the inspiration and guide. Old age, perhaps guided by wisdom in its common western sense, brings a diminution of desire. Kephalos, the aged host of Socrates at the beginning of *The Republic,* quotes with approval a conversation on sex with the aged Sophocles, who said, "I feel as if I had escaped from a mad, cruel slave driver." Since sexual activity of any kind is forbidden in the first of the Sangha's four Parajika rules, violation of which calls for permanent expulsion, clearly arhantship is easier for the aged. The usual justification for the rule is not puritanism or asceticism, but the various hindering attachments that accrue from sexual relations: the woman herself, then the children and the family obligations, as well as domination by sexual need.[24]

Kephalos is "philosophical" (perhaps too much so) about the departure of lust. A quality of age is acceptance, a sense of proportion, of the relatedness of things and the inevitability of some. "A philosophical attitude" affords detachment of the kind (but not the degree) required by the Buddha; it sees "nothing personal" in the violence of nature or of an enemy, weakness in friends, accident. It is a pale suggestion of the "even-mindedness" of the fourth Unlimited, the ideal of the arhant's emotional state.

Yogic discipline, which seems to have antedated the foreign Aryan invasions of India, has its own procession of stages leading up to samadhi, the state of realization; it is interpreted by orthodox brahmins and Vedantists as the blissful merging of atman and Brahman. Christian mystics, following similar meditative disciplines, strive to achieve what they call the ecstatic union, if not identity, with God; Jewish mystics, diffident and mindful of the terrible transcendence of God, go no farther than being in "the presence of the Throne." Sénart declared in 1889, "Buddhism is not a philosophic sect; it is a system of Yoga. . . . This path, though it begins with right views, is in fact a Path for the Mystic, and ends in right ecstasy. It is in fact a rational mysticism."[25]

But the mystic's trance can come without deliberate training or even desire, as it did to the child Siddhartha sitting under the tree in the field his father was ceremonially ploughing.[26] As psychologists study the phenomenon in itself or in the context of psychedelic drugs used with or without reference to religious practices, it becomes clear that the enstatic state is related to the religious experience only by definition. Ancient yoga is atheistic; the Ishvara (deity) of Patanjali is not essential to yoga.

Enlightenment, bodhi, nirvana, arhantship can be taken, then, as a resultant of any or all of the above components. What they bring, together or severally, is a lessened concern with the passions, the events, the conditioned crosscurrents of daily life. The arhant of the Old Wisdom discipline appears, despite all the injunctions of friendliness and sympathy for all, a remote and forbidding figure, detached from craving and cooled away from the warmth of this world. The growing numbers of people, especially the laity, needed a different psychological type for immanence, a more engaged ideal. The word and the concept of the bodhisattva grew to fill the need.

FOUR

Orthodoxy, Heterodoxy, and Buddhism

A man seeking a way out of an intolerable situation must use the means available. Gautama's given was life as he knew it, the social and political structure of his day, the attempts of others to explain, exploit, or escape the conditions of life. As thinker, as a member of a ruling oligarchy, he had to face the spreading power of the brahmins as a caste, as priests, as cultural determinants. As a seeker of personal peace he had to learn what the lush forest growths of ascetics, mystics, materialists, agnostics, and other heretics were saying. The closely dependent tribal structure of many regions (janapada) was breaking down, requiring a search for new norms of social relations, and at the same time affording opportunities for independent economic activity and accumulation of personal rather than tribal wealth.[1]

Some assumptions of the day he too assumed, such as karma and rebirth, presumably because they bespoke a system of active personal responsibility. The practice of yoga, which he had learned from Arada and Udraka on first "leaving the house," likewise made for discipline and the state of mental control aimed for in the eighth step of the Path. A degree of asceticism that brought freedom from family and social distractions, without subjection to extreme austerity, the very process of self-assertion by negation, would fit into the way of life he would live and teach.

The old gods, whether of the Vedas or the ancient, pre-Aryan, ever-renewing local cults, were not rejected; they were merely given an auxiliary role in the dharma. But the ritual of worship of the gods, the arrogated and by now exclusive role of the brahmins, was scorned as ineffectual; and sacrifice, the traditional fulcrum of brahmin power, was rejected as worse than ineffectual. The pretensions of the brahmins to social, intellectual, and moral pre-eminence were refuted; and caste was washed away at the vihara door.

As we have seen, the Buddha trod two middle paths in guiding his followers to liberation. The first was the one proposed to the five original disciples in the deer park, rejecting both the pursuit of desires ("base, common, leading to rebirth") and the way of austerities. Extreme austerities were practiced by munis, the silent ones, vratyas, priests of primitive cults, and assorted solitary psychotics; all of whom sought the magical powers bought by severe penances. Some achieved a power beyond magic: the trance of insight into ultimate mystery, the bliss of oneness of self-and-not-self, the state that was identified as mukti, liberation from mortal limitations. The Buddha's program included a form of liberation, for which he borrowed the term nirvana, but he rejected as "grievous, ignoble, and useless" the pursuit of pain and hardship.

The second path was on a more abstract level, and concerned the nature of liberation. Did the soul put on immortality? Or was liberation of a less glorious order, the gross disintegration of the temporarily associated physical elements of the now dead mortal?

The simple logic that later developed into the web of causation and the skandhas-bundle should have thrown the man who felt anitya, duhkha, and anatman with every breath, into the easy void of the annihilationists. The belief in rebirth was so recently accepted among the more culturally pretentious, the brahmins and their followers, that Gautama need not have allowed it a place of contention in discussing the afterlife.[2] It was probably of wider and more ancient acceptance among the non-Vedic believers in Buddha-country in the eastern Ganges region, but still not so strong as to demand acquiescence.

The Responsible Buddha

But if anything is clear at 2500 years' distance, it is that Sakyamuni, the man who "left the house," left wealth, favor, a loving wife, and a new baby at the undue age of twenty-nine, was sooner a moralist and teacher than a rationalist. His philosophical training, at Kapilavastu and Rajagriha and Sravasti, was thorough enough to make him suspect that rigid logic applied to the modal world must lead to contradiction. More important, as an altruist, the Buddha could not offer his hearers an end that was an unpromising full stop, with no reason for virtue or hope of compensation for the misery of this life. His world was not yet ready for an existential heroism that declared the reward of virtue to be ataraxia and aesthetic rightness. He held forth nirvana, achieved by the synergism of morality, meditation, and wisdom—nirvana which was not the utter disintegration of the skandhas, nor yet an eternal stasis of the soul.

But before the newly transfigured Buddha took up his ministry he had to face a doubt that was profoundly apt, historically and psychologically: Why bother?

"Now if I proclaim the doctrine and other men are not able to understand my preaching, there would result but weariness and annoyance to me. . . . With great pains have I acquired it. Enough! why should I now proclaim it? This doctrine will not be easy to understand to beings that are lost in lust and hatred. Given to lust, surrounded with thick darkness, they will not see what is repugnant, abstruse, profound, difficult to perceive, and subtle."

When the Lord pondered over this matter, his mind became inclined to remain in quiet, and not to preach the doctrine. Then Brahma Sahampati . . . thought: "Alas! the world perishes! Alas, the world is destroyed! if the mind of the Tathagata, of the holy, of the absolute Sambuddha inclines itself to remain in quiet, and not to preach the doctrine." (Mahavagga 1, 5)

Rishis who had gone to the forest and found their truth did not come back to the town grove or stoa to profess their wisdom. They would do as the new Buddha, who "sat cross-legged at the foot of the Bodhi tree uninterruptedly . . . enjoying the bliss of emancipation," and declare, "Happy is the solitude of him who is full of joy, who has learnt the Truth." They might manifest love or indulge their remnant of human vanity and enjoy some human companionship by letting pupils sit before them, as did the Upanishadic seers and Sakyamuni's teachers, Arada and Udraka. But unlike modern international, jet-propelled maha-swamis, they felt no urge to make a lion's roar of their message. Another reason it would have been natural for the Buddha to let the world go by is the nature of the mystical experience and its aftereffects. Clearly, whatever ratiocinations went on in Sakyamuni's brain that night under the bo tree, the climax was the ultimate trance, the dhyanas. It is a well-known fact that one of the sequelae of such an achievement or seizure is a reapportionment of values, often antinomian—"all is dross that is not Helena." Human concerns pale into pettiness after the blaze of supernal light, the meeting with God (as the Christian mystics saw it), or with one's own being.

But the Master defied the example of the Wanderers and his own strong desire to remain undisturbed in mukti, the blessed state of nirvana. He returned to the painfully living, to teach them duhkha and the cessation of duhkha, taking his nirvana with him to teach as the more proper end than nullity when the skandhas were loosed, a brighter light when the lamp was shattered. The logic of phenomenalistic causation? But he had been there! And he remained "cooled," liberated. But it was not the soul, the atman that inhabited, or experienced, or rejoined nirvana. Nirvana was not a place, like Heaven, or a state of bliss, or another term for the Absolute of the Upanishadic seers. The Buddha's Middle Way called for a new definition of the After-This-Life, because his This-Life was so different from the notions of his brahmin adversaries. If, as Foucher puts it, "the molds through which our perceptions of things flow are no less of an illusion than the perceptions themselves," how could the Buddha let his followers talk of a Soul, an Ego?

Atman Rejected

This is the fundamental "heresy" of Buddhism from "orthodox" Brahminism.[3] But the doctrine of atman rejected in Buddhist nairatmya was, by an irony that was to find rebirth in many similar doctrinal cooptations in Hindu history, not yet orthodox. Orthodox brahmin doctrine at that time was concerned with ritual and sacrifice, and speculation thereon probed the origins of their power over the gods. Knowledge of the symbolism took its place beside the mastery of words and procedures as a way of gaining cattle and offspring and power over enemies. Knowledge about the soul was sought by recluses at the far edge of the Vedic camp. The main body was the hymns themselves in their wonderful variety: celebrations of the gods, philosophical ponderings, riddles, charms, medical lore, with historical, polemical, anthropological content. Then grew the body of commentary, the Brahmanas, which give the rules for the sacrifices and explain the samhita, the collection of mantras used in the sacrifice. At the next level of abstraction are the Aranyakas, the "forest treatises," supposedly for those who have retired into the forest and are unable to perform full-scale sacrifices; they learn instead the symbolism of the rituals and meditate on them. Even more abstruse are the Upanishads, which, though nominally attached to one or another of the four Vedic collections, moved off to their own level. Their primary subject was Brahman, the Ultimate, the Absolute, the only reality behind appearance and change. And identified with Brahman was atman, the Self, the true soul.

ORTHODOXY, HETERODOXY, AND BUDDHISM 51

The Upanishads developed the quest for knowledge in two directions: the kind of power desired, and the kind of knowledge. The conquest of death by knowledge of one's true nature was the goal. In the Chandogya Upanishad (6, 16) the sage Uddalaka reaches, by a process of reasoning, the conclusion that those who know the truth about Being are merged in it never to be reborn. Rebirth is touched on in this work and treated more specifically in its companion, the Brhadaranyaka.

What was the relation between these two Upanishads, generally accepted as the earliest, and Buddhist thought? They are usually assigned to no later than the sixth century[4] and therefore could have made their way to the ears of Buddha or his disciples. But there are two reasons why this is unlikely. First, the Upanishads were secret. The term implies "a secret sitting for instruction," available only to the proved initiate. "Therefore only to his eldest son shall the father as Brahman communicate it, but to no one else, whoever he may be"[5]—"or to a worthy disciple," translates Nikhilananda (Chandogya 3, 11, 5) (*Upanishads*, p. 297). "This shall be communicated to no one, except the son or the pupil" (Brhadaranyaka 6, 3, 12). Even religious secrets can leak out, however, and in time the Upanishadic teachings were taken over by brahmins from their kshatriya originators (who had not been preoccupied with rituals and sacrifices and the perquisites thereof). And brahmins were among the Buddha's earliest converts. Might they not have presented the new version of immortality in the debates leading to conversion?

Here the second reason enters. The Buddha-country was quite remote from the original center of brahmin culture. Thomas says:

> This centre was in the West, chiefly in the region between the Ganges and Jumna. It gradually permeated the East of India, but there are indications to show that the East, and Magadha especially, were long considered unfit for the habitation of brahmins. But at least as a sacrificial system Brahminism had established itself there before the development of Buddhism. There was not the same reason why the study of the secret doctrine should have spread as early as the brahmin cult, which performed the sacred rites for individuals at every stage of life. (*History of Buddhist Thought,* p. 83)

Although the Pali term for the opponents is samana-brahmana, not all of them are real shramans, recluses. "The brahmins are never referred to as living an ascetic life," says Thomas (p. 86); rather, Majjhima 3, 167, refers to people "running like brahmins at the smell of a sacrifice."[6] It seems unlikely that any converts had been Upanishadic sages, or knew their teachings. A key test of this is whether the scriptures manifest any real understanding of the Brahman–atman mystery.

Buddhism makes no mention of Brahman (neuter) as the one reality, or of any identity of this with the atman. The Brahma that we find so often mentioned in Buddhist writings is a personal god ruling over a separate region of the universe, and born and reborn as inevitably as any other being. But this Brahma is never brought into relation with the Buddhist theory of the self. (Thomas, p. 96)

On the other hand, there is a clear confrontation between Upanishadic and Buddhist thought on this matter of the soul (without direct reference, of course) in the Chandogya. Prajapati tries to locate the atman, which is free from death and sorrow, and has real thoughts, in the body. By elimination, it is not in the physical personality, the dream state, deep sleep; so the conclusion is, "the body is mortal but is the support of the immortal bodiless atman" (8, 12, 1). The Buddha, however, showed that none of the various aspects of the personality can be related to the atman, mainly because of their impermanence (Majjhima 1, 232). Jayatilleke says:

The main difference in the attitude of Prajapati and the Buddha is that the former assumes the existence of an atman and on failing to identify it with any of the states of the personality, continues to assume that it must exist within it and is not satisfied with the results of the purely empirical investigation, while the latter as an Empiricist makes use of the definition of the concept of the atman without assuming its existence (or nonexistence) and is satisfied with the empirical investigation which shows that no such atman exists because there is no evidence for its existence. (*Early Buddhist Theory of Knowledge*, p. 39)

A possible reference to Prajapati appears in the Brahmajala Sutta's analysis of various theories; one theory has it that "the soul after death has form, is without defect and is conscious [Digha 1, 31]. Prajapati's theory assigned all these characteristics to the soul after death." There may also be reference to Uddalaka's different theory, that the soul would be without form, defect, or consciousness. (Chandogya 6, 10, 1) [7]

Rebirth Without Atman

Rebirth would be rejected, it seems, along with the atman. Without a soul, what is there to be reborn? This is the question which Theravadins still strive to answer, and which the Mahayana steers around. Why did the Buddha accept rebirth as the fate of the unenlightened? An easy answer is that the belief was in the air, perhaps as the idea of the

Creation existed in Newton's time. But the Buddha could not have accepted rebirth easily, for two reasons.

First, it was not in the air. It was of only recent growth. The early Upanishads speculated much on the afterlife, including rebirth, which is ruled out at one point: "The world of men is obtained through a son only, not by any other means" (Brh. 1, 5, 16). Jayatilleke says:

The first clear reference to the theory of rebirth or the return to earth to become man or animal is found at Brh. 6.2.15–16, Ch. 5.10.1–8 and Kaus. 1.2. It is only in the Katha Upanisad that for the first time the theory is generally accepted (1.2.6; 2.2.7) and thereafter we find its acceptance in the Mundaka (1.2.10), Svetasvatara (5.12), Prasna (5.3–5) and Maitri (3.1). (Pp. 373–74)

Sakyamuni may have been a contemporary of the composers of the earliest parts of Brhadaranyaka and Chandogya, or a generation or two later. His successors grew up with the doctrine of rebirth, but we must assume that the fundamental acceptance came from the Master. We can trace or conjecture extension or development or even ignoring of early teaching in later Buddhist thought, but not a direct reversal and elision of the Master's thought. And rebirth is firmly embedded in the earliest scriptures.

The second reason for the difficulty of the Buddha's decision was the obvious materialistic tendency in the basic doctrines of causation and body components. There was a strong skeptical and materialist movement in that period of free and intense inquiry. Many thinkers declared the impossibility of knowing anything about survival, and the Buddha acquiesced in their doubts by refusing to describe nirvana or the mechanics of rebirth. In taking the Middle Path between the Eternalists and the Annihilationists—who were materialists—he gave the latter equal place with brahmin orthodoxy. He was aware that his own followers as well as opponents accused him of materialism. His doctrine of anatta caused people to say "the recluse Gotama declares the cutting off, the destruction and the annihilation of a real being" (Majjhima 1, 140), using the same language he used to describe materialism.

There must have been strong compulsion to make the Master reach out for a doctrine fostered by his main intellectual and organizational opponents, the brahmins, one that was and remains difficult to reconcile with his basic ontology. We can only conjecture what made up his mind.

First, we must remind ourselves of his primary impulse. He was a moralist, a prophet, and a physician probing the behavior and spiritual health of his people. Sila was the first of the three guides to salvation; because lower in order than samadhi and prajna, it was more universal. Even those who could not become arhants in this existence could be placed on the road by sila. The Teacher of the wiping away of Ego and desire accepted Even-mindedness, the self-control beyond emotion of the arhant, as the last of the Unlimiteds, the four stations of Brahma; but the first three were the warmly outgoing qualities of Friendliness, Compassion, and (most difficult for petty, insecure mortals) Sympathetic Joy in the happiness of others.

The implications of karma, the working out of individual responsibility that bespoke the spiritual maturity of his message, joined with the moral teachings to urge rebirth on the Teacher. The first civilized cry against God is that He is not just. The best that the Book of Job can do is to state man's protest that the good are not rewarded and the evil do not suffer, and to reply that man must simply have faith that God's universe, which he did not see created and which he cannot understand, will in time work out, even for man's welfare. With rebirth, God's plan has time to work. A standard formulation of one pragmatic justification for rebirth is Swami Nikhilananda's:

> In the narrow span of a single life we cannot possibly reap the fruit of all that we do. It is reasonable to admit the existence of a transmigrating soul in order to substantiate the general belief in moral requital. . . . Our present acts and thoughts are the result of our past and create our future. Man is the architect of his own fate and the builder of his own future destiny. This conviction makes the believer in the doctrine of rebirth responsible for his present suffering and also gives him an incentive for habitual right conduct to build up a happy future. As he accepts with serenity his present ill fortune, he can also look forward to the future with joy and courage. (*The Upanishads,* pp. 57–58)

A second argument for rebirth is a version of Pascal's formula: "You can never know, so you might as well believe." The Buddha voiced purely rational appeals to elite brahmins called "reasonable people" in the Apannaka and Sandaka suttas; if we believe in an afterlife and it does not exist, we are at least praised by the wise in this life; if it does exist, our belief has furthered our progress toward it. If we do not believe, we are condemned in this life, and if it does exist, we will suffer in it. This is "skill in means" for conversion, adaptation of the argument, for whatever it is worth, to the audience. The brahmins had no strong belief in any direction, so an appeal to reason rather than to truth or need was in order.

Buddhists found a verification of rebirth within their own doctrine. In the process of enlightenment, after achieving the eighth jhana, one recalls one's past existences. "I was in such a place with such a name. ... Dying there I was born in such a place. ..." (Digha 1, 81) Since one's reports of trance states, which are essentially indescribable, are conditioned by one's cultural background, one can understand why this evidence of trance content would carry conviction.

Yoga, we have seen, was essential to both Buddhist practice and fundamental theory. It is impossible to establish the time relationship between the various stages of Buddhist yogic theory and the classical statement by Patanjali, the Yogasutras, in probably the second century B.C. Both are formulations of a still-growing body of techniques that date back behind the Indus Valley culture. Thomas Berry sets Buddhist and classical yoga side by side: "For Yoga, liberation is the disengagement of the Purusha, the inner spirit of man, from its seeming contact with phenomenal order. For Buddhism, it is a pure experience of transcendence in which there is no subjective experiencer." *(Religions of India*, p. 77)

It can be assumed that the numerous yogins of Gautama's day, including the two with whom he studied, had individual applications and rationalizations of the basic discipline of yoga, "a conscious, studied, sustained effort at disciplining man's body and mind"; Berry adds, "so that the inner self of man (Purusha) is released from time into eternity, from the conditioned world into the realm of the unconditioned, from multiplicity into unity" (p. 76). Such modern verbalization may apply to those in the devout Patanjali tradition; for many in Gautama's day yoga was simply "for kicks," as it is for many today. And Kosambi, a westernized rationalist, says; "Yoga within limits is a good system of exercise in a hot climate for people who do not live by muscular exertion and hard physical labour. The most that one can attain by it is some measure of control over normally involuntary functions of the body, and good health; but no supernatural powers" (p. 105).

Yoga and Knowledge

Supernatural powers seem to have been the main objective of the non-Vedic recluses who developed yoga, a magic distinct from that of the holy Word of the hymns and rites. These powers were incorporated into the Buddhist meditative system as a subordinated benefit incidental to the performance of the eighth step of the Path, samadhi. These siddhi, which were acquired after achieving the eight dhyanas, were the ability to materialize one's shape, to project an image of oneself to appear anywhere, to levitate, to hear distant sounds, and to know the minds and spiritual states of other individuals. The Buddha also, in the vijja stage, could remember his former existences and could know the passing away and rebirth of others—the "verification" of rebirth mentioned above.[8] The Buddha discouraged the use of siddhi as he scorned magic, sacrifice, and ritual, as irrelevant to the true development of spiritual power for salvation, and a cheap way to make converts (although he used magic to advantage in converting the Jatila Kassapas, as we shall see).

The role of yogic trance, whether in classical yoga or in Buddhism, cannot be appreciated without a preliminary analysis of western attitudes to thought and psychic processes. Only recently have we begun to broaden our notion of the way to knowledge by including more than empirical evidence and discursive reasoning, and returning, after three centuries of the scientific revolution, to the contributions of intuition, the unconscious, and the conditions called altered states of consciousness.[9] In India both the sramanic and the orthodox Vedic traditions have given priority to processes that evoked the identity of being and thought, that fused the self and the world in a state of enhanced consciousness.

But to assume a "non-rational" source for certain kinds of knowledge is to imply that this kind of thinking is somehow inferior to "rationality" itself. A logic of symbols such as India's proceeds not only on assumptions but on modes of perception which happen to have been suppressed in Western thinking for many centuries through specialization in a certain kind of consciousness. There is nothing "mystical" or "uncanny" in this kind of thought if one uses the word "mystical" in the sense which Santayana gives it: the most *natural* mode of thinking. (Lannoy, *The Speaking Tree*, p. 273)

In contrast, Max Weber's approach is typically "western": he traces "technologies of contemplation," one of which is Yoga, to

the ancient magical experience of auto-hypnosis and related psychological states, [which] is induced by physiological effects of controlled regulation and temporary stoppages of breathing and its reaction upon brain functions. The emotional states resulting from such practices were valued as holy and cherished as blissful removal of the soul. They formed the psychological basis of the philosophical holy teachings which in a framework of metaphysical speculations sought rationally to establish the significance of these emotional states. (*The Religion of India,* p. 163)

In what way can we attribute intellection to samadhic states? In the Nikayas the Buddha is a jnana-vadin, one who "knowing, knows and seeing, sees, having become sight and knowledge," says Jayatilleke (p. 418), who relates this kind of knowing to that of the later Upanishads, in which the "traditional ways of knowing hitherto accepted are discarded as far as the knowledge of the atman goes and 'seeing' acquires the new connotation of extrasensory perception.... One *sees* (pasyate) while in meditative rapture (dhyamanah) by the purification of knowledge (jnana-prasadena) and not by any of the sense organs." Knowledge derived from this means of perception is called jnana (pp. 61–62). But this direct intuitive knowledge was not sufficient for Buddhist enlightenment. Like the materialists, the Buddha recognized the need for sense perception and objective validation, as well as discursive inference based on the belief in causation. As a teacher and practicing moralist, he knew that the higher reaches of jnana were available only to the few, and then only rarely without intense discipline, both intellectual and meditative. If Sariputra and Maudgalyayana achieved arhantship quickly, they brought to their new teacher long philosophical training. "I do not say that one can win the final knowledge at the very beginning; it is had from a gradual discipline, a gradual mode of action and conduct" (Majjhima 1, 479). And for the great majority of his disciples, who could never hope for enlightenment in this existence, the beginning moral disciplines, the early steps in the forty objects of meditation, and an elementary intellectual grasp of the Four Noble Truths provided a salutary start on the path to liberation.

Both the Buddha and the yogins knew that meditative discipline brought much profit even without the final victory. If, as the Quakers say, "God speaks in the soul only when the person is silent" (Weber, p. 163), even the early stages of training prepare a quiet place for the troubled mind, a lowering of confusing tensions. Then the intuitions, always at work in the unconscious, have less surface tension to break through with answers to problems both superficial and deep-seated. In equanimity and mindfulness achieved through control of the ego, objectivity can prevail and "facts" can be seen in new relations and proportions. So, while Weber's and Kosambi's reflections on the doubtful intellective content of yoga are justified, the salubrious effects of meditative discipline even apart from its religious context are attested by many cultures. The relation of yoga to religion becomes a matter of choice and definition. Patanjali inserted Ishvara, the personal Lord, into his system because yoga is a spiritual discipline that "in the highest state of seedless Samadhi should be interpreted as man's entry into the world of the sacred out of the profane, into the unconditioned world . . . , into the absolute, the blissful world of eternity beyond the world of changing phenomena" (Berry, p. 108). But yoga could stand as well without the presence of the Lord, nor does it require religious devotion to arrive at its complete spiritual fulfillment. Ishvara is outside the tradition of Samkhya, from which Patanjali's yoga derives. Samkhya is part of the strong naturalist and atheistic movement in early India that also includes the Ajivika, Carvaka, Jain, and Buddhist versions. Patanjali, by calling Ishvara one of many Purushas, broke the pure Purusha-Prakriti dualism of Samkhya and opened the way for the eventual identification of the personal deity with the absolute Brahman.

In early Buddhist times the samadhic experience of the Materialists did not move them out of their nonspirituality. They disavowed that yogic rapture proved anything but itself. The Brahmajala Sutta refers to "a class of Materialists who, while valuing the attainment of yogic states from a purely pragmatic point of view, denied the epistemic claims made on their behalf."[10] Ajita Kesakambali seems to have been one of these. As a positivist and empiricist, he is said to have denied both the existence of the soul and the value of morals or religious practices. His reliance on sense perception as the ultimate basis of knowledge raises an interesting question of the nature of jnana, the knowledge that comes from higher intuition. Vivid as it is, is it sense perception? Are the "higher knowledges," the abhinnas, knowledge? Of the six abhinnas (magic power, the divine ear, knowledge of others' thoughts, remembrance of former existences, knowledge of the passing away and rebirth of beings, and knowledge of the destruction of the asavas), the Buddhists regarded the three last, the vijja, as the verification of rebirth. "When the defilements of the mind [asavas] are eliminated and the mind is prone to dispassion and is developed by dispassion, it becomes supple as regards the things verifiable by higher knowledge" (Samyutta 3, 232). But the disrespectful yogin Ajita remarked that "there are no well behaved recluses and brahmins of good conduct who can claim to know the existence of this world as well as

ORTHODOXY, HETERODOXY, AND BUDDHISM

the next by realizing this themselves with their higher intuition" (Jayatilleke, p. 99).

The empirical argument that the soul cannot exist apart from the body because it cannot be seen separate from the body is brought to bear against attempts to describe the shape and color of the soul as observed in trance states. Such observations could not be demonstrated for all to see;[11] no matter how "real" they are to the beholder.

The Disputants

Santayana's phrase "the cockpit of learning" would apply to the intellectual vitality of the Buddha's time, in which brahmins, skeptics, empiricists, eternalists, annihilationists, and determinists swirled in debate and temporary alliances, while the Buddha himself stood outside and took on a disputant only when directly attacked. The actual ideas at issue are suggested, rather inadequately, in the first two sutras of the Digha Nikaya. The "net of Brahma" presents what were supposed to be all of the sixty-two possible views about the beginnings of things and the future held by various schools. Some positions are included to exhaust all the logical possibilities (it is held in eight ways that the self is neither conscious nor unconscious after death), and Thomas holds (p. 77) that not one of the sixty-two doctrines mentioned can be certainly identified with any brahmin school—an overstatement, but understandable in view of the Buddhists' lack of concern for exact statement about rival systems, and for refuting them. The second Digha sutra, on the fruits of asceticism, has the interest of personality in its empaneling and interrogation of six samana-brahmana (not all of them brahmins) by King Ajatasatru. The treatment of these historical figures is less factual and less analytical than that in the Jain work, the *Sutrakritanga*.

Of the six heterodox thinkers the last, Sanjaya Belatthiputta, receives the roughest treatment, being set down for dullness, stupidity, verbal jugglery, and eel-wriggling. He is a careful skeptic who irritated the Buddhists not by his opposition but by his denial of the possibility of knowledge.

If you ask me whether there is a next world, . . . I do not say so, I do not say thus, I do not say otherwise, I do not say no, I deny the denials . . . there is a result and a consequence of good and evil actions, there is no result or consequence, . . . there is and is no result of good or evil actions, the Perfect One (Tathagato) exists after death, the Perfect One does not exist after death, the

Perfect One both exists and does not exist after death, the Perfect One neither exists nor does not exist after death. (Digha 1, 27)

The passage, from its tone and content, is generally considered satirical, but it does indicate that the skeptics had already proceeded (by the time the sutra was composed) to the formulation of the four-cornered question that would be basic in the approach of Nagarjuna the Madhyamikavadin in 150 A.D. Sanjaya is believed to have been the teacher of the brilliant logician Sariputra, who left him not because of his stupidity but because of the greater appeal of the Buddha.

Sanjaya represents the purely intellectual skeptic, the fourth type mentioned in the Brahmajala. The first three adopt skepticism through fear of falsehood, through fear of involvement, or through fear of interrogation and embarrassment in debate. They are likened by Jayatilleke to the Greek Pyrrho, who was said to have chosen skepticism out of a desire for ataraxia. Sanjaya risked conflict on questions of metaphysics and morals. He granted the possibility of the truth of propositions, but denied the means of knowing. His approach harks back to Yajnavalkya of the Brhadaranyaka Upanishad, who posed the entire question of the rational unknowableness of the atman, which can *not* be described (*neti, neti*) by any but negative epithets, and which he accepts by rational extension. Yajnavalkya may be credited also with an early version of the principle of indeterminacy, the fallibility of the instrument in reaching certain judgments:

For when there is duality, then one smells another, one sees another, one hears another, one speaks to another, one thinks of another, one knows another. But when everything has become the Self, then what should one smell and through what, what should one see and through what, what should one hear and through what, what should one speak and through what, what should one think and through what, what should one know and through what? Through what should one know That owing to which all this is known—through what, my dear, should one know the Knower? (Brh. 2, 4, 14)

Deussen explicates the passage thus:

On careful consideration two thoughts will be found to be implied here: (1) the supreme atman is unknowable, because he is the all-comprehending unity, whereas all knowledge presupposes a duality of subject and object; but (2) the individual atman also ("through whom he knows all this") is unknowable, because in all knowledge he is the knowing subject ("the knower"), consequently can never be object. Essentially these two thoughts are one; for the individual atman is the supreme atman, and in proportion as we rise to this knowledge the

ORTHODOXY, HETERODOXY, AND BUDDHISM 61

illusion of the object vanishes, and the knowing subject alone remains without object. (Pp. 79–80)

Sanjaya's skepticism at certain points runs parallel with the Buddha's principle of avyakrta, the undiscussable. He refused to make any of the four alternative judgments on whether the Tathagata exists after death (Digha 1, 27), a position that, as we have seen, leads to the logic of the Sunya of the Madhyamika.

The Samannaphala sutra uses Ajita Kesakambali ("of the hair blanket") as the paradigm of materialism, empiricism, and positivism. Unlike Sanjaya he is assigned a definite stand on the state of the soul and the value in morals and religious practices: there is none. He believed in the four elements (and perhaps a fifth, ether, akasa), and "the soul is the same as the body" (the elements), and therefore he rejected survival. He rejected the authority of the Vedas and of extrasensory abhinna. He is the typical annihilationist (ucchedavada):

> A man consists of the four elements, and when he dies and is cremated the elements return to their places. Both fools and sages with the dissolution of the body are cut off and destroyed, and after death they are not. (Thomas, p. 72)

There is no evidence of Ajita supporting his empiricism with experiment, but another materialist, Payasi, tells the Buddhist disciple Kassapa about his disbelief in the unseen gods (he is unimpressed by the evidence of "clear, paranormal, clairvoyant vision"), and then he tells of a series of rather grisly experiments he has performed to test whether a soul escapes from the body at death. He weighs a body before and after death; it is heavier after death. He flays a man alive and keeps cutting; no soul anywhere. He puts a thief alive in a jar, makes the mouth airtight, and when the man is dead he opens the jar quickly; he sees no soul emerge. (Digha 3, 332, in Jayatilleke, pp. 73, 105)

Purana Kassapa, the first philosopher on King Ajatasatru's list, was a determinist (niyativadin) who proceeded logically to deny karmic influence and therefore responsibility, guilt, and merit. His rigid notion of overall causation left no room for causality on the individual level. A less obvious consequence of his determinism was his claim to omniscience: he claims "with his infinite intelligence he has a direct knowledge of a world that is finite" (Anguttara Nikaya 4, 428, in *ibid*, p. 245). This direct knowledge, we are told in the commentary to the Brahmajala sutra (and we could have guessed), comes from yogic experience. We must assume that, given the complete interrelatedness of events in a finite, determined cosmos, a single breakthrough into the structure at any stage will empower extrapolation into knowledge of the entire system.

Makkhali Gosala, like Purana, was primarily a determinist. He denied free will and told the king of a fantastic series of lives, over millions of years, that would eventually work out in salvation. He is best known as the leader of the Ajivikas, a term loosely applied to many kinds of determinists and atheists. Jayatilleke uses the term to specify sramanas who were neither Jains, materialists, nor skeptics (p. 142). Gosala seems to have been a broad-ranging eclectic with a hold on primitive practices. He practiced austerities in the old-fashioned way "to acquire magic power and superhuman insight . . . and it appears that he was capable, either honestly or by fraud, of producing psychic phenomena," says Basham (*History and Doctrine of the Ajivikas,* pp. 50–51). "Gosala also [like the Jains] went naked, but drank and practiced orgiastic sexual rites which doubtless originated in contemporary primitive fertility cults. . . . It should never be forgotten that there always existed a marginal population to whom sorcery, fertility rites and secret tribal cults seemed essential," Kosambi comments (p. 105).

The fourth doctrine the king described is made memorable by being carried to logical absurdity. Pakudha Kaccayana is reported as stating that one who splits a head with a sword does not kill anyone; he merely makes a separation among the seven indestructible bodies (to the four elements, earth, air, water, fire he adds pleasure [sukha], pain [dukkha], and life or soul). There is no slayer or causer of slaying, no bearer, knower, or causer of knowing. The explanation is that Pakudha is a realist: the soul is separate from the body and therefore indestructible. This opinion is contrary to the unifying principle of the materialists, that the soul is identical with the body. Pakudha is supposed to be the a priori thinker described in Brahmajala:

> Herein a certain recluse or brahmin is a reasoner or speculator. By the exercise of reason and speculative inquiry, he arrives at the following self-evident conclusion: the soul and the world are eternal, independent, steadfast as mountain peaks and as firm as pillars—these beings transmigrate and fare on, die and are reborn and exist for ever and for ever. (Digha 1, 16)

Pakudha is considered a precursor of the Vaisesika (particularist) school of philosophy because of his predication of multiplicity and indestructibility of elements. Once the soul is made independent of the body, logically it cannot be destroyed by another combination of elements, a sword. Then death becomes a matter of definition, and the king's report comprehensible.

The Jain

The remaining one of the six philosophers is Nigantha Nataputta (Jnatriputra the Nigrantha, the unfettered one). He is known to us as Mahavira, the great one, the historical founder of Jainism,[12] the rival sect that is closest to Buddhism in background, motivation, and doctrine. The confusion that besets the Nigantha's version of his fourfold vow in the sutta might tempt one to attribute sectarian malice rather than simple ignorance to the composers.

The man who became the Jina (the conqueror) and the last of twenty-four Tirthankaras (masters of the ford passage) was like Gautama a high-born kshatriya. He too earned the designation of "heterodox" for rejecting the authority of the Vedas, along with their gods, priesthood, and social structure. The rules of behavior garbled in the sutta are almost identical with the Buddhist rules for novices. The Jain tradition of the predecessors was borrowed by later followers of the Buddha who made his antecedents other Buddhas or earlier incarnations of himself. Parsva, the legendary immediate predecessor of Mahavira, was probably historical and is placed by the Jains two centuries earlier; he is supposed to have handed down the first four rules: the prohibition of taking life (ahimsa); limitation of possessions; truthfulness; and the prohibition of taking anything not freely offered. When Mahavira set up an order of ascetic monks, he added a fifth rule, celibacy. The vow of the monks substitutes the renunciation of love for the milder "limitation of possessions," and is close to the Buddhist mindful struggle to put down desire.

The significant difference between the two doctrines is the teaching on atman. The Jains accept the soul as the only perfection. It is the active vital principle opposed to the inertia of matter. The soul monads, equal and eternal essences, are capable of infinite wisdom (Weber, p. 194). The process toward salvation is the clearing away of soul-obscuring karma-dust from the jiva, the spirit sullied by life. After the seventh step of the stages of knowledge to final clarity, "the soul of the perfectly redeemed is qualityless, bodyless, soundless, colorless, tasteless, without feeling, without resurrection, without contact with matter, knowing and perceiving 'without analogy,' hence directly and without imagery leading an 'unconditional' existence" (*ibid.*, p. 195).

Comparing the Jain to the Buddhist conceptions of nirvana, its nature and the process of attainment, may help demonstrate the basic differences between the two spiritual disciplines. Both Jains and Buddhists, especially the Theravadins today, emphasize daily practice to reinforce spiritual states, but the Buddhist scriptures stress the need for basic perception of the way things are, an understanding of pain and the cessation of pain, as the guide on the road to liberation. And at the peak of the process, after sila and samadhi, comes prajna, a radical remaking of understanding. At the achievement of nirvana, there is a transmutation into an indescribable state. The Jains specify nirvana as the state of omniscience, when the atman is free from obscuring karma accumulation. The way to liberation is primarily sila. By rigorous obedience to rules for karma-reducing action, the atman, over many generations of integral rebirth, can free itself. The intrinsically omniscient atman is blinkered by eight kinds of karma-particles, the three most important being knowledge-obscuring, perception-obscuring, and intellect-and-morality-obscuring. At the end of the purification process the soul is free to exercise the highest form of knowledge, the paranormal, the omniscience of kaivalya (Pali, kevala). It was a doctrinal requirement for Mahavira to claim omniscience when after many years of rigorous asceticism he achieved liberation.

The Jains have a complex epistemology based on the intellection of the atman. They believe in the independent existence of the material world, and in that sense are pluralists and realists. The highest kind of knowledge is immediate perception obtained by the consciousness of the atman itself. Ordinary sense perception is not immediate, since it depends on the fallible mediation of the senses. Immediate perception is that of samadhic trance, and includes, at the highest level, kaivalya (alone, absolute), or omniscience. Also included in paranormal perception are manahparyaya, entering another mind, or clairvoyance, and avadhi, clairvoyance and clairaudience, similar to the lower abhinna of the Buddhist stages to nirvana. Included in mediate knowledge are sense perception, inference and analogy, and scripture and tradition.

In contrast to the absolute knowledge of the cleansed soul, things on earth are seen as through a glass, darkly. The Jains recommend noncategorical assertion or relativism. One talks of truth guardedly: conflicting statements may be partly true, partly false, or both true and untrue, depending on the point of view. Is a man who is sitting in the library telling the truth when he says he is writing a book? (A "trope of the final cause.") When Mahavira was asked whether the body was identical with the soul or different, he replied, Both. "It is only when 'one understands the true nature of all substance by all the standard means of knowledge (pramana) and all the points of view (naya) that one's knowledge is comprehensive' " (Jayatilleke, p. 164).

Such relativism does not induce a laodicean attitude toward religious duties. Weber points out the interplay of the commandments in fixing the Jains' place in Hindu society. Ahimsa bars them from agriculture and industrial activities dangerous to life, such as those using fire or sharp instruments, and masonry. So they go into commerce and intellectual pursuits. Strict truthfulness involves the Protestant observation that in business "Honesty is the best policy"; so they achieve a solid position in the world of trade. "As with Protestantism, 'joy in possessions' (*parigraha*) was the objectionable thing, but not possession or gain in itself" (Weber, p. 200). So the limitation of possessions prevents ostentatious consumption or display, and Jains support hospitals for both man and beast, public institutions, and charity. But perhaps charity is not the correct word, because, even more strongly than the Buddhists, the Jains beware of "love" and other human involvements. "The heart of Jainism is empty."

What defines heterodoxy in Indian thought is rejection of the authority of the Vedas, whether by the Jains and Buddhists or by the other thinkers of the Samannaphala. Rejection of the Vedas meant rejection of the brahmins, who alone knew the orally transmitted verses and the rituals and sacrifices they include. The social and economic reasons for the widespread defiance of the ceremony-multiplying and fee-seeking priests, especially in the Gangetic plain, are discussed by Weber, *passim*, and Kosambi (pp. 100 ff.). The reasons Buddhists give are narrower.

Buddha, Brahma, and Brahmins

The need to explain one's own origins was one of several reasons for the growth of the Vedic commentaries, the Brahmanas, Aranyakas, and Upanishads. The earliest questionings come in the hymns themselves. The primordial sacrifice of the universal Purusha in Rig 10, 90, gave forth both the Vedas and the castes—with the brahmins at the head:

From that wholly offered sacrificial oblation were born the verses and the sacred chants; from it were born the meters; the sacrificial formula was born from it. . . .

His mouth became the brahman; his two arms were made into the rajanya; his two thighs the vaishyas; from his two feet the shudra was born.

In the Brahmanas Prajapati the personal divinity is the creator of the Vedas, and he is also identified with Brahma. In the Upanishads Prajapati and Brahma are the source of the Vedas and also the first teachers. Thus begins the tradition of the authoritative succession of brahmin teachers from the divine source. In little more than a century after the Parinirvana the Buddhist schools were tracing their origins through a line of teachers back to Ananda and Kassapa and thus to the Buddha himself.

It is this claim to brahmanic succession that the Buddha questions. In the Tevijja Suttanta a young brahmin, Vasettha, states that various brahmins teach different paths to union with Brahma, "as near a village there are various paths, yet they all meet together in the village." The Buddha asks whether any of these, or their teachers back to the seventh generation, or even the ancient rishis versed in the Three Vedas, the very "authors and utterers of the verses, whose ancient form of words so chanted, uttered, or composed the Brahmans of today chant over again or repeat. . . speak thus: 'We know it, we have seen it, where Brahma is, whence Brahma is, whither Brahma is.' " So the brahmins versed in the Three Vedas are like a string of blind men clinging one to the other, and not even the foremost can see. Neither can they point out a way to a state of union with the sun or the moon they pray to and worship. After a few more critiques of unreasonable claims by brahmins, it is clear that the Vedic tradition cannot claim to be revelation.

The Tevijja Suttanta presents also a principled attack on the validity of householding brahmin priests' invocations to the gods (Indra, Soma, Varuna, Isana, Pajapati, Brahma, Mahiddhi, Yama). Living in the world, possessed of wives and wealth, priests are subject to the five things leading to lust (forms, sounds, odors, tastes, substances) and the five hindrances (lust, malice, sloth, pride, and doubt). But Brahma has none of these possessions, sensual appeals, and hindrances. It is absurd "that these Brahmans versed in the Vedas and bearing anger and malice in their hearts, sinful and uncontrolled, should after death, when a body is dissolved, become united to Brahma, who is free from anger and malice, sinless, and has self-mastery."

Here the Buddha has shifted the source of sacerdotal authority from tradition and revelation to the discipline of the priest himself. Then he carries it further: only a Tathagata has the wisdom to teach others. A man listens to the truth, has faith in the Tathagata, then renounces all worldly things, goes into the homeless state, and "passes a life self-restrained according to the rules of the Patimokkha." Such a bhikkhu will be like Brahma, free from anger and malice, pure in mind and master of himself; and after death, when the body is dissolved, it is every way possible that he should become united with Brahma, who is the same.

Here the Buddha is playing fair with his two young brahmin interlocutors: he answers their questions, and ends up in their eschatological context, the atman-Brahman reunification at death (although he refers to the masculine Brahma, not the neuter Brahman). But of course they ask him to accept them as disciples, and they betake themselves for refuge to the Lord, the Truth, and the Brotherhood (Buddha, dharma, sangha).

The Buddhist attitude toward the old Vedic gods cannot be inferred from the Tevijja Suttanta because the strategy there is to handle the questions put by the young brahmins on their own terms, which illustrate the intellectual ambience of the early Upanishads, Jayatilleke believes (Appendix). The Buddha seems to have allowed the gods a place in his mythic structure because they were indispensable phonemes in popular vocabulary, like the gods who put an idea in Achilles' head, or the force in our "God bless you." When directly questioned, his answer is almost a shrug:

You reply "It is clearly observable whether there are gods." Then is it false and untrue?

Anyone who, when asked if gods there be, answers that there are gods, and that this is clearly observable—why an intelligent man will arrive at the same conclusion as to whether there are gods.

Why did you not make this clear at the outset, Lord Gautama?

The world is loud in agreement that there are gods. (Majjhima 107)

In the Buddhist dispensation, the gods can have no real function. In nontheistic ontology, which dispenses with even the late and poetic creation myths of the Vedas, gods must be subject to the same laws of karma and cyclical decay as all other substances and beings, though perhaps on a longer time scale than man. They have lost their Vedic function as personifications of natural forces. They have a poetic function. Before the onslaught of Mara, deities throughout the ten thousand worlds were busy singing the praises of the Great Being; Sakka (Indra), the king of the gods, was blowing the conch-shell; the great black snake-king sang more than a hundred laudatory verses; then they all fled

(Jataka 1,72). Later, Brahma intercedes for man and begs the newly Enlightened One to proclaim the truth. In the Mahayana, Nagarjuna reflects the elaborate superstructure of the other world: Shakra (Sakka), Mara, lord of the Kamadhatu, the six realms of desire, and the Devaraja Mahabrahma in Brahmaloka (the Brahma world). But his real opinion is

> The gods are all eternal scoundrels,
> Incapable of dissolving the suffering of impermanence. . . .
> We know the gods are false and have no concrete being;
> Therefore the wise man believes them not.
> The fate of the world depends on causes and conditions;
> Therefore the wise man does not rely on gods.[13]

In practice, Buddhists find place for local divinities in their art and other conceptualizations (e.g., the yakshis on the Sanchi gates). Tantric Buddhism introduced new gods and goddesses, mainly as personifications. One of the main causes for the decline of Buddhism in India was its gradual loss of separate identity from Hindu devotional practices.

Brahma is the leading god in contact with the world. Like the others, he is part of samsara, and impermanent; he is subject to karmic law and cannot grant liberation. He thinks he is the creator because in one of the world cycles he was the first reborn, and because later beings think so (Digha 2,1; 2,5). But he really knows nothing. Asked by a monk where the four great elements cease, Brahma recites his string of titles (the Supreme, the All-seeing, the Controller, the Creator, etc.), but when pressed for an answer he admits he does not know. "Go now to the Exalted One (the Buddha), ask him your question, and accept his answer" (Digha 2,11,81–3).

Under the aspect of eternal cyclic change (the given of both Hindu and Buddhist belief), the names of divinities that seem to hold sway at any one time "are purely accidental and transitory, mere ripples on the surface of manifoldness in the immense protracted drama. God is therefore *subject* to the inexorable laws of samsara and *karma,* rebirth and causality, . . . the idea of an Almighty responsible for good and evil is alien to Indian thinking" (Lannoy, p. 283). Here is a recent Theravadin statement:

Buddhists do not believe that there is any creator god who has made his laws so imperfectly that they require continual rectification through the prayers of men. If one believes that the universe is governed by a changeable and a changing god—rather than by eternal laws—one will have to try to persuade him to make it better.[14]

Sacrifice, the ultimate instrument of human power over nature and the gods, was also the expression of brahmin dominance. For this reason alone it was scorned by all the Materialist schools, and by the Buddha and his followers. The Buddha also condemned the elaborate rituals as wasteful of effort and material, and immoral for its slaughter of animals. The Upanishadic seers also advocated ahimsa, but could not question sacrifice without denying the authority of the Veda.

Profound social and economic change in Buddha country helped reduce the power of the sacrifice and its officiants. Kosambi reminds us:

Obviously, the simultaneous rise of so many sects of considerable appeal and prominence in one narrow region implies some social need that older doctrines could not satisfy. . . . The existence of new classes in the Gangetic basin of the sixth century is undeniable. The free peasants and farmers were one. The neo-Vedic pastoral class of vaisyas within the tribe was replaced by agriculturists for whom the tribe had ceased to exist. Traders had become so wealthy that the most important person in an eastern town was generally the sreshthi. (P. 100)

The break-up of the psychological security of the Aryan tribal and caste structure is often mentioned as a reason why people turned to the anti-brahminical schools. Behind the dissatisfaction with the sacrificial cult "and the growth of pessimism, asceticism, and mysticism, lay a deep psychological uneasiness," according to Basham (p. 246). "The feeling of group solidarity which the tribe gave was removed, and men stood face to face with the world, with no refuge in their kinsmen." He cites a king in Maitrayani Upanishad 1, 1: "the Pole Star is shaken, the Earth founders; the gods perish. I am like a frog in a dry well."

The new classes benefited from the loosening of bonds. The man of the new propertied class, farmer or merchant, could do what he liked with his wealth, unhampered by tribal duty.

Both agriculturists and traders suffered from the constant warfare which was regularly preceded by Vedic *yajna* fire sacrifice. The trader had to be on good terms with people beyond the territory of his tribe and state; but he also needed safe trade routes, free from robbers. A part of this demand could be satisfied only by the growth of a "universal monarchy," a single state that would end petty warfare and police the entire countryside. But trade always extended beyond political frontiers. (Kosambi, p. 101)

Besides benefiting from the social changes, Buddhism was instrumental in their spread. Visitors to the cave temples and viharas at Ajanta, Bharhut, and Karle are likely to remark at the isolation of the sites and the unascetic quality and quantity of the paintings and sculptures, so full of vitality and the joy of both this world and the next. Some of the donors were merchants from far off. We now know that the viharas were located not only at sacred and perhaps prehistoric sites for pilgrimages but were also placed as travelers' rests along trade routes. The next development was that the monasteries served as depositories for traders' funds and, inevitably, as sources of investment capital.

The old system was restrictive of new farming methods and trade.

> Yajurvedic kingship was a powerful deterrent to unlimited agrarian production by individual householders, and an insupportable burden for the peasantry. Peace and lower taxes were essential. Cattle and other animals were requisitioned in increasing number for the *yajna* without payment. This is shown by Pali stories of royal fire sacrifices. The strain upon regular agriculture was intolerable. (*Ibid.*, pp. 101–2)

From earliest Vedic time fire was the essence of worship, and Agni, whether literally the fire or the personification thereof, was the center of the rite. The Buddha tweaked the brahmins with fire as the instrument of their pretensions and greed. The Jataka stories contain much antiestablishment satire. In Story 144 the Bodhisattva was a brahmin. He is given a sacred fire and an ox by his parents. He decides to sacrifice the ox to Agni, but he needs salt for the ritual and goes off to the village. When he returns he finds the ox has been roasted in Agni's fire and eaten by a band of hunters. They have left only tail, hide, and shanks. The young man says, "My lord of Fire, if you cannot manage to protect yourself, how shall you protect me? The meat being gone, you must make shift with what remains." Then he puts the fire out with water, renounces the world, and attains the Brahma world (von Glasenapp, pp. 151–52).

Another Jataka (543) has the Bodhisattva deflating Vedas, sacrifices, and brahmins:

> If he wins merit who to feed the flame
> Piles wood and straw, the merit is the same
> When cooks light fires or blacksmiths at their trade
> Or those who burn the corpses of the dead. . . .
> These Brahmins all a livelihood require,
> And so they tell us Brahma worships fire;

Why should the increate who all things planned
Worship himself the creature of his hand? (*Ibid.*, pp. 153–54)

The Master is said to have disdained the use of miracles, but the conversion of the brahmin recluse Kassapa was accomplished mainly through fire magic. First he conquered the savage Naga who guarded Kassapa's sacred fire by returning smoke for smoke and fire for fire; next morning he handed over the serpent in his alms bowl. Then Kassapa's followers couldn't split their firewood or light their fires or then extinguish them until the Buddha permitted. In all, the incident (Mahavagga 1, 20) counts 3500 miracles; but the great Kassapa was worth it. And the next item is the terrifying Fire Sermon.

Not only can the householder Mendaka perform the loaves-and-fishes miracle, but so can his wife, his son, and his daughter-in-law. And his slave can plough seven furrows at once with one ploughshare. Mendaka's generosity to the Blessed One and his bhikkhus is the occasion for the Vinaya rules allowing the five products of the cow, and making provision for journeys. "But I do not say that you may, on any pretext whatsoever, accept or seek for gold" (Mahavagga 6, 35). Mendaka is clearly an example of the successful agriculturalist mentioned above (sreshthi; Pali; setthi) who, in an intact tribal structure, would not have been permitted to squander his wealth (which he could not have accumulated in the first place) on nonsacrificing dissidents.

The Master also scorned augury, divination from marks on the body, and interpretation of dreams and omens, and refrained "from seeking a livelihood by such low arts, by such lying practices." He also scorned fortunetelling, astronomical as well as astrological predicting, predicting rainfall and harvest, giving advice on marriage, removing sterility, imparting virility and rendering impotency, etc. These and other paragraphs on conduct in the form of Three Silas are inserted toward the end of the Tevijja Suttanta, perhaps with the implication that such were the legacy of the Vedas.

FIVE

Lamps Unto Themselves

> One has put the emphasis on compassion, universal good will, selfless devotion, and love of one's fellow man extended to all living beings to the point of forgetting one's self completely. The other advocates above all the withdrawal into the self, concentration of spirit, constant vigilance over acts and words and thoughts, solitary meditation, and the complete suppression of all emotion. In short, . . . the first imitates the Bodhisattva but the second the Buddha.
> —Alfred Foucher, *The Life of the Buddha* (p. 245)

This is a rather extreme setting off of the bodhisattva, the benign ideal of the Mahayana, from the arhant, the realization of the Old Wisdom schools' discipline, here derived from the Buddha himself. In working out this contraposition we must consider the nature of the Buddha as human model or superhuman guide; the growth of Buddhism from a discipline to a religion; the relation of the Sangha to the laity; the changing meanings of the terms "Buddha," "bodhisattva," and "nirvana," and the diminishing importance of nirvana as a goal.

It seems safe to conclude that for two or three centuries after the Parinirvana the dominant image of the Master was as a man, no matter what intimations of the supernatural appeared in the stories of his miraculous birth and his past and future existences. He was a man who had achieved a state called Enlightenment, preached a new insight into man's painful existence, organized his followers into an Order, and pointed the way toward their enlightenment. On achieving this state of nirvana they were called "arhants," a term meaning "worthy, deserving," but which they thought was derived from "killing the enemy," i.e., craving.[1]

When he died his followers mourned, although the arhants proved their worth by conquering their *desiderium*.

Of those of the brethren who were not yet free from their passions, some stretched out their arms and wept; and some fell headlong on the ground, rolling to and fro in anguish at the thought: "Too soon has the Blessed One died! Too soon has the Happy One passed away from existence. Too soon has the Light gone out in the world!"

But those of the brethren who were free from the passions (the Arahats) bore their grief, collected and composed at the thought: "Impermanent are all component things!"[2]

Thus they recognized his mortality. He had built well. With Sakyamuni gone, the Dharma and the Sangha remained. Three months before he died he warned Ananda and the others, exhorting them, "Be a lamp unto yourself, be your own refuge." He would not be an intercessor, a savior, he would not be with them alway, except in the figure, "I am the Dharma."

Samadhi and Beyond

The way to enlightenment was well marked. The signposts were the monastic rule and the sermons, which were later summed up under three main headings, sila, samadhi, and prajna. These summed up the monks' way of daily life toward each other and toward the laity; the practice of meditation; and a transformation of personality marked by intuitive, immediate response, free of craving and discursive thought. Enlightenment can be discussed more effectively after another look at Gautama's sramanic predecessors and contemporaries. They too were seeking liberation. The orthodox brahmin priesthood performed rituals and sacrifices, promising themselves freedom from rebirth and their lower-caste patrons rebirth into brahminhood and eventual moksha. The Upanishadic seers, many of them kshatriyas, envisioned moksha as the union of atman (the soul) with Brahman (the That, the Absolute). But they, like the five ascetics of the Uruvela grove, and the three naked, matted-hair Kassapa brothers, and the pretantric Makkhali Gosala, and even the materialist Ajita of the hair blanket, who believed in neither soul nor afterlife, wanted the experience of liberation *in this life*. Indeed, like Gautama and the arhants ("unspotted in the world are they, Brahma-become, with outflows none"),[3] they would live out their lives, assured of nonreturning.

What did they all have in common? Even at this distance it appears that as yogins and ascetics their goal was the state of samadhi, in which they transcended their human limitedness and experienced Oneness—with their inner being, with the entire creation, with the Absolute (however their ontology was phrased). To this day the most important parts of the Indian saddhu's, or recluse's, day are the periods of meditation which, according to the most adept, are periods of bliss. Deep samadhi, the unitive or mystical experience, has been described in different terms according to the cultural context of the practitioner, but the images are remarkably uniform: the oceanic unity; the vividness of light and color (if any); the all-happening-together, past, present, and future; the vividness of detail in vision, as of the world seen for the first time. This is the top rung of the Ladder of Bliss in the Taittiriya Upanishad (II, 8, 1). If we take a healthy, vigorous young man, with the whole world at his command, as the unit of bliss, and multiply one hundred times for each ascending level—human gandharvas (insatiable satyrs), celestial gandharvas, Manes, various levels of gods, Indra, Brihaspati, Prajapati— we shall arrive at the bliss "of a man versed in the Vedas and free from desires," in Swami Nikhilananda's disarming translation (p. 270).

However exquisite the bliss of the "zero-experience" (Bharati's term), there was another dimension which validated it for the Buddha and the Jain Mahavira, both realized yogins (although legend has it that the latter had to strive many years for his enlightenment). This was the higher order of knowledge it bestowed. The Jain claimed omniscience; the Buddha claimed less; but before too long, to all realized ones psychic and magical powers were attributed as well as gnosis. The Pali scriptures formalized the steps to enlightenment into the eight stages of trance (jhanas), the three iddhi, the three knowledges (vijja), and the ultimate panna (prajna), full intuitive wisdom.

What the Buddha added to the various methods of achieving zero-experience was so rich, encompassing all human striving, that the meditative base and the mystical culmination are often forgotten by students of Buddhism. The Mahabodhi is presented to us not only as the bliss of trance but also as a complex of intellectual and psychological discovery. His message, which at first sounds so chilling in despair, is full of counsel on how to live decently in the world. He gave guidance to husbands, to merchants, and to kings.

But as long as the main purpose of the teaching was surcease from pain in samsara, and the achievement of nirvana through depersonalization of the individual, the abolition of Ego, then the arhant could do no other than seek withdrawal and concentration, solitary meditation and suppression of emotion in the awareness that "impermanent are all composite things." We must regard the Buddha's social and moral teachings as incidental and instrumental to his higher purpose: direction of his followers to the state of the detached mystic, manifested in a qualitative, unmistakable experience. The relation of Buddhist nirvana and yogic samadhi and other mystical experience will be discussed in Chapter 8. But now we must treat the arhant's training and personality.

That arhantship was attained at first in a distinct experience, rather than by certification after a long apprenticeship, is clear from the scriptures. Poor Ananda, beloved of the Master, could not be dubbed arhant. He did not break through, according to the eleventh Skandhaka, until the eve of the First Council, where he (nominated not by Kassapa but by the bhikkhus themselves) was to recite the Sutras.

And the venerable Ananda—thinking, "Tomorrow is the assembly, now it beseems me not to go into the assembly while I am still only on the way"—spent the whole night with mind alert. And at the close of the night, intending to lie down, he inclined his body, but before his head reached the pillow, and while his feet were still far from the ground, in the interval he became free from attachment to the world, and his heart was emancipated from the Asavas (that is to say, from sensuality, individuality, delusion, and ignorance).[4]

Growth of the Sangha

Others did not wait so long. When the new Buddha moved from Gaya to the deer park at Issipatana, his refulgence overcame the coolness of his five former companions, he proclaimed his Buddhahood, and they listened to the First Sermon. As he spoke, first Kondanya "obtained the pure and spotless Eye of Truth, 'Whatsoever is subject to the condition of origination, is subject also to the condition of cessations,'" and was ordained. In later formalizations, this condition would be called "entering the stream." Then two more caught on, and the first three went out for alms while the Teacher gave instruction to the last two, about how the noble hearer of the word becomes weary of body, sensation, perception, samkharas, consciousness (the skandhas), divests himself of passion, and becomes free. "The five bhikkhus rejoiced at the words, . . . and their minds became free from attachment to the world, and were released from the Asavas. At that time there were six Arahats in the world" (Mahavagga 1, 6).

Since our physiological and psychosomatical data on what triggers the zero-experience are rudimentary, we cannot reject the story as pious legend. We may conjecture that the five, as long-time practitioners of tapasya and yoga, knew what they were looking for and were integrated into fulfillment by the charisma of their preceptor and the force of his message. But what are we to make of the next conversion, that of Yasa, the pampered son of the Benares setthi? Yasa had the same revulsion of surfeit that Siddhartha had had on the night of the Great Renunciation (and in the same words: the drooling spittle and muttering of the music-girls, the image of the charnel house); he walked out to the deer park and met the Buddha who was walking there. His mind was "prepared, impressible, free from obstacles"; he heard the principal doctrine of Suffering and the Path, and "just as a clean cloth free from black specks properly takes the dye, thus Yasa, the noble youth, even while sitting there, obtained the pure and spotless dye of the Truth"—as Kondanya had a few days before.

The setthi came looking for his son, whom the Buddha, with a small miracle, kept invisible while talking with the father. The father saw the light and spoke for the first time the triratna (the three jewels), "I take my refuge in the Lord, in the Dhamma, and in the fraternity of Bhikkhus" (the Sangha), and became "the first person in the world who became a lay disciple by the formula of the holy triad." Then the Buddha made Yasa visible and said that he could not return home because, as he had been listening, "his mind has become free from attachment to the world, and has become released from the Asavas." So Yasa was ordained, and "there were seven Arahats in the world."

Then four of Yasa's friends came and heard the Dhamma, and then fifty more friends of the family, and "there were sixty-one Arahats in the world."

The next group of converts did not become arhants. They were the thirty young men, all with their wives, except one who brought along a prostitute, who went sporting in the Uruvela grove back near Gaya. The loose girl snatched some valuables and ran. Searching for her, they met the Buddha, who asked, "Which would be the better for you; that you should go in search of a woman, or that you should go in search of yourselves?" They listened, reached the truth, and were ordained. It is assumed that the twenty-nine wives went home.

The next conversions in the Mahavagga (Chap. 15) are those of the three Kassapa brothers, the jatilas, or matted-hair brahmin ascetics. In an apt display of gamesmanship, the Buddha requested permission to enter the first Kassapa's fire room, the symbolic and magical center of Vedic power, and then applied siddhi to overcome with fire the firebreathing guardian serpent. Then he staged several more miracles, some involving light and fire, and finally overwhelmed Kassapa by reading his mind and breaking down his only defense, "He is not, however, holy like me." Kassapa's five hundred followers joined him in flinging their hair and materials for the fire sacrifice into the river, and receiving ordination. Then the second brother, with three hundred followers, and the third, with two hundred, did likewise. Then, after some more fire miracles, the Buddha preached the Fire Sermon to his thousand new followers.

Everything, O bhikkhus, is burning. The eye is burning; visible things are burning; the mental impression based on the eye . . . ; the contact of the eye, be it pleasant, be it painful, be it neither pleasant nor painful, that also is burning. With what fire is it burning? . . . with the fire of lust, of anger, of ignorance; it is burning with birth, decay, death, grief, lamentation, suffering, dejection, and despair.

The ear is burning, sounds are burning, etc. The nose is burning, odors are burning, etc. The tongue is burning, tastes are burning, etc. The body is burning, objects of contact are burning, etc. The mind is burning, thoughts are burning, etc.

Considering this, O bhikkhus, a disciple learned, walking in the Noble Path, becomes weary of the eye, weary of visible things, weary of the mental impressions based on the eye, etc.; he becomes weary of the ear . . . , the nose . . . , the tongue . . . , the body . . . , the mind. . . .

Becoming weary of all that, he divests himself of passion; by absence of passion he is made free; when he is free, he becomes aware that he is free; and he realizes that rebirth is exhausted; that holiness is completed; that duty is fulfilled; and that there is no further return to this world.

And then "the minds of those thousand bhikkhus became free from attachment to the world, and were released from the Asavas"—became arhants, in short, and reached nirvana. The communal samadhic trance that the legend here proposes is interesting to imagine, but the wonder tales do suggest the impact of the exultant confidence of the new Master, and the integrating effect of his many-sided message on those who had already left the world of sense and selfhood or were, like Yasa, ready to leave it.

The last arhants to be mentioned here are historically the most important. Sariputra and Maudgalyayana were young brahmin followers of Sanjaya the skeptic, according to the Mahavagga legend (1, 23). One day Sariputra saw Assaji, the last of the first five, and liked his decorous manner. "Your countenance, friend, is serene; your complexion is pure and bright. In whose name, friend, have you retired from the world?" Assaji told him of "the Samana Sakyaputta, an ascetic of the Sakya tribe," and modestly responded to the request for the spirit of the doctrine with the famous quatrain, inscribed on stupas and columns wherever Buddhists go on pilgrimage:

> The Buddha hath the causes told
> Of all things springing from a cause;
> And also how things cease to be—
> 'Tis this the Mighty Monk proclaims. (Warren, p. 89)

Sariputra on hearing the text "obtained the pure and spotless Eye of the Truth" and went to inform his friend. Maudgalyayana, seeing him from afar, said, "Your countenance, friend, is serene; your complexion is pure and bright. Have you then really reached the immortal?"[5] Sariputra repeated Assaji's words, and his friend also obtained the Eye of the Truth. Then, followed by all two hundred fifty of Sanjaya's pupils, they went to join their new master, who saw them coming from afar, and said, "These will be a most distinguished, auspicious pair."

Auspicious indeed. Conze says, "As Saint Paul stands to Jesus, as Abu Bekr to Mohammed, as Xenocrates to Plato, as Stalin to Lenin, so does Sariputra stand to the Buddha. . . . With less genius the successor produces a kind of portable edition of the Gospel which accords more with the needs of the average man and his capacity for comprehension" (*Buddhism,* p. 90). Sariputra is given credit or blame for the intellectual framework that trained the Elder, the rigid arhant who would not bend for the Mahasanghikas and was scorned by the Mahayana.

Toward the Abhidharma

From the day of Enlightenment the Teacher knew what would happen to his doctrine: most could not understand it, and even the few could understand only part. His contribution was so complex yet so unified, so firm yet so flexible, that only his own presentation could be trusted. He who organizes the teaching for broad or systematic teaching, he who translates the Word into words, traduces. To Sariputra fell the task—self-assigned, probably.

Of course the Buddha's immediate objective was to teach Dharma to those who could understand it, to bring them "into the Stream" and then into complete bodhi. But the Path traversed all psychology (including the working of sense perception and the use of after-images in meditation), physiology (including its more repulsive aspects as subjects of meditation), morality (especially the noble Brahma-viharas), etiquette (in accepting invitations to dinner and keeping appointments), and political theory (in his unprecedented reminder to kings that their first duty was to their people). As summed up by Sariputra or later formulators, the Path became Moral Discipline, Trance, and Wisdom. Sila included Right Speech, Right Action, and Right Livelihood; samadhi included Right Effort, Right Mindfulness, and Right Concentration; prajna included Right Thought and Right Understanding.

The organization of information into lists is a device to help memorization, like versifying. Sariputra is credited with many of the lists that centuries after his death (which preceded the Buddha's by six months) were included in the third Pitaka, the Abhidharma. This was a collection of commentaries, definitions, and formulas. Some were supposed to be chanted in unison, all were to be memorized. The Abhidharma books are concerned with Wisdom, specially defined. The Abhidharma canons of two schools are extant, the Sthavira in Pali and the Sarvastivada in Chinese translated from the Sanskrit.

The special definition of wisdom in the Abhidharma schools (the Old Wisdom schools) is that which contributes to Depersonalization. Here we are reminded of the single-mindedness of the arhant. The last step before nirvana is the destruction of the asavas, which include desire for existence and delusion about the soul. "I am" is a forbidden word. "Wisdom alone is able to chase the illusion of individuality from our thoughts . . ." (Conze, *Buddhism*, p. 110). Buddhaghosa, the prolific fifth-century organizer of Sthavira doctrine, summarized the implications of the skandhas memorably:

> Suffering exists, but there is no one who suffers;
> Deeds are, but there is no doer of deeds.
> Nirvana is, but no one is blissful;
> The path is, but there is no traveler on it. (*Visuddhimagga* 16, 90)

Such is the road to nirvana for the No-person! To *live* cognizant of such a depersonalized state requires lifelong training in mindfulness. The terrifying discipline of the arhant, "the withdrawal into the self, the constant vigilance over acts and words and thoughts, the complete suppression of all emotion," results in one who "has shed all attachment to I and mine, is secluded, zealous, and earnest, inwardly free, fully controlled, master of himself, self-restrained, dispassionate and austere" (*Buddhism,* p. 94).

Ecstasy and Organization

Perhaps the Buddha was mindful of this austere dispassion when he foretold the waning of the Sangha in five hundred years. We can attribute his foresight to the omniscience of a Tathagata, or simply to a realism aware of what an organization can do to the ideals it was formed to promote. The spirit became letter; the long encompassing vision of the Buddha became the lowered glance of the arhant avoiding distraction from his goal—to achieve and retain his own salvation. The early arhants, mindful of being a lamp unto themselves, built an organization that soon had no place to go, except inward. It continued to spread, teaching good things like nonharming and compassion. But it lost the élan of the Teacher. It separated the monks from the laity, and when the test came a hundred years later, when the Mahasanghikas wanted to open some windows on a changed landscape, the Elders, the third generation after the Disciples, said No. Meditation continued to be the main occupation but was formalized in techniques later summed up by Buddhaghosa as the Forty Objects of meditation; and yet fewer gained enlightenment than in the early days.

What authentication could there be for so paradoxical a turning away from the warmth of the Buddha's own personality, so flat a fixing on "even-mindedness" over the other Unlimiteds—friendliness, compassion, and sympathetic joy? It is irony that it was the quest of ecstasy that led away from the Buddha's joy to the arhant's formula. In establishing an ontology that left no room for the individual abiding personality, the Buddha had more than the courage of his intellectual convictions, the rationalization of Dependent Genesis and the Five Components. He had the strength of his own experience, and also that of most of his philosophical adversaries, whether materialistic yogins or Upanishadic atmavadins. That was the undifferentiated bliss of the zero-experience, the mystical samadhi itself:

The ecstatic feeling involved in the transcendent state is a conviction of a safe loss of personal identity, usually rationalized as a sense of continuity into the divine presence. . . . In the universally appearing reports of the mystic experience, the characteristic described is that of an ecstatic loss of the differentiation between self and other, between subject and object.[6]

Or, in Plotinus' words,

Having freed itself of all externals, the soul must turn totally inward; not allowing itself to be wrested back toward the outer, it must forget everything, the subjective first and, finally, the objective. It must not even know that it is itself that is applying itself to contemplation of The One.

Plotinus, the Buddha, and Yajnavalkya moved on from the bliss of merging to create ontological systems. Modern investigators measure brain waves and insert probes to find the ecstasy center of mice (and soon of men). The divine malady, epilepsy,[7] is traced to an imbalance of electrical potential, and its God-filled aura may spare some of its light for research into the Beatific Vision, or at least into the physiological ground of the mystic's bliss as a creative escape, like rapid-eye-motion dreaming, from the rational confinement of wakefulness. The rational Buddha, back among faulty mortals, was wiser than to rely on samadhi alone as the way of liberation for mankind. He elaborated a complete way of life that started with a single begging bowl and rags taken from the village scrap heap, and moved *ad hoc* into abstract epistemological disputation and the techniques of meditation. In later generations samadhi was neatly placed between sila and prajna, and arhants fortified the momentary merging of subject and object in trance with the utmost purgation of the Ego in a lifelong discipline.

But how many monks actually achieved enlightenment? And, after all the memorizations on the nine body-apertures and charnel-yard watches and the mixed messes in the begging bowl and the studied externalization of the ego, was the achieved repression of the craving for separate existence qualitatively the same as the state of the mystic in samadhi? We are aware that this is an academic question and, to a serious Buddhist, probably an irritating one. Since the Buddha, Buddhists have been concerned with present actions for liberation, not hypothetical speculations. Yet our study is not directed toward salvation but toward understanding. It may shed light not only on the past but on our own thought. As interest in occultism, astrology, and other dubious exercises[8] waxes, we must separate out the definition and the operation of mysticism and its role in creative work, so long neglected or denied. (Christopher Smart, a potentially great poet, was clearly a mystic, and tried to communicate the vividness of his experience, so he was locked up in "rational," eighteenth-century England.) If it is true, as Shands suggests, that "the mystic state, in its simplest description, appears to be one in which a primal unity is momentarily re-attained with the most powerful spiritual feelings of which man is capable" (p. 18), then it should be useful to compare Gautama's creative trance with the psychic state of the arhant. Such a study would help us understand the upsurge of the other-directed ideal of the bodhisattva to be dealt with in the next chapter.

One practical reason for the discipline of the arhant was an understandable confusion in the Buddha's day over the implications of samadhi, whether yogic or jatila-sramanic or Upanishadic or Buddhist. Was the achieved mystic thenceforth a man of God or, in less loaded terms, a man set apart from ordinary social requirements? To this day in India the wandering saddhu, who walks naked against city traffic lights, or even the householder who gets religion and spends his time meditating rather than earning a living, is indulged as attuned to a different drum playing the age-old rhythm of the arch-saddhu Siva. The question became: Is the man who has seen ultimate truth capable of committing a crime?

There was a strong tradition that he was not. Having escaped the bondage of the senses, the ordinary means of perception and ratiocination, having merged with the ultimate source of things as they are, having broken down the distinction between the ordered sequence of time and the extension of space, how can the numinous "realized one" be held to the standards of the earthbound householder?

The Buddha, as a leader and observer of men, must have been aware of another fact about yogic adepts: the zero-experience of itself does not really change the personality, does not make the mystic saintly, even though his culture may regard him as holy. The Buddha observed many forest dwellers, some of them probably "realized" mystics, like the jatila Kassapas of the early conversions. Those who joined him were not exempt from the oaths of ordination and the infinitely detailed Vinaya rules of the Sangha. They had to shave their heads, for one thing, and learn a new morality.

The suicide of Godhika presents an interesting illustration of the relation of trance, nirvana, and rebirth in orthodox Buddhist practice, and a *casus* for the Master's judgment on the conduct of an arhant. Buddhaghosa applied the story in the Samyutta sutra 1, 109, as commentary on stanza 57 of the Dhammapada (translated by P. Lal as "And Mara stands helpless / before the clear thinker and perfect knower, / the good man"). Godhika

attained release for his mind in ecstatic meditation, and then through the power of a disease which beset him, the trance was broken up. A second time, a third time, up to the sixth time was his trance broken up. He thought, "Doubtful is the fate of those who fail in trance. This time I will resort to the knife." And taking a razor for shaving the hair, he lay down on a couch in order to cut his windpipe. Mara, the Slayer, perceived his intention, and thought, "This monk is about to use the knife; but they who do so are indifferent to life, and such attain to insight and saintship. If I should attempt to dissuade him, he would not heed me. I will get the teacher to dissuade him."

As Mara, in disguise, was telling of Godhika's intentions, the elder used the knife, and the Teacher, recognizing Mara, said, "Thus verily, the valiant act, / Nor think to hanker after life! / Lo! Godhika uproots desire, / And, dying, has Nirvana gained." Mara "was searching in all directions for the elder's rebirth consciousness." But the Teacher told his followers, "Godhika has attained Nirvana, and his consciousness has not fixed itself."

What of the Commandment of ahimsa? The arhant's attainment of nirvana was the higher law. In practical terms, suicide was useless as a way to escape duhkha, because one immediately re-entered the round of rebirth and continuing pain. But if the suicide was an arhant and died in the odor of sanctity (literally the theme of Dhammapada 57), the way of death seemed not to matter. As Elder Rahula puts it, "An Arahant, though he acts, does not accumulate karma, because he is free from the false idea of self, free from all other defilements and impurities *(kilesa, sasava dhamma)*. For him there is no rebirth."[9]

The Disciplined and the Independent

The Buddha, founder of a holistic ethical-social-devotional system predicating many cycles of existence, had to settle for human nature as it was, and so permitted a formalization of rules on several levels: for the arhants, for the rest of the Sangha, for lay adherents. Unlike Jesus, who as God wanted to save all and gave himself as the once-for-all sacrifice for the spiritual nourishment of all, the Buddha was in this context only a man and welcomed the salvation of those who could prove by authentic trance and depersonalized Wisdom that they were off the wheel of rebirth. Through leadership in the Sangha, they were to show the way of Dharma to others who would grow ripe for liberation over the generations. So, inevitably, the charisma of the founder, so potent in bringing disciples into the stream, was replaced by the organization, which gave structure and techniques.

So the lists to memorize and the stages of progress and the levels of stream-winners were established. The disciplines can be formally viewed as performing distinct but related functions. First, of course, was to guide the aspirant to climactic trance, such as Ananda achieved late and poor Godhika could not maintain long enough for full effect. Here the arhants served the essential function of guru and Zen master.[10] Second was the induration of even-minded detachment. With continued awareness of the need to keep craving at a safe distance, or dissolved, a new personality structure was developed that could not conceive of relapse into karmic accumulation.

A third reason for the stress on lifelong discipline was, we must assume, the ambiguous nature of the zero-experience alone. It came to children and to women (who, indeed, were accepted as nuns, bhikkhunis, but with misgivings). Shri Anandamayi, "currently regarded as the most distinguished living exemplar of Hindu mysticism," according to Lannoy (*The Speaking Tree*, p. 357), "frequently fell into trance, burning herself at the kitchen stove" as a child. Agehananda Bharati has related his first experience as a boy of twelve in Vienna. Hindus accept the holiness of ecstatic conduct in itself, as in the case of Anandamayi. But in Buddhism samadhi is not the end; it is a stage, a manifestation, and must fit into the context of Dharma and Sangha. The spirit of the Buddha gave life to Dharma and Sangha, and the letter of Kasyapa and Sariputra did not take life away but merely dried it up a little.

Yet there were fully enlightened ones who were not members of the Sangha and whose very existence in the fold of the Master needs discussion at this point. The claim of superiority of the Mahayana is summed up in this statement: "The Disciples and Pratyekabuddhas do not think that they should, after winning full enlightenment, lead all beings to Nirvana." The Disciples (sravaka) were, of course, the Elders, the Arhants, the Abhidhammika reciters, and they are given credit for "the meritorious work founded on giving, morality, and meditational development."[11] Who were the Pratyekabuddhas (Pali, Paccekabuddha)? The term means "independent" or "separate" Buddha. Here is a modern Theravada explanation:

Concerning the beings who have arrived at the supramundane plane, that is to say, *sotapannas* and beings of still higher development, those who have reached the Goal may be *Sammasambuddhas, Pacheka* Buddhas, or Arahants. A *Sammasambuddha* is a Fully-Enlightened One who comprehends the Truth by his own intuition, without the help of any others, and who can preach and make others understand the Truth. A *Pacceka* Buddha also comprehends the Truth by his own intuition only, but he is unable to preach to others. An Arahant realizes the Truth after first hearing it from another; he is able to preach and so make others understand the Dhamma. The Buddhas, *Sammasambuddha* and *Pacceka,* are not members of the Sangha; the Arahants and the persons on the three lower stages of the Path comprise the *ariyasangha.*

Bhikkhus of the *sammutisangha* lead the religious life intending to attain to the *ariyasangha,* first "entering the stream" or becoming *sotapannas,* then rising to the higher stages.[12]

The Pratyekabuddhas pose questions that cannot be answered. How can anyone reach so complex a Truth as the Dharma by his own intuition—except the Buddha himself? We can assume that they were ascetics who had reached trance and depersonalization and remained apart—but so did many brahmins. How Buddhist were the Pratyekabuddhas? And, for that matter, what Truth did the Sammasambuddhas preach?

The Second Council

At any rate, the Elders were not the sole heirs of the Master. They could not excommunicate those who were not among them, but they did try to maintain authority over those who were in the fold but tried to stretch the fence a little. So we move to the story of Vaisali, the Second Council, and the schism of the Mahasanghikas.

We do not have the Mahasanghikas' version of the schism (in fact, only their Vinaya remains). The Sthavira side is found in the Twelfth Skandhaka attached to the Pali Cullavagga, and in the Ceylon chronicles, the *Dipavamsa,* and the *Mahavamsa,* the latter derived from but modifying the former. They say that a century after the Parinirvana the controversy took place over ten practices that the Vaisali monks had introduced. These included accepting money as gifts, keeping salt in a horn for future meals, eating when the sun's shadow was two finger's breadth past noon (the rule was that no solid food be taken after noon) and relaxing the rules so that not all the monks in a parish need attend the same Uposatha ceremony (confession at the new and full moons) and so that a rug longer than prescribed could be used if it had no fringe. The elder Yasa, identified in the chronicles as the Buddha's sixth convert, and now therefore about 165 years old, objected and through the elder Revata arranged a council, at which a jury of eight elders, four from the east and four from the west (because the dissidents were trying to make it look like a regional split), all of whom incidentally had seen the Buddha, rejected the ten revisions. So the "wicked monks," said the *Dipavamsa,* "made a reversed teaching, they broke up the original collection of the scriptures and made another collection, . . . they broke up the sense and the doctrine in the five Nikayas. . . ."

Conze says that the actual split did not occur until about Ashoka's time. Vasumitra, the historian, lists as the real reason for the split five points of doctrine proposed by the monk Mahadeva. Three were directed against the arhants: that they could be tempted by Mara and others (they could still have nocturnal emissions), that they were to a degree ignorant, rather than omniscient, and that they could still have doubt.

The two bills of disagreement indicate the real significance of the Vaisali monks' protest: it was to loosen the hold of the established Vinaya rules as set and policed by the elders, and to open out the doctrine and reduce the gulf between the Assembly of the arhants (the ariyasangha), on the one hand, and the lower monks (the sammutisangha), the laity, and women, on the other. In so doing the protesters developed ideas about the bodhisattva ideal and (as the ten theses showed) went beyond what was conceived as the final word of the man-Buddha. With such statements as "The form-body of the Tathagata is boundless; so is his power, and the length of his life," they moved into doctrinal revisionism, and the further unfolding of Dharma; by emphasizing the supernatural qualities of the Buddha they prepared the way for worship and for the docetic belief that his appearance on earth was really an illusion in order to place Dharma before mankind.

The Diverging Schools

The number eighteen for the doctrinal schools suffers from a kind of momentariness: the list keeps changing with time and the source, whether the fourth-century Pali *Dipavamsa* or the late Sarvastivadin *Mahavyutpatti*, centuries later. Five are of interest for our purpose.[13]

The two Abhidharma, or Old Wisdom, schools are the Sarvastivada and the Sthavira (Pali, Theravada—a term still used for the doctrines of Ceylon and Southeast Asia). The mission of elders to Ceylon under Mahinda established the Theravada; a small counterpart on the mainland retained the name Sthavira after the more dominant Old Wisdom school became known as Sarvastivadins. The difference in doctrine was metaphysical and slight: The name means "all exists" (*sarvam asti*). The Theravadins simplified the doctrine to mean, "the past exists, the future exists, the present exists," but in fact the existence is latent or potential. The basis of the doctrine is the Abhidarma listing of the twelve bases of cognition (the ayatanas): the six senses (five external, sight, sound, touch, taste, and smell; one internal, mind), and the corresponding sense data (form, sound, etc.). Stcherbatsky says,

When the principle "everything exists" is set forth, it has a meaning that nothing but the twelve bases of cognition are existent. An object which cannot be viewed as a *separate* object of cognition or a *separate* faculty of cognition is unreal, as *e.g.* the soul, or the personality. Being a congeries of separate elements, it is declared to be a name and not a reality, not "a dharma." (*The Central Conception of Buddhism*, p. 7; quoted in Thomas, *History*, p. 164)

All objects or all dharmas can act as an object of perception, and all dharmas whatsoever can act as object-conditions (alambana pratyaya) of the sixth, the mind-sense. In this way even the dharmas of the past and future can function as object-conditions of perception, and in that sense can be said "to exist" (Murti, p. 170).

Because of our habitual reliance on the more easily available Pali versions of the Abhidharma, we may tend to overestimate the importance of the Sthavira in India; we must remind ourselves that when the leading early Mahayanist, Nagarjuna, attacked the Vaibhasika (the "naive realists" and "existential dualists" according to Guenther), he is referring to the Sarvastivadin texts, not Sthavira (Theravada). The Sarvastivadins, who were the most powerful Old Wisdom group, almost never referred to the Sthavira.

The Sautrantika, also critical realists and offshoots of the Sarvastivadin, are so called because they are supposed to have rejected the validity of the Abhidharma Pitaka, relying rather on the sutras, which were closer to the word of the Buddha. (The Sarvastivada Abhidharma texts were not claimed to be the word of the Buddha, as the Pali were, but of known men, such as Sariputra and Maudgalyayana.) The distinctive tendency of the Sautrantika was a recognition of the role of the mind in the perception and relation of phenomena, in the theory called "conceptual construction" (vikalpa).[14] They questioned the legitimacy of the inflated lists of categories in the Abhidharma; for example, they reduced the number of dharmas from seventy-five to forty-three. Murti says, "The Sautrantika by his insistence on the creative work of thought and the doctrine of Representative Perception directly led to the Idealism of the Yogacara" (the outright idealist Mahayana school).

The Vatsiputriya, related to the Sammatiya, are the prime target of all other schools because of their clinging to the notion of a person or individual (pudgalatman) as "a quasi-permanent entity, neither completely identical with the mental states, nor different from them" (Murti, p. 81). Theirs was a kind of dogged honesty in their discomfort with the skandhas as a way of accounting for "the basic facts of experience, memory, moral responsibility, spiritual life, etc." Vasubandhu, the great commentator on Abhidharma, devotes a dialogue to answering a Vatsiputriya's question: "If the individual represents exactly the elements he is composed of and nothing else, why then did the Lord decline to decide the question, whether the living being is identical with the body or not?"—a reference to the discussion with Vacchagotta (see above, Chapter 3). The response explains the avyakrta approach, and the need to consider the questioner's (Vacchagotta's) state of mind. Eventually the Mahayana gave in and came around with a much more sophisticated version of the abiding individual than either the pudgala or the atman.

The Mahasanghika group that came closest to Mahayana positions was the Lokottara ("out of the world"—referring to the Buddha), whose book, the epic-romance *Mahavastu* ("The Grand Occurrence") is "a storehouse of Jatakas, edifying stories, and dogmatic Sutras. Buddha is treated as God who had descended into the world and who underwent penance etc. as a sort of make-believe. To some extent the *Mahavastu* also anticipates the Mahayana spiritual discipline, especially its conception of the ten bhumis of the Bodhisattva. According to Vasumitra, Mahasanghika schools "maintained that (1) The Blessed Buddhas are all supermundane (lokottara). (2) The Tathagatas have no worldly attributes (sasrava dharmas). . . . (5) In the teachings of the Bhagavan (Buddha) there is nothing that is not in accordance with the Truth. (6) The physical body (rupa-kaya) of Tathagata is limitless. (7) The majestic powers of Tathagata also are limitless. (8) Lives of Buddhas too are limitless. (9) Buddha is never tired of enlightening living beings and awakening pure faith in them. . . ."[15]

It is in this last quality that the Mahayana centered its rejection of those whose lamp was for themselves. By one definition the enlightened attitude was "the training in thinking of sentient beings."

When a Bodhisattva possesses one virtue, he has all the most excellent Buddha qualities. Which one? The attitude which does not exclude sentient beings from his thoughts.[16]

One should not exclude even a person who has wronged one, sGam.po.pa says, "Should you ask whether we can speak of excluding from our thoughts all sentient beings or only one, the answer is that except for Sravakas and Pratyekabuddhas not even eagles or jackals can do it" (*ibid.*).

SIX

The Paradoxes of Mahayana

Human understanding is a continuing tension of contradictions. The talking member of the animal kingdom contrives survival by response to his environment on several levels: adrenalin reaction by animal instinct to sudden challenge or change; conditioned or learned response in evading or controlling environment; long-term planning to accomplish destruction of possible competitors, or cooperation for survival. The broadening of the realm of cooperation from the tribe to the entire human race started as an impractical ideal in such as Mo Tzu but has become a desperate necessity to offset the now-outdated guarantor of survival, parochial grasping.

A related dialectical progression is the reception of sense data from external and internal phenomena; the unconscious development of receptive patterns and response to such; and finally the "conscious" grasp and imposition of order by memory and a long attention span—the manipulation of noumena. The thriving human animal feeds in three fields: instinctual physical response, conditioned response, and the noetic. Restriction in nourishment produces variously the slug and the bookworm. Our post-Freudian, post-Jungian culture is aware of the need to resolve contradiction in wholeness: to coordinate unconscious and conscious, conditioned and intellectual, physical and spiritual.

The Buddha, a whole person balancing compassion and analysis, love and discipline, said he taught only one thing: sorrow and the cessation of sorrow. But that is two things. Recognition of sorrow and the urge to overcome it constitute compassion. Teaching to overcome it is technique. The Old Wisdom is primarily concerned with the technique. Mahayana moves to the other side.

Friendliness and compassion, from being subordinate, become cardinal virtues of prime importance. Compassion, in particular, impels the Bodhisattva as strongly as wisdom, and provides the motive why, not content with personal salvation, he strives to advance to full Buddhahood. The Abhidharma tradition had set up an opposition between friendliness and compassion on the one side, and wisdom, the highest virtue, on the other.[1]

The man who became the Buddha found himself in a practical situation, with a message to teach to specific people, whom he met by chance, like Yasa, or whom he sought out, like the five ascetics and the three jatila Kassapas. He taught only the metaphysics needed to support the practical psychology that would train his disciples to dissolve their Egos. Such dissolution led to liberation from rebirth and the condition of nirvana. The goal-directed trivium of the arhant-in-training included sila, morality, the objective being the unselfing of the self, and only incidentally the improvement of social relations and the benefit of others; samadhi, the mastery of trance almost as a demonstration that nirvana, the ultimate unconditioned, nonmaterial realm, is achievable; and prajna, the wisdom of Abhidharma, the stages and steps of depersonalization that assured permanent dissolution of the asravas.

So the arhants were not ecstatic mystics like the Hindus Anandamayi and Ramakrishna; they minded their eyes and thoughts. They dutifully taught the younger aspirants in the Order the techniques of self-control and meditation and bestowed merit on the laity by accepting, while the Master was alive, food in their begging bowls and viharas for sojourn in the rainy season, and in later centuries, gold and silks and temples and universities. But for the immediate salvation of the laity there was not much concern; they would await their turn through however many rebirths would be necessary for them to become ready to enter the stream.

An Establishment Grows

What of compassion? Not the narrow Unlimited karuna from which one stepped up to Even-mindedness, but Mahakaruna, the true sign of "the enlightened attitude," concern for the salvation of all mankind, such as the newly enlightened Gautama, urged by Brahma, took upon himself?[2]

As long as the Buddha was a man teaching his way of salvation to his fellow men, he flexibly applied skill-in-means not as the Tathagata, pitying and playing illusions on men for their own good, but as a leader of backsliding men, less violently exasperated than Moses and more confident than Lincoln, cajoling, threatening, inspiring, meeting each person's questions with humor or scorn or direct analysis, considering what would be best for him and for Dharma too. Because his psychic

THE PARADOXES OF MAHAYANA

perception and inspiration were powerful, this guru led many to quick realization of their potential arhantship.

But after he was gone, the disciples had only the rules and the memory of his words. Without his artful wisdom, they formalized, memorized, and dogmatized what he had said, to tread deeper the one path they had to liberation. Each rule in the Vinaya, perhaps as Upali recited it, emerged from a specific incident. The Buddha was going to relax or rescind some of them, but Ananda, never quick on the uptake, forgot to ask him which, so the dutiful disciples, not trusting their own judgment, kept them all.

As time passed, the Order grew and took on organization. Despite the complaints that "The Samana Gautama causes fathers to beget no sons, wives to become widows, families to become extinct"[3] (Mahavagga 1, 24, 5), the Order became a stabilizing force in society, and accepted support from the wealthy and from royalty.[4] No longer typical was the mendicant who went into town in the morning and collected leftover scraps in his begging bowl and suffered from dysentery: a sick monk whom he had to clean up was the occasion of the Master's expostulation, "If ye, O bhikkhus, wait not one upon the other, who is there indeed who will wait upon you? Whosoever would wait upon me, he should wait upon the sick" (Vinaya, Mahavagga 8, 26, 3). Random food-foraging had to be supplanted by institutional feeding, with contributions in cash instead of in kind—one of the Mahasanghika innovations. Centuries later the Mahasanghikas established cave colonies or monasteries in both India and China, which became centers of cultural and economic activity. For example, the monastery at Karle:

> The sculpture is beautiful and even voluptuous, of handsome couples, of opulent men and women dressed in the height of style, riding horses and elephants; hardly what one would expect in an assembly place for monks, but precisely what rich merchants would have liked. The artists must have been specially brought from some distance and employed at considerable expense. Moreover the whole complex took a few centuries to complete, but the plan remains unitary. This means a continuity of design, finance, and administration. The connection with merchants and bankers (*sresthi*) from many different places is obvious from the names of donors inscribed on various pillars, statues, and caves which they donated. (Kosambi, pp. 183–84)

Kosambi also points out the connection of the monasteries with trade routes and their involvement with investment. They "all lie handy to the trade routes running from the western estuarial harbours . . . through the well-marked passes of the sheer Deccan scarp that leads up to the plateau. The new terminus Junnar, soon a second Jatavana capital, is similarly ringed around with no less than 135 Buddhist caves." (Pp. 184–85)

Formerly, the entrant into the Order had first distributed all his worldly possessions and then renounced the worldly life. Now he brought his money and experience of money-making into the monastery. . . . It is also obvious that these abbeys were important stages on the journey, resting places for the caravaneers, as well as supply houses and banking houses. (P. 185)[5]

Another Mahasanghika departure from the narrow view of the Elders, more important doctrinally if not socially than the use of cash, was the new look at the nature of the Buddha. Even the Theravada had hinted at the comparative unimportance of the physical Gautama: "What is there, Vakkali, in seeing this vile body? Whoso sees Dhamma sees me; whoso sees me sees Dhamma." Unfortunately we do not know directly the views of the Mahasanghika; we have only the Vinaya and the noncanonical *Mahavastu* of the Lokottara. But the reports of the historians and commentators like Vasumitra and Bhavya are clear and dependable. Quite early, probably before Ashoka, some basic Mahayana teachings were developing, as we have seen (Chapter 2), especially that of the transcendental Tathagata, omniscient, unlimited in power and the way of leading to enlightenment.

A basic modification of early doctrine was the transformation of the bodhisattva. According to Theravada, the term described the Buddha in his former existences, imbued with the will but not yet the achievement of Enlightenment: "Before my awakening, monks, when I was not yet fully awakened but only a Bodhisattva, I perceived radiance, but I saw no forms."[6] The new bodhisattva embodied the Mahakaruna of the Tathagata. Having earned nirvana far beyond the merit of "a Disciple or a Pratyekabuddha," he remains immanent to inspire and guide all mortals, "to become capable of pulling others out of this great flood of suffering," in the words of the Sarvastivadins, as presented in the *Abhidharmakosa* of Vasubandu. Just as some people find pleasure in the suffering of others, even if it is not useful to them, why should not bodhisattvas, confirmed in pity, find pleasure in doing good to others?

One must admit that the Bodhisattvas, by the force of habit, detach themselves from the Dharmas which constitute their so-called "Self," do no longer consider these Dharmas as "I" or "mine," growing in pitying solicitude for others, and are ready to suffer a thousand pains for this solicitude. (Conze, *Buddhism*, p. 126)

Via Dhyana to Emptiness

In the Mahayana construct, the bodhisattva did more than serve as the immanent instrument of the Tathagata's limitless compassion. He also served to illustrate how the fundamental principles of selflessness and victory over passion were to be merged into the new metaphysics of Sunyata, "emptiness," or, like zero and "bindu," the seed or point, the infinitely potential.

> He has gone beyond all that is worldly, yet he has not moved out of the world;
> In the world he pursues his course for the world's weal, unstained by worldly taints.
>
> As a lotus flower, though it grows in water, is not polluted by the water,
> So he, though born in the world, is not polluted by worldly dharmas.
>
> Like a fire his mind constantly blazes up into good works for others;
> At the same time he always remains merged in the calm of the trances and formless attainments. (Ratnagotravibhaga I, slokas 71–73, in *BT,* p. 130)

The last line seems to be a reference to the four higher "formless" dhyanas, the arupavacara jhana of the Pali Old Wisdom progression leading to prajna; but friendliness and compassion and good works are earthbound to the rupa-jhanas, the trances relying on matter. In the New Wisdom progression of the Six Perfections, which is a reformulation of sila-samadhi-prajna, trance (dhyana) is the fifth, after generosity (dana), morality (sila), patience (ksanti), and vigor (virya), and all five are given validity by the last, wisdom. The first four require studied application in the realm of the conditioned and the composite, where sorrow reigns. Dhyana, trances, on the contrary,

> discloses new facets of reality unsuspected by the average worldling, and at the same time convince him (the bodhisattva) of the insufficiency and unreality of all merely sensory experience.
>
> The perfection of wisdom finally is the ability to understand the essential properties of all processes and phenomena, their mutual relations, the conditions which bring about their rise and fall, and the ultimate unreality of their separate existence. At its highest point it leads right into the Emptiness which is the one and only Reality.[7]

Trance, then, unhinges the mind from the things of heaven and earth that are talked about in philosophy and lets wisdom in. It breaks down the duality of seer and seen, subject and object, the daily forms of predication and discussion, limited to the senses and the words men make up to report on them. Such reports are inexact and misleading because the reporter assumes an improper identity of I and mine, which cannot exist; and while he takes his stance for a sighting, the matter he is made of and the matter observed do not stand still. Man can escape from his predicament only by the extinction of karma and of the asravas, the karma-inducing fourfold grasping (at sense desire, false views, reliance on mere rule and ritual, and the theory of self). Nagarjuna, the great Madhyamika philosopher—and antiphilosopher—throws down the challenge:

Karma and the defilements derive from discrimination.
They spread as a result of discursive ideas, they are stopped by emptiness.

Discrimination means making observations and distinctions; discursive ideas are those which move step by step. Similarly dangerous is thought-construction (as of "the daughter of a barren virgin"), which springs from and intensifies this-worldly dualism. If one could resist such thought activity, "one would not experience the jungle of Samsara." One way of resistance is in trance.

But the Yogins who abide in the vision of emptiness do not at all apprehend the skandhas, elements and sense-fields as if they were something in themselves; in consequence they do not enter upon discursive ideas with these as objects, make no discriminations, by inclination to the ideas of I and mine do not give rise to a host of defilements. . . . It is thus, when one resorts to emptiness, characterized as blissful and as the appeasing of all discursive ideas, that all the discursive ideas, which are a net of thought construction, disappear. . . . Discrimination comes to rest, and with it all karma and defilement, and all kinds of rebirth. Hence one calls emptiness Nirvana, as it brings to rest (nirvriti) all discursive ideas.[8]

Such talk makes sense only on two premises: first, that it takes the basic teaching of the Buddha seriously, in that the physical world, the multiplicity of dharmas, the world of bodies and their thoughts and words, is the world of frustration, and is to be escaped or circumvented; second, that the trance experience is a form of cognition that is not a discursive setting off of viewer against object, but manifests unity and conquers samsara.

In the discussion of the avyakrta in Chapter 3, the Buddha's refusal to hold views that could not be proved or disproved, in the matter of eternalism or annihilation of the soul, was referred to as the origin of the Madhyamika dialectic. Nagarjuna's central thesis is the vanity of holding views about the phenomenal world.

A view, because of its restriction, determination, carries with it duality, the root of samsara. Nagarjuna states this dialectical predicament thus: when the self is posited, an other (para) confronts it; with the division of the self and the not-self, attachment and aversion result. . . . "A position (paksa) begets a counter-position (pratipaksa) and neither of them is real." (Murti, p. 270)

What *is* real is the indeterminate, sunya. Sunyata, emptiness, is the negation of standpoints. "Correctly understood, Sunyata is not annihilation, but the negation of negation; it is the conscious correction of an initial unconscious falsification of the real." In the Heart Sutra, the shortest of the Perfection of Wisdom sutras that enunciated the doctrine of emptiness, the bodhisattva Avalokita, the compassionate one, looked down from on high: "he beheld but five heaps; and he saw that in their own being they were empty." Severally and together, form, feelings, perceptions, impulses, and consciousness—all skandhas are emptiness, and "all dharmas are marked with emptiness, they are neither produced nor stopped, neither defiled nor immaculate, neither deficient nor complete . . . "there is no decay and death, no extinction of decay and death; there is no suffering, nor origination, nor stopping, nor path; there is no cognition, no attainment, and no non-attainment" (*BT*, p. 151).

Even more strikingly paradoxical than the Heart Sutra is the Diamond-Cutter Sutra, the Vajracchedika, which has the same purpose: to warn against conceptualization. "But Subhuti, as soon as I have spoken of these Buddhas and their Dharmas, I must recall the words, for there are no Buddhas and no Dharmas."[9]

The doctrine of Sunyata originated, Berry reminds us, in the Hinayana, in the ten sutras of the Majjhima headed "Division of Emptiness." The Buddha announces, "Dwelling in emptiness, I now dwell in its full perfection." To realize the notion, one must go through the discipline of meditation. First, to eliminate perception of one's surroundings and move to the infinite realms and achieve "awareness of the plane of infinite space." Then, in the higher jhanas, one "attains the true, unmistaken, completely clarified and highest realization of emptiness."[10] Yet jhanic emptiness, leading to the paradoxes of nirvana, about which nothing can be conceived or stated, is a simple matter compared with the Void of the Prajnaparamita sutras, which cut off all conceptualization, including that of the Tathagata.

Beyond Being and Non-Being

But the Mahayana warns that no matter what the Disciples and Pratyekabuddhas believed, such trance realization was not really nirvana, but merely an encouragement on the way to it. The Lotus of the Good Law Sutra (Saddharmapundarika), the best beloved of the Mahayana writings, reminds us of the Tathagata's skill:

> 61. A Teacher, skilled in means, he demonstrates the good Dharma:
> To those most advanced he shows the supreme enlightenment of a Buddha;
> 62. To those of medium wisdom the Leader reveals a medium enlightenment;
> Another enlightenment again he recommends to those who are just afraid of birth-and-death:
> 63. Disciples, who have just escaped from the triple world, and who are given to discrimination,
> May believe that they have attained Nirvana, the immaculate and serene.
> 64. But now I reveal to them that this is not what is meant by Nirvana.
> For it is through the full understanding of all dharmas that the deathless Nirvana must be attained.

But as for "someone who discerns dharmas as in their own-being" (suchness),

> 81. Since all dharmas are the same, empty, essentially without multiplicity,
> He does not look towards them, and he does not perceive any separate dharma,
> 82. But, greatly wise, he sees nothing but the Dharma-body. . . .
> 83. All dharmas are the same, all the same, always quite the same.
> When that has been cognized, Nirvana, the deathless and serene, has been understood.[11]

How can one get beyond the "medium wisdom" of the Pratyekabuddhas, the self-achieved (sloka 62)? How obtain a cognition of the Void, lacked by the Disciples "afraid of birth-and-death"? The first prescription is to avoid defining and naming, which are duality in action. "Suchness," tathata, is the more positive term than sunyata, but together they point beyond the world of describable things. Manjusri, the bodhisattva of wisdom, says,

> Through the mode of Suchness (tathata) do I see the Tathagata, through the mode of non-discrimination, in the manner of non-observation. I see Him through the aspect of non-production, . . . of non-existence. But Suchness does not attain (enlightenment)—thus do I see the Tathagata. Suchness does not

become or cease to become. . . . Suchness does not stand at any point or spot. . . . Suchness is not past, future or present. . . . Suchness is not brought about by duality or non-duality. . . . Suchness is neither defiled nor purified. . . . Suchness is neither produced nor stopped. . . . In this way the Tathagata is seen, revered and honoured.[12]

In Nagarjuna's realm of nonideas, absolute truth is transcendental or "void" because "it contains nothing concrete or real or individual that makes it an object of particularization."[13] Suchness, bhutathata, falls outside the category of being and nonbeing. Nagarjuna says in his Madhyamika-shastra, reminding us of our discussion in Chapter 3,

> Between thisness and thatness
> Between being and non-being,
> Who discriminates,
> The truth of Buddhism he perceives not. . . .
>
> To think "it is" is eternalism,
> To think "it is not" is nihilism:
> Being and non-being,
> The wise cling not to either.

Nagarjuna's drastic conclusion is the Eight Nos: "There is no death, no birth, no destruction, no persistence,/No oneness, no manyness, no coming, no departing." This cannot be understood literally, but rather in the light of Vimalakirti's response to Manjusri's request for an explanation of duality: a resounding silence. Manjusri admiringly exclaimed, "Well done, well done! The Dharma of Non-Duality is truly above letters and words!" (Suzuki, *Outlines,* p. 107)

The weight of Nagarjuna's argument rests on the intractability of terms. If they are to have any use, they must refer to a specific situation as understood by a mortal user, himself a creature of time and place, "conditioned." But this "discrimination" is unfreedom. So if even nirvana must be apprehended with word-conceptions, it joins this world. If we can change our outlook and not think of nirvana as a positive entity, a dharma without samskaras, then we escape the dilemma by describing nirvana in negative terms (as Yajnavalkya described Brahman with neti, neti), and nirvana is "what is not abandoned nor acquired; what is not annihilation nor eternality; what is not destroyed nor created" (Murti, p. 273). But then nirvana has no more "reality" than samsara, the realm of Contingent Origination. Nagarjuna asks, "Where there is no attribution of reality to Nirvana and no withdrawal of samsara, how can samsara and Nirvana be there distinguished in thought?" The conclusion is the four-way negation: that nirvana is neither (1) existent; (2) nor nonexistent; (3) nor existent and nonexistent; (4) nor nonexistent and not nonexistent.

So the Madhyamika dialectic, an outcome of the Prajnaparamita celebration of the Void, ends up in skepticism. But it gets back into the real world (else what would the Buddha say?) by setting up the category of "conditional truth," samvrtti satya, which is set parallel to absolute truth, paramartha satya. Thus a certain status is granted to the realm of illusion and opinion and sense perception, all the expedients of man to give order to the flux he floats in.

The Bodhisattva: Dispassionate Compassion

The Prajnaparamita sutras were inspirational works that seem to have been directed primarily against the Disciples' and Pratyekabuddhas' dedication to nirvana. In the Old Wisdom, prajna meant primarily the conquest of Ego-delusion. Mahayana's new meaning for prajna was the denial of the self-existence of everything. Nirvana, as a haven for well-behaved arhants, became intellectually untenable as well as socially limiting. The new ultimate, the Void, became the stage for a new drama of liberation for all mankind, with a new set of protagonists, the bodhisattvas, and a new expansive poetry and art.

What of the first five perfections, the ideals of human behavior? Generosity, morality, patience, vigor, and trance are worthy disciplines for growth toward full attainment, as the Old Wisdom arhants knew and practiced. But in the Mahayana sutras it is the bodhisattva who strives, both for himself and as an example to Sariputra and other hostage Disciples who gain courage to look beyond nirvana to Buddhahood itself. In the earlier Buddhism a person becomes a bodhisattva when he puts aside imminent liberation and resolves to spend many incarnations to become a Buddha and lead many to nirvana, as Sumedha in the time of Dipankara took the first step toward becoming Gautama. In Mahayana likewise, as Conze explains,

A person turns into a Bodhisattva when he first resolves to win full enlightenment for the benefit of all beings. Thereafter, until Buddhahood, he passes many aeons in the practice of the Paramitas. . . .

The Mahayana distinguishes *ten stages* through which a Bodhisattva must pass on his way to Buddhahood. . . . These "stages" refer to fairly exalted conditions, for Nagarjuna, the greatest thinker of the Mahayana, was a Bodhisattva of the first stage only. The first six stages correspond to the perfections,

THE PARADOXES OF MAHAYANA

and with the sixth the Bodhisattva has by his understanding of Emptiness come "face to face" with Reality itself.[14]

Although entitled to nirvana at this stage, he renounces it. Through the last four stages he can be called a celestial Buddha, and he becomes an object of worship, like Avalokitesvara, the compassionate one, and Manjusri, whose sword of wisdom cuts through error.

The bodhisattva of the Prajnaparamita sutras speaks the paradoxes to which Nagarjuna later gave formal dialectical structure. From the simple statement in the Heart Sutra ("Here, O Sariputra, form is emptiness and the very emptiness is form") we can move on to the elaborate teasing games that the lay bodhisattva Vimalakirti plays with the Elders and his fellow bodhisattvas:

Subhuti, if without cutting off carnality, anger and stupidity you can keep from these (three) evils; if you do not wait for the death of your body to achieve the oneness of things; if you do not wipe out stupidity and love in your quest of enlightenment and liberation; if you can look into (the underlying nature of) the five deadly sins to win liberation, with at the same time no idea of either bondage or freedom; . . . if you do not regard yourself as a worldly or unworldly man, as a saint or not as a saint; if you perfect all Dharmas while keeping away from the concept of Dharmas, . . . then can you receive and eat the food.

Hey, Aniruddha, when your deva eye sees, does it see form or formlessness? If it sees form, you are no better than those heretics who have won five supernatural powers. If you see formlessness, your deva eye is non-active (wu wei) and should be unseeing. . . .

So, if you, Maitreya, received the Buddha's prophecy of your future attainment of Buddhahood, all living beings (who are absolute by nature) should also receive it. Why? Because that which is absolute is non-dual and is beyond differentiation. If you, Maitreya, realize supreme enlightenment, so should all living beings. Why? Because they are the manifestation of bodhi (enlightenment). . . . Bodhi is unseeing, for it keeps from all causes. Bodhi is non-discrimination, for it stops memorizing and thinking. Bodhi cuts off ideation, for it is free from all views. . . . Bodhi puts an end to desire, because it keeps from longing. Bodhi is non-dual, it keeps from (both) intellect and its objects. . . .[15]

The Mind, Conserving and Creating

The Madhyamikas, it seems, felt no need to resolve their paradoxes, to go beyond analysis and to establish control over the Void in the age-old way of India, the way of Yoga. But Yoga was the starting point of the Madhyamikas' successors and rivals, the Mind-only school, the

Vijnanavada, also called the Yogacarins because of their foundation in samadhi.

The brothers Asanga and Vasubandhu, prime theoreticians of the Mind-only school, had in yoga an authentication of their doctrine that could not be applied by their modern counterpart, Bishop Berkeley, whose ontological idealism is summed up in the phrase *esse est percipi.* The self-constructions or the super-knowledges of the yogic trance were legitimized by universal social acceptance and the specific testimony of the Buddhist scriptures. In Berkeley's day "enthusiasm" was to madness near allied, and the mystical experience betokened possession not by God but by demons. The yogin, or Yogacarin, could start from samadhi as a serious demonstration of the diminished authority of reason and ordinary sense perception, and could proceed to a realization of the inner self by projected vision.

The error of duality, according to the Yogacarins, lay not in the vain attempt to differentiate and define objects that had no own-being, as the Madhyamika thought, but in regarding objects as independent of the mind which gave them being. The question of permanence or impermanence of dharmas, so important in early Buddhist thought, fades away. In the Lankavatara sutra the Buddha tells the bodhisattva Mahamati (Manjusri):

I am neither for permanence nor for impermanence. . . . External existents are not admitted; the triple world has been explained as mind-only; . . . the combination and separation of the great elements does not take place and does not disappear, and there are no primary and secondary elements; a duality of what is discriminated takes place in spite of the fact that object and subject cannot be defined; one comprehends duality as a result of false discrimination; one has moved away from false views about external existents or non-existents, and one has understood that they are merely one's own mind. *(BT,* p. 208)

To vaporize the stone that Dr. Johnson kicked (with closed eyes) in order to refute Berkeley's *esse est percipi,* an elaborate verbal and metaphysical structure is required. The Yogacarins work up to a version of undifferentiated awareness called store-consciousness (alaya-vijnana) or, in Suzuki's term, the All-Conserving. In addition to the six avenues of consciousness (the sixth is mind-consciousness), there is manas, a directing self-conscious mind, which marshals the data of the standard six awarenesses. Manas is capable of volition and discrimination between subject and object. It is a double-edged sword, says Suzuki:

It may destroy itself by clinging to the error of ego-conception, or it may, by a judicious exercise of its reasoning faculty, destroy all the misconceptions that arise from a wrong interpretation of the principle of ignorance. The Manas destroys itself by being overwhelmed by the dualism of *ego* and *alter*, by taking them for final, irreducible realities, and by thus fostering absolute ego-centric thoughts and desires, and by making itself a willing prey of an indomitable egoism, religiously and morally. On the other hand, when it sees an error in the conception of the absolute reality of individuals, when it perceives a play of Ignorance in the dualism of me and not-me, when it recognizes the *raison d'être* of existence in the essence of Tathagatahood, i.e., in Suchness, when it realizes that the Alaya which is mistaken for the ego is no more than an innocent and irreproachable reflection of the cosmic Garbha (the cosmic womb), it at once transcends the sphere of particularity and becomes the very harbinger of eternal enlightenment. (*Outlines*, pp. 134–35)

It is permissible to discern beneath this complex structure the simple outlines of an earlier foundation, the unity of the realized yogin and godhead, of Sakyamuni achieving enlightenment in victory over duality. Because there is no substance independent of its attributes, a "no soul-in-itself considered apart from its various manifestations such as imagination, sensation, intellection, etc.," thought processes are like the waves on the surface of the ocean of the Tathagata-Garbha:

> So with the Mind All-Conserving.
> When stirred, therein diverse mentations arise:
> Citta, Manas, and Manovijnana (mind-consciousness).
> These we distinguish as attributes,
> In substance they differ not from each other. . . .
> (Lankavatara, *ibid.*, p. 131)

It is ignorance that makes a false construction of experience and posits an external world. "But, says Vasubandhu in his 'Thirty Verses' (28), 'When cognition no longer apprehends an object, then/It stands firmly in consciousness-only, because, where there is nothing to grasp there is no more grasping."

The state in which "cognition no longer apprehends an object" is, in the Old Wisdom meditative disciplines, that of the higher dhyanas, the "trances without support." The Yogacarin applied similar discipline but with a more sophisticated epistemological superstructure. The early Buddhists, sensitive to the Master's distrust of theorizing and especially his dissociation from eternalism, steered away from any suggestion of an Absolute. The Mahayanists veer very close to Brahman in the abstractification of the Buddha. No matter how direct or elaborate the doctrinal structure, what all Indian ontological analysis after Samkhya comes down to is the qualitative difference, unbridgeable by rational activity, between the Absolute and the Actual. The alaya-vijnana, the manifestation of the undifferentiated tathata, is as close to an Atman as a Buddhist will permit himself to go (it is, after all, endowed with the potential of recognizing particularity). So, starting *comme il faut* with the distinct planes of Absolute and Phenomenon, the Void and the Conditioned, the Vijnanavadins offer their own device, the projecting Mind, and thus effect an interplay of the parallel planes. In practice, this is usually done by a dogmatic act of faith ("The Way begets one; one begets two . . . ") or by reference to the other-worldly quality of mystical trance. The Yogacarins did both and, in a further attempt at explaining the unexplainable, they refined the Three-body theory, the Trikaya.

The final sloka of Vasubandhu's "Thirty Verses" is:

This is the element without outflows, inconceivable, wholesome and stable,
The blissful body of emancipation, the Dharma-body of the great Sage.

(*BT*, p. 211)

This seems to be a deliberate confounding of three elements: the liberated arhant, marked by the stopping of the outflows (asravas); the blissful body that is aware of and enjoys its state of freedom; and the Ultimate, the Dharma itself, nirvana itself, where all is one, conceived as a form of the Tathagata.

The Three Bodies

The Dharma-body is not a body, but Buddhahood, the teaching itself conceived as the Buddha discarnate. It is the Tao, the Logos, svabhavika, from which all is derived. The other two bodies are the Buddha in visible action. The nirmana-kaya, the transformation-body, or apparitional body, as Conze calls it, is the body that Suddhodana thought was his son, and Yasodhara her husband. It was really another of the Tathagata's manifestations of skill-in-means, an appearance at a certain place at a certain time, as the Buddha chose Jambudvipa for his mission. But the clouds of glory that he trailed gave cause for wonderment. How could a *man* have been so wise, so noble? His wisdom and nobility grew, like any mythification, after his death, so that within a century the Masanghika docetism was under way.

The sambhoga-kaya, the body of enjoyment, tests the faith and the patience even of Manjusri the wise, because, as Suzuki says, "the conception of Sambhogakaya is altogether too mysterious to be fathomed by a limited consciousness," as we must agree on hearing that it is "a corporeal existence and at the same time filling the universe and that there are two forms . . . , one for self-enjoyment and the other as a sort of religious object for the Bodhisattvas" (*Outlines,* p. 263). For example, the magnificent Buddha who addresses the Panbodhisattvium at the opening of the Lotus sutra (having prepared for his discourse with samadhi) must have been enjoyable to both himself and his audience. Asanga and his commentator Vasubandhu tell us that on such occasions the enjoyment-body assumes as many forms as will satisfy the infinitely diversified inclinations of the bodhisattvas assembled; and that it is also a creation of the alaya-vijnana, which can be understood as another term for the Dharmakaya. Suzuki places the "lotus flowers with thousand-fold petals and each flower as large as a carriage-wheel," and kotis of acres of jewels in all the Sukhavatis, the Pure Lands, in proper perspective. "Modern Mahayanists in full accordance with this interpretation of the Doctrine of Trikaya do not place much importance on the objective aspects of the Body of Bliss" (*ibid.,* pp. 268–69).

A Religion for the Laity

Suzuki, the modern Buddhaghosa to the gentiles, speaks as a scholar to scholars. But the history of Buddhism tells how a discipline grew into a broad religion, and many more Buddhist hearts were given to sambhoga-kaya than minds to dharma-kaya. Whatever divergence may have been implicit in the message of Gautama, whether human or nirmana-kaya, his first disciples interpreted karma narrowly and would win freedom by their own merit—not as a reward, but by self-strengthening; and the lay folk could accumulate their own merit by removing obstacles on the path of the candidates for arhanthood—providing food and shelter, especially in the rainy season, in the hope that in future lives the same would be done for them—and by following a half-scale model of the monks' discipline, the first five of the ten rules. The laity, uninspired by the inward-looking elders, found imaginative expression in building stupas, making pilgrimages, and worshiping the numinous Buddha and his bodhisattvas.

The new larger-than-life Buddha filled the need of the laity for an active part as members of the Sangha, and the need of the religious establishment for a brighter face to turn to kings and for missionaries to carry abroad. The Mahasanghikas' ubiquitous Tathagata and the acceptance of cash were more than a symbolic breakthrough. The way was opening for universal worship, the magnificence of Ajanta, the growth of great colleges and monasteries and their participation in business enterprise and the affairs of state. The people's need to change the

Sakyamuni thus-gone-to-nirvana into the undying Tathagata enabled Buddhism to meet—for a time—the competition of the brahmins, who had moved from ritual and sacrifice, incorporated the Upanishadic vedanta, and benefited from an unorthodox and potent popular movement, the bhaktic cult of Krishna. The new blue god could apportion himself one to each of thousands of love-filled milkmaids in the Krishnalila dance, and each thought he was hers alone. So, less erotically (until Tantra blossomed), the new Buddha was all things to all men and women.

All beings are potentially Tathagatas:

Because the Buddha-cognition is contained in the mass of beings,
... all animate beings have the germ of Buddhahood in them. . . .

It pervades, as a general mark, the vicious, the virtuous, and the perfect.

(Ratnagotravibhaga I, 27, 50, in *BT*, pp. 181–82)

Or, as the monk said when rebuked for spitting on the image of the Buddha, "Where is there not the Buddha?"

The laity were promised more immediate rewards than potential Tathagatahood.

Speedily he wins fortune after he has circumambulated a Stupa. . . .
If he here gives a pointed tower, he will there be waited upon by Apsaras.

(Sikshasamuccaya 299, in *BT*, pp. 186–87)

There are as many Buddha-fields as there are Buddha-manifestations of the dharma-kaya, but surely the one most sought in prayer and dream was Sukhavati.

This world Sukhavati, Ananda, which is the world system of the Lord Amitabha, is rich and prosperous, comfortable, fertile, delightful and crowded with many Gods and men. And in this world system there are no hells, no animals, no ghosts, no Asuras and none of the inauspicious places of rebirth. . . .

All beings are irreversible from the supreme enlightenment if they hear the name of the Lord Amitabha, and, on hearing it, with one single thought only raise their hearts to him with a resolve connected with serene faith. (Sukhavativyuha 15, 26, in *BT*, pp. 202, 206)

This is the heaven of the Pure Land faith, which developed in China and survives, much spiritualized, in the Shin school in Japan. Amitabha, the Buddha of Infinite Light (or, as Amitayus, of Infinite Life), has his kingdom or world-system in the west. In the east rules Akshobya (the Imperturbable).

There were tutelary Buddhas for all ten points in space (the eight main compass points, zenith, and nadir) as well as for all the world systems. The idea of a multiplicity of Buddhas started early, a natural conclusion from the belief in rebirth: Sumedha, the first of a line that culminated in Sakyamuni, was inspired by Dipankara, who was in a different Buddha-line. But in the later centuries, especially in Tantra, five Buddhas took a foremost position as the heads of Buddha-families, around which prayer and ritual and psychological healing processes took form. Thus the loving Amitabha, with whom the compassionate bodhisattva Avalokitesvara was associated, is supposed to preside over the "greed" family in Tantric (Vajrayana) doctrine. The faith of bhakti, which centers on Amitabha, is a sublimation of greed, Conze points out. Similarly, Akshobya, with his related bodhisattva Vajrapani, presides over the "hate" family, and the gnosis of Prajnaparamita is an antidote for hate. Conze quotes Buddhaghosa:

> As on the unwholesome plane hatred does not cling, does not stick to its object, so wisdom on the wholesome plane. As hate seeks for faults, even though they do not exist, so wisdom seeks for the faults that do exist. As hate leads to the rejection of beings, so wisdom to that of all conditioned things.[16]

The others of the five Jinas (victorious Buddhas) are Vairocana the Brilliant (bodhisattva Samantabhadra), Ratnasambhava the Jewel Born (Ratnapani), and Amoghasiddhi, the Unfailing Success (Visvapani). The five Jinas are the centers, in Vajrayana thought and meditative practice, of elaborate correspondences with nature, the senses, the cardinal points, letters of the alphabet (for mantra), colors, sounds, emotions, and each has a fairly distinctive iconography for meditation on the mandala. In time, each group acquired female divinities, as Tara for Amitabha, and Prajnaparamita for Akshobya.

In actual devotional practice the bodhisattvas, whose very definition promised help for man, were called upon more frequently than the more distant Buddhas. Avalokitesvara, the divine one who surveys the world (for those in need of compassion),[17] was probably the earliest bodhisattva to be adored, and with the most widespread cult. He is prominent in the chapters (22–26) of the Lotus of the Good Law Sutra devoted to bodhisattvas, and the Karandavyuha sutra is devoted expressly to him (in it he takes worshipers to Amitabha in Sukhavati). He became popular in China, and in the later T'ang he became Kwan Yin (in Japan, Kwannon), a female figure of repose and mercy, possibly as a result of the association with Tara.

> He who is now so compassionate to the world,
> He will a Buddha be in future ages.
> Humbly I bow to Avalokitesvara
> Who destroys all sorrow, fear and suffering.

He is represented with a lotus in his hand, and is therefore called Padmapani (lotus in hand) and Padmadhara (bearing a lotus); a famous depiction is the Padmapani in Ajanta Cave 1.

Manjusri, the patron of wisdom, whose icon shows the sword and the book, is also prominent in the Lotus sutra, and is the main interlocutor with the Buddha in the Prajnaparamita sutras. His epithet, Kumarabhuta, is sometimes taken to mean "handsome youth," but more likely it refers to his vow, as King Amba, to become a bodhisattva. He is prominent in Vajrayana iconography.

Maitreya, the single bodhisattva mentioned in the Pali scriptures (as a future Buddha), is, like Avalokitesvara, in the ninth stage toward Buddhahood. His name indicates friendliness, and he is depicted with the wheel, the stupa, and a flask filled with the elixir of immortality. He receives instruction from Manjusri in the Lotus sutra, and there is a messianic quality in the belief that his coming will unify the world in righteousness.

Other prominent bodhisattvas are Samantabhadra (All-Good), like Avalokitesvara an embodiment of compassion; Mahasthamaprapta (Attained to Great Strength), a successor of Vajrapani in some cults as a symbol of power; Kshitagarbha (Earth-Womb), popular in China and Japan as the deliverer of souls from hell or spiritual torment.

Besides the mythical celestial bodhisattvas there is also the category of sainted humans, such as Nagarjuna, the philosopher; Hsuan Tsang, the pilgrim and translator; Kumarajiva, the translator; Milarepa, the singing recluse and teacher; Tsongkhapa, the reformer; Shotoku, the prince who introduced Buddhist thought to Japan. Sangharakshita points out that some of these are regarded not as men become bodhisattvas but as bodhisattvas who became men.[18]

In a class by himself is Vimalakirti (Immaculate Reputation), the wealthy upasaka (layman) of Vaisali, the bodhisattva who came from the realm of Profound Joy of Akshobya to do his work on earth. The Vimalakirtinidesa sutra, dated by its translator Charles Luk at about the beginning of the Christian era, touches several lines of Mahayana thought: the critique of the arhant's preoccupation with salvation; com-

THE PARADOXES OF MAHAYANA

passion as the commanding quality of the bodhisattva; the vanity of words in grasping nonduality; the state of mind as the decisive quality in striving for buddhahood, rather than the details of action in samsara. Vimalakirti is presented as a walking contradiction of the arhant ideal. He is warm, engaged in life, yet its master.

Living in the house, yet without desire, with wife and children, yet practicing purity; . . . ornamented with jewels, and with spiritual splendor too; enjoying food and drink, and also the taste of meditation; in the gambling house, leading the gamblers into the right path; in the house of passion, yet making clear to all the fault of passion; . . .

His life exemplified the six perfections, but he warns against accepting the fruits thereof:

He should speak of the impermanence of the body but never of the abhorrence and relinquishment of the body. He should speak of the suffering body but never of the joy in nirvana. . . . He should speak of the voidness of the body but should never cling to the ultimate nirvana. . . .

Although he practises samatha-vipasyana which contributes to the realization of bodhi (enlightenment) he keeps from slipping into nirvana. . . . Although he has realized ultimate purity he appears in bodily form to do his work of salvation; this is Bodhisattva conduct. (Vimalakirti Nirdesa sutra, Chap. V, pp. 52, 60)

Manjusri alone accepted the Buddha's suggestion to visit him in his contrived illness, after all the other disciples and bodhisattvas had begged off in trepidation at the upasaka's sharp dialectic. Both describe the paradoxical nature of the Buddha-path. Manjusri reminds his companions on the visit that, just as a lotus grows only in marshy land, "living beings in the mire of klesa (troubles) can eventually develop the Buddha Dharma," but "he who perceives the inactive (wu wei) state and enters its right (nirvanic) position, is incapable of advancing further to achieve supreme enlightenment" (p. 84). Mahakasyapa, speaking for the Disciples present, admits that "Even those committing the five deadly sins can eventually set their minds on the quest of the Buddha Dharma but we are unable to do so." Vimalakirti chants a description of the true bodhisattva at work in the world:

> He meditates amidst desires,
> Which also is a thing most rare.
> Or he appears as a prostitute
> To entice those who to lust are given.
> First using temptation to hook them

> He then leads them to the Buddha wisdom.
> He appears as a district magistrate
> Or as a chief of the caste of trader,
> A state preceptor or high official
> To protect living beings. (P. 90)

The illness itself was an example of skill-in-means in an act of compassion. After greeting Manjusri with a recognition of the proper even-mindedness of the visit ("Welcome, Manjusri, you come with no idea of coming and you see with no idea of seeing"), Vimalakirti explains his illness:

> Because all living beings are subject to illness I am ill as well. . . . when the only son of an elder falls ill, so do his parents, and when he recovers his health, so do they. Likewise a Bodhisattva loves all living beings as if they were his sons . . . (P. 50)

In Chapter IX of the sutra Vimalakirti gets his guests talking about the nondual dharma. Even Manjusri almost falls into the trap. After thirty-one bodhisattvas have given brief but learned discourses on the subject, Manjusri says,

> when all things are no longer within the province of either word or speech, and of either indication or knowledge, and are beyond questions and answers, this is initiation into the non-dual Dharma. (P. 100)

Manjusri knew his Nagarjuna, but Vimalakirti knew his Gautama Buddha. When Manjusri said, "Your turn," the layman kept silent. Then Manjusri exclaimed, "Excellent, excellent; can there be true initiation into the nondual Dharma until words and speech are no longer written or spoken?" It is said that the Ch'an masters enjoyed the Vimalakirti Nirdesa sutra.

SEVEN

Tantra and Zen: The Restorers

Vimalakirti, who was even-spirited in the sickroom and the marketplace and the brothel, was the logical outcome of Mahayana's view of samsara and nirvana as equally without self-being, just as the asceticism of the arhant was the logical conclusion of Hinayana belief in the reality of dharmas in samsara and their conquest in nirvana. Vimalakirti, the versatile layman who dismayed the disciples and put bodhisattvas on their mettle, embodied the reaction against an asceticism that sought both ecstasy and quiescence by wrenching the body and psyche from their dulling (karma-dust-gathering, the Jains said) pattern of eat-sleep-love-acquire. Freedom from desire, freedom from *things* had for long conferred prestige on the practicing ascetic.[1] Rejection of the world had indeed brought even-mindedness, victory over samsara, and had led to the highest intuitive knowledge of the Absolute; but Vimalakirti was the proof that it was not the only way. He was *in* but not *of* the welter of things. By the act of supreme cognition he saw samsara as the arhants and Caliban saw it: "It is but trash." But he conquered it not by flight but by going beyond; for what it was he made the most of it. By a continuing act of conscious will he was free from Mara's daughters even while enjoying them—*and in whatever guise he chose to see them.*[2]

Tantra and Zen continue Mahayana by going through Sunyata. If Madhyamika identified samsara and nirvana by destroying both with dialectic, Tantra and Zen revive them in the union of compassion and wisdom, skill-in-means and Sunyata, Hevajra and Nairatmya, and (in Tantra) yogin and yogini. They approach samsara with loving curiosity rather than fear of pollution. The intense concern of Old Wisdom with the senses as *memento mori,* as experiences to be transcended (e.g., by meditating on the animal functions of the living body and the dissolution of the dead one) is paralleled on a different plane by Tantra and Zen taking sense experience as a direct vehicle toward enlightenment, equipped with the wheels and wings of informed teaching.

Both Tantra and Zen, in stooping to play in the creative clay, risk much. They can be mired in samsara if the earth is not firm enough for the leap to liberation. In Tantra, the wine and the complaisant yogini may be no more than a snare for fools, and in Zen a koan may remain a silly question and a kick a kick and not a breakthrough to satori. But when successful, both integrate man's equipment and experience in an enduring way of daily life more joyous than that of the arhant, who is ever-mindful of his precarious state of upadhisesa, nirvana-in-life.

Tantra

Tantra (says Murti, who takes his stand at the Madhyamika, a stage which Tantra used as an intellectual base) is

the unique combination of mantra, ritual, worship, and yoga on an absolutistic basis. It is both philosophy and religion, and aims at the transmutation of human personality, by tantric practice suited to the spiritual temperament and needs of the individual, into the Absolute. (P. 109)

The transmutation takes place by a complex and deep working of many influences on the prepared personality: the symbolism of the mandala; the self-hypnosis of *japa,* the repetition of the mantra; the intense involvement with the "symbols" and "abstractions" of the Buddha-gods and their female counterparts not as symbols and abstractions but as deeply felt and shared actualities; the sexual act as ritualized embodiment of the creative potential and actuality of the universe, the union of Wisdom and Means, nirvana and samsara, lotus and vajra, the Sunya as potential, the seed as point and universe.

Toward Direct Aesthetic Experience

According to the foremost western proponent of Buddhist Tantra, Herbert V. Guenther, the superior person is one who has taken the three major steps of the noetic enterprise: (1) detachment from practical concerns (including disgust with the pleasures and riches of the world); (2) development of an enlightened attitude (concern for others); and (3) unbiased outlook (end of belief in an ego). He is now ready for direct experience of reality in full joy and immediacy. (*Treasures on the Tibetan Middle Way,* p. 10)

We have spent much time discussing Buddhist dissatisfaction with dualistic, categorized, egocentric patterns of ordinary cognition, and the

TANTRA AND ZEN: THE RESTORERS

quest of yogins, Buddhist and other, for immediacy and certainty. Guenther, unlike most writers on Tantra, minimizes mystical experience and directs our attention to a way of perception open to all:

> many of us have lost the capacity of understanding that, apart from an intellectual apprehension of the world, there is another one which yields truths just as valuable and valid. This is the aesthetic apprehension of intrinsic perception by the artist, the poet, and the seer, whose words are a commentary on a vision rather than a futile attempt to establish a system of supposedly universal truths over and above man's cognitive and sensible capacity. . . .
>
> Aesthetic experience belongs to the core of man's Being; it is more fundamental than any intellectual experience. Being basic to man's striving, it is the *terminus a quo,* enlightenment being the *terminus ad quem* which is nevertheless permanently grounded in aesthetic experience. Inasmuch as every experience is a living process, it is not reducible to anything else. (*Buddhist Philosophy in Theory and Practice,* pp. 160–61)

"Enlightenment" here is not the climax of samadhi; it is a joyous appreciation of every moment, "grounded in aesthetic experience." It is the permanent state of Milarepa:

> I am a yogi who lives on a snow-mountain peak.
> With a healthy body I glorify the Mandala of the Whole. . . .
> Happy and natural I live
> Without forethought or adjustment. . . .
> Where'er I go, I feel happy,
> Whate'er I wear, I feel joyful,
> Whatever food I eat, I am satisfied. I am always happy
> Through Marpa's grace,
> I, your old father Milarepa,
> Have realized Samsara and Nirvana.
> The Yoga of Joy ever fills my hermitage.[3]

Guenther expresses vigorously the distinction between discursive, interested perception of daily activity and the immediate, disinterested way of aesthetic perception:

> Ordinary perception is ego-centred, harsh, aggressive, imposing; aesthetic perception is object-centred, receptive, appreciative. In it the object becomes the guide, and the subject submits to its lead. This submissive union of the subject with the object, an aesthetic union, is undertaken for a more intimate appreciation of the object's intrinsic value and being which is, paradoxically, the subject's very being. (*The Tantric View of Life,* p. 84)

Appreciation of the object's intrinsic value is seen to have an ethical component when the "object" is a human relationship.

A person who is attached to, or hates, another, remains not only ignorant of the other, who for him is not a genuine person, but a segment that is selectively, classificatorily distorted by his own feelings, but he remains equally ignorant of himself. Treating others as mere objects he turns himself into a mere object for others, dispensable, and the quicker done away with the better. Inter-personal relationships require existential knowledge rather than categorical, "objective," knowledge. (*Ibid.*, p. 95)

It would be misleading to imply that Guenther ignores the immediacy of samadhic experience. He quotes a leading Tibetan thinker, Klongchen rab-'byams-pa:

Tantra as essence is intrinsic perception (rig-pa), because when in aesthetic experience the thing-in-itself is directly seen, the continuity of Nirvana is upheld, while when in the absence of a Guru's instruction no such vision obtains, continuity in Samsara is guaranteed.

Tantra is said to blossom because anyone who sees "the four lamps" and has an intuitive understanding belongs to a type of man who is immediately aware of the thing-in-itself, while he who does not so understand continues in a pattern of karmic action and reaction and emotional instability. [Guenther's note: "The 'four lamps' are symbolic terms for certain mystical experiences."] (*Buddhist Philosophy*, p. 164)

Because all experience, physical and mental, is an experience of the body, all bodily activity is the subject of intrinsic appreciation. Saraha reminds us of both the Buddha and Milarepa:

Seeing, hearing, touching, thinking,
Eating, smelling, running, walking, sitting,
Idly talking, talking back—
Know all this to be the mind and do not run from this oneness.
To see Being is not to see it as something. (*The Tantric View of Life*, p. 94)

Sexual activity as both a normal human activity and as a profound symbol of polarity and unity has brought distracting connotations to Tantra in India, its place of origin, as well as in the West. But first we must place Buddhist Tantra in relation to Hindu.

Tantra (from a root meaning "expand") is an Indian development that spread to Tibet with Buddhism. An amalgam of ancient magic, mother-goddess cult, fertility rite, and symbol and sound incantation to achieve self-deification, it is practiced on both a primitive and an extremely sophisticated level. As investigation and disclosure of its symbolism develop, it becomes apparent that the Tantra embodies many psychological truths, such as the techniques of transference, catharsis, and insight. Until recently descriptions of Hindu Tantra have expressed either apologetic dismay or awe.

It has, of course, been very loosely taken by some scholars to denote the literature of the mystical worship of female deities (Sakti) alone, with which are associated various revolting and apparently depraved and immoral rites. . . .

The most interesting development appears to be the utilization of Vedic mantras in apparently revolting Tantric rites, e.g. *pancatattva sodhana* or the purification of the five tattvas, viz. madya (wine), mamsa (meat), matsya (fish), mudra (fried grain) and maithuna (sexual intercourse).[4]

More abstract is this statement about Buddhist Tantra (Vajrayana):

The way of the Vajrayana is the Way of Power which leads to the mastery of good and evil. It is also the Way of Transformation whereby inward and outward circumstances are transmuted into weapons by the power of mind. (John Blofeld, *Tantric Mysticism of Tibet*, Foreword)

This is a more circumstantial statement by an academic who is an authentic initiate in Hindu Tantra:

There is decidedly such a thing as a common Hindu and Buddhist tantric ideology, and I believe that the real difference between tantric and non-tantric traditions is methodological: tantra is the psycho-experimental interpretation of non-tantric lore. As such, it is more value-free than non-tantric traditions; moralizing and other be-good cliches are set aside to a far greater extent in tantrism than in other doctrine. By "psycho-experimental" I mean "given to experimenting with one's own mind," not in the manner of the speculative philosopher or the poet, but rather in the fashion of a would-be psychoanalyst who is himself being analysed by some senior man in the trade. . . . All tantrics flout traditional, exoteric orthodoxy, all put experiment above conventional morality, . . . and all agree that their specific method is dangerous, and radical, and all claim that it is a shortcut to liberation.[5]

Tantric mysticism, according to Bharati, is not "the search for divine truth within the mind" (Blofeld, p. 9), but a way of practice to achieve a psychic state of being that is related to the "divine" only by the specific verbal context. St. Teresa and Meister Eckhart talk of union with the Godhead, Hindu yogins talk of escaping from the conditioned world, Buddhists after the Madhyamika would talk of rising above the realm of definition and distinction. The target of tantric *sadhana* (devotional practices) is freedom from the irksomeness of attachment, as it is for all Hindu and Buddhist belief. The method of tantrism is more radical than any other method, and the immediate aim of the tantric ritual is to achieve enstasy.

Enstasy . . . is a non-discursive, quasi-permanent condition of the individual agent, and it is highly euphoric. In Indian theological parlance—Hindu, Buddhist, and Jain—it is tantamount with supreme insight or wisdom, and all other knowledge attained by discursive processes is thought to be vastly inferior; formal learning of any kind is, by implication, essentially opposed to enstasy, marring its voluntary repetition and intensification. (*The Tantric Tradition*, p. 286)

Prajna, we have seen, is nondual cognition, intuition of the Real. Learning and reason, working through differentiation and distinction, cannot dispense with the duality of subject and object. After the arhant ideal failed, the problem of the schools was to provide a way of unity such as the arhants had achieved precariously through self-restriction and meditation, but a way more catholic and benign. Madhyamika gave backhanded recognition to samsara as no less real than nirvana—which was itself indeterminable. Yogacara offered more possibilities. Snellgrove sums up the movement toward the new experientialism of Tantra:

Both [Madhyamika and Yogacara] are equally convinced of the reality of the mystical experience, but whereas the one asserts the non-substantiality of all experience and the indeterminability of any absolute itself, the other asserts the absolute existence of the one unity which contains potentially the twofold division into this and that, into subject (grahaka) and object (grahya), and so on into ever greater diversity. (*The Hevajra Tantra*, pp. 19–20)

Guenther moves the subject–object identity of Yogacara into a new relationship, that of the aesthetic transaction:

Aesthetic awareness is certainly subjective in the sense that it must be "felt," experienced by the apprehending subject, but it is not "merely subjective" in the widely held sense of the phrase as being a passing personal whim. Beyond its subjective accessibility as a vividly moving experience the aesthetic fact is the matrix from which all conscious life emerges. (*Buddhist Philosophy*, p. 160)

Tantric practice, Bharati points out, exercises the creative subjective response of the individual to his mantra and other devices to raise him to his desired enstatic state. Guenther reminds us that

awareness ranges from the aesthetic fact or experience as the first instant of mental activity and as the matrix of all other cognitions, through a disentanglement of the aesthetic experience from the "ordinary" and confused manner of cognition, to the mature and pure aesthetic experience which is known as "enlightenment," a persisting is an intuitive attitude. (*Ibid.*, p. 165)

Female–Male Symbolisms

All mysticisms that make public profession of their mystery must find images for the two elements of their experience, the goal and the starting place, the Absolute and the phenomenal, the Unconditioned and the limited. In Buddhism the Prajnaparamita sutras established the dominant image of the Ultimate as female, just as in the Tao the receptacle, the patient, the eventually prevailing is yin. The Emptiness of Sunyata is all potential. But then, of course, a personification must be found for the actual, the practical. In early Buddhism Wisdom was balanced with compassion (karuna) or skill-in-means (upaya), to accomplish the Tathagata's work among men. Later, the Tathagata himself became the male functioning element, the god achieving the intention of the unmoved Godhead—a distinction that Eckhart himself made in facing the problem of an Absolute Godhead behind a Yahweh-moved phenomenal world.

Guenther, following the sunyata tradition, calls the potential for aesthetic encounter "nothing."

This basic nothing is termed "ancestress" which is a verbal symbol for pure transcendence. In the fine arts this nothing is presented as a female figure whose color depends on the interpretation given to the nothingness of transcendence. This conception of the ground of man's being as female has important consequences for the whole attitude of Buddhism. It recognizes the female principle in the nature of things as valid in its own right and attributes to it an inspiring and emotionally moving character of friendliness, tenderness, and intimacy, the greatest one being the union of two lovers. This recurrent theme in Tibetan painting is therefore a symbol of aesthetic awareness in which inspiration and appreciation have become united in wedlock. (*Ibid.*, p. 166)

In Buddhist Tantra the female is the potential element. The Hindu Tantrist Bharati points to a historically significant fact:

The main speculative difference between Hindu and Buddhist tantrism is the Buddhist ascription of dynamicity to the male and of "wisdom" to the female pole in the central tantric symbolism, as opposed to the Hindu ascription of dynamicity to the female and (static) wisdom to the male pole. . . . (P. 31)

The relevant Hindu symbol is the shakti of Shiva, the consort Durga or Kali, dancing on the supine Shiva and imparting energy to him (his eyes are open), and the Hindu phrase, "Shiva without Shakti is a corpse."

Guenther extends and deepens the space between the two Tantras:

Hinduist Tantrism, due to its association with the Samkhya system, reflects a psychology of subjectivistic dominance, but tempers it by infusing the human with the divine and vice versa; Buddhist Tantrism aims at developing man's cognitive capacities so that he may *be,* here and now, and may enact the harmony of sensuousness and spirituality.[6]

In all Tantra, woman has an important role in sadhana, either in person or as abstraction, depending on the mode.

The Prajnaparamita and Tara were the first autonomous Buddhist deities. . . . Tara was a creation of the popular mind. The Prajnaparamita, on the other hand, originated among small groups of ascetic metaphysicians. In the Mahayana, the Prajnaparamita was not only a virtue, a book, and a mantra, but also a deity. (Conze, *Buddhism,* p. 192)

The delicacy of the following passage indicates a presentation of the Tantra of the right hand:

Adepts are instructed to think of perfect wisdom with the intensity and exclusiveness that characterize a young man's thoughts of a young and lovely girl. This is a purely Tantric technique which has often proved effective in stimulating adepts to unflagging zeal. (Blofeld, p. 244)

Nowhere in this book does Blofeld mention maithuna, which is to right-minded commentators the most shocking of the "various revolting and apparently depraved and immoral rites" (see above) of the pancatattvas. But one cannot do justice to the theory and practice of Tantra without a clear statement of its utilization of sexual symbolism and practice. A fairer statement of the matter is M. N. Dutt's comment on a quotation from Agamasara:

The purpose of this sloka is: Cohabitation is at the root of creation, preservation and destruction. It achieves all ends and confers the most difficult knowledge of Brahma. The esoteric meaning of Maithuna, in the language of Yoga, is the recitation of the various attributes of God. (*A Prose English Translation of the Mahanirvana Tantram,* p. 23)

The *Mahanirvana Tantra* is, despite the name, a Hindu work mainly in the form of a conversation between Shiva and Parvati, his consort in her lovely form. This passage suggests the quality of a tantric ritual "of the left hand."

There sitting himself in company with the devotees who worship the Supreme Brahma, a worshipper should gather and fetch the Tatwas, and O Siva, place them before him (212). Then uttering for a hundred times, the mantra Om, Hansa on all the Tatwas, he should recite the following *mantra.* (213) "The libation itself is Brahma, the thing by which the libation is offered is Brahma, the offerer of the libation is Brahma, the vessel in which the libation is offered is

TANTRA AND ZEN: THE RESTORERS 117

Brahma . . . and the devotee who worships in this way the Supreme Brahma becomes merged in or unified with the Brahma."

Dutt explains the place of the five forbidden practices in the Hindu ritual in the traditional way, more simply than but without contradicting Guenther's Tibetan metaphysics of the aesthetic transaction:

All these, wine, meat, fish, and women are objects of temptation. If a worshipper can overcome this temptation, the road of eternal bliss is clear for him. It is not an easy affair for a man to have a youthful and beautiful damsel before him and worship her as a goddess without feeling the least lustful impulse within him. . . . Thus we see that in Tantrik religion, a worshipper is to approach his God through diverse objects of pleasure. He is to relinquish his desire and self and convert the various pursuits of enjoyment into instruments of spiritual discipline. (P. 21)

Two classical passages of similar effect:

Just as water that has entered the ear may be removed by water and just as a thorn may be removed by a thorn, so those who know how, remove passion by means of the passion itself. Just as a washerman removes the grime from a garment by means of grime, so the wise man renders himself free of impurity by means of impurity itself. (Cittavisuddhiprakarana, in *BT*, p. 221)

By that act by which the beings boil in terrible hell for 100,000,000 kalpas, by that very deed the yogi is released. (*Advayavajrasamgraha*, in *The Tantric Tradition*, p. 301, n. 9)

Or, in the words of Saraha,[7] who is supposed to have given expression in the ninth century to then-current tantric ideas,

Enjoying the world of sense, one is undefiled by the world of sense.
One plucks the lotus, without touching the water.
So the yogin who has gone to the root of things,
Is not enslaved by the senses although he enjoys them. (Sloka 64)

One may worship a divinity, and (in trance) even his form may be seen.
(Sloka 65)[8]

Saraha, somewhat like Omar, despairs of the efforts of the schools, whether the Brahmins who "vainly recite the Vedas four," masters who "smear their bodies, And on their heads they wear matted hair," Jain monks for whom "there is no release, deprived of the truth of happiness, they do afflict their own bodies," bhikshus of the Old School, who "wither away in their concentration on thought," those of the Great Vehicle, those who just meditate on mandala circles, or those who "strive to define the fourth stage of bliss." Saraha sums up,

Do not discriminate, but see things as one.
Making no distinction of families.
Let the whole of the threefold world become one in the state of Great Passion.
(Sloka 26)

Here there is no beginning, no middle, no end,
Neither samsara nor nirvana.
In this state of highest bliss
There is neither self nor other. (Sloka 27)

Clearly, Saraha is no unlearned ecstatic going his idiosyncratic way to liberation. He has gone through the ways of all the schools and urges a deceivingly simple way, the shrine of one's own body (Sloka 48). But he does not omit the basic commandment of Tantra, dependence on the guru.

Abandon thought and thinking and be just as a child.
Be devoted to your master's teaching, and the Innate will become manifest.
(Sloka 57)

The central position of the Master in Tantra is made explicit in the work by a contemporary of Saraha, "The Attainment of the Realization of Wisdom and Means," by Anangavajra. Wisdom, which realizes the nonsubstantiality of things, and Means, or Compassion, the passionate devotion to relieve the suffering of man, are wed.

The mingling of both, which is like that of water and milk, is known as Wisdom-Means in a union free of duality. It is the essence of Dharma. . . . it is the final stage of Enjoyment and Release. . . . it is here that those intent on the good of the world become Buddhas now. . . . (*BT*, pp. 241–42)

The method cannot be expressed in words, "since there is no connection between the sound and the true meaning. . . . So a wise man must resort to a good master, for without him the truth cannot be found. . . ." The master gives instruction in the esoteric doctrine, and then presides over "that sacramental experience of Vajrasattva."

And so a son of the Conquerors for the sake of this consecration strives with all his might, and with the observation of all due ceremony approaches his vajra-guru, that ocean of all good qualities. Having found a yogini with wondrous eyes and endowed with youth and beauty, he should deck her with fair raiment, and garlands and the scent of sandal-wood, and commit her to his master, and together with her he should honor and praise him with all his might, using scents and garlands and milk and other kinds of offerings. (*BT,* p. 244)

TANTRA AND ZEN: THE RESTORERS

Then, in a set hymn, he beseeches the master for the vajra-consecration. The guru calls the pupil into the mandala, which is strewn with delectable things, resounding with bells, and pleasant with flowers and perfumes:

it is the most wondrous resort of Vajrasattva and other divine beings and is prepared for union with the yogini. Then joining with the yogini the most worthy master places the Thought of Enlightenment in the lotus vessel, which is the abode of the Buddhas. Next he consecrates the pupil, now joined with the yogini, with chowries and umbrellas held high and with propitious songs and verses. Having thus bestowed upon him the consecration, that excellent gem, he should give him the five-fold sacrament. . . . It consists of the precious jewel, with camphor, red sandal-wood and vajra-water, and as fifth component the empowering mantra. (BT, p. 245)

In his edition of the *Hevajra* tantra D. L. Snellgrove stresses the occurrence of sexual symbolism at every turn. "Vajra and lotus derive their whole significance from their masculine and feminine connotations." In the name Hevajra, the syllable *he* symbolizes compassion, *vajra* (the thunderbolt) is Wisdom. Snellgrove reminds us of the essential identity of the female and male, symbolizing that of nirvana and samsara, the two-in-one, made explicit in the maithuna ceremony.

Bharati, as a practitioner, presents the matter in a slightly different fashion. To adepts, "all the complexes which tantric Buddhism personifies in its deities, populating the universe with psychoexperimentally necessary and highly ingenious anthropomorphic hypostases of philosophic 'non-entities,' for example the Goddess *Nairatmya*"[9]—all these are frankly and playfully psychic games one plays with oneself to help break down the barrier between the rational and the intuitional. The siddhi that the adept can conjure up are known to be constructs, but the psyche moves in its ancient ways to the ultimate reality:

Enstasy is reached when the adept succeeds in suspending, temporarily at first, but in increasing spans of time, all object-thought, and in concentrating on the non-discursive, interiorized object of his meditation, which is variously described in anthropomorphical terms as the *istam* (Tibetan *yid dam*), the chosen deity, or in absolutist speculative terms as the case may be. (Bharati, p. 297)

Guenther, who explains tantric doctrine on a more conceptualized level than Bharati, sums up the sexual component in Tantra at its most elevated:

The symbol-term *mudra* also signifies "woman" who must be understood as a "way of doing," a "mode of activity," a typical manner of conduct rather than as a typical kind of thing.... The *mudra*-woman thus actualizes Being and is its actuality, just as my body expresses my existence and as the concrete actualization of Being is both the "expression" and the "expressed." When further it is said that no understanding is possible without the *mudra*-(woman), the dialectic of lived experience is indicated. This lived experience is the tension of one existence towards another existence. It is essentially equivocal; everything which we live or think always has several meanings. Since existence, indeterminate in itself, manifests and expresses itself in the individual's body as sexuality and is manifested and expressed by the sexuality of the body, Mahamudra as absolute Being is equally indeterminate but manifests itself as masculinity or femininity which becomes *embodied* in a man or a woman. Masculinity and femininity belong to a plane of reality where male and female have little meaning. Male and female are only the adaptation to organic life of a basic polarity pertaining to the very process of becoming. As the higher Tantras deal with an individual's lived existence they quite naturally include sex, not because they advocate what other disciplines bashfully try to conceal but because they realize that sexuality is coextensive with the life of man. They are aware of the fact that sexuality cannot be reduced to existence nor can existence be reduced to sexuality. Man as embodied Being is sexual because he is the concrete expression of a basic polarity. (*Buddhist Philosophy,* pp. 194–95)

From Saraha down to Guenther, there is agreement that it is not the act itself, but the quality of the understanding of the experience, the richness of the transaction, that leads to enlightenment. The sexual act can be the occupation of fools and, as the Buddha put it, "the common way," or it can be the *Liebestod,* the death of the self (Nairatmya) in union that is ecstatic both in itself and as mystical experience, the cognition of Being as the solution of the mystery of the joining of the Absolute and the Actual.

Pancatattva, Mandala, Mantra, Chakra

The basis of tantric theory and practice, then, is to increase the import of the senses by imparting symbolic and spiritual significance to them as aesthetic experience, then to harness them in the achievement of lasting enstasy, in a positive, joyous appreciation of the wondrous world-as-it-is. Here it is unlike classical yoga, which fell in line with the Upanishadic forest-dwellers and the Old Wisdom arhants in working to subdue the craving senses as the way to its form of enstasy. Snellgrove has this to say of the arhants:

In so far as the early Buddhists (sravakas) had sought nirvana in a deliberate stopping of the process of samsara, such mystical experience as they achieved was limited and imperfect. It was not the end as they had thought, but merely a stage. Moreover it was limited because it was personal and therefore selfish. To bring about a cessation (nirodha) of phenomenal existence (=duhkha) for oneself amounted to disregard of the sorry plight of others. (P. 23)

The most troublesome manifestation of tantric defiance of respectability is the practice of the pancatattva or the pancamakara, "the five M's" (madya, mamsa, matsya, mudra,[10] maithuna) as an integral part of left-handed tantric old ritual (they are not mentioned by Blofeld). The rationale, as we have seen, is that only in making dualistic distinctions does man think of actions as either good or evil. Man remains a "rational animal" until he can transcend his limitations by obtaining intuitive insight. The five M's were employed literally in left-handed practice (which is illegal and has been practically eliminated in modern India), metaphorically with substituted materials and actions (worship with flowers instead of sex) in the right-handed. Both Bharati and Blofeld outline actual rituals, the former stressing physical details and comparisons between Hindu and Buddhist procedures, the latter giving the verbal content of prayers and incantations. Bharati mentions the taking of *cannabis* (vijaya, that gives victory) about an hour and a half before the five-M ceremony, just the right time for it to work to release inhibitions.

The mandala serves a double purpose in Tantra. As an object of contemplation, mandala deities come alive and help bring the adept to the special world that is not rooted in daily life. Second, the mandala is laden with intellectual and emotional symbols that summarize much of man's conscious and unconscious experience: the inverse triangles depicting male and female interrelation, the sounds, colors, physical senses, varieties of wisdom, types of evil, times of day—and endless combination of conceptions and actualities reduced to order, but always with the reserved understanding that the order is imposed by the mind on what is actually formless; in sunyata all is merged, and enstasy is its manifestation.

The mantra is even more obviously an instrument, a device for the modification of the psyche. Some mantras, containing what seem to be nonsense syllables, go back to primitive magic; others have sophisticated order and reference, such as palindromes and syllables arranged in order of their vowels in fixed pattern. In mantra, words are deeds; it is verifiable by what it effects, a complex feeling tone in the person, a magical force that confers existential status upon imagination contents. Omitting the purpose of the mantra, Bharati defines it thus:

A *mantra* is a quasi-morpheme or a series of quasi-morphemes, or a series of mixed genuine and quasi-morphemes arranged in conventional patterns based on codified esoteric traditions, and passed on from one preceptor to one disciple in the course of a prescribed initiation ritual. (P. 111)

The purpose is "propitiation, acquisition, and identification, or introjection." Propitiation, the most ancient, would ward off unpleasant powers and bring support from favorable ones. Acquisition includes not only things but powers of control, such as magical skills. Identification is exemplified by the Upanishadic "I am Brahman" or the Vajrayana "I am of the nature of the *vajra* through the intuition of *sunya*."

The key of the mantra is the bija, the seed syllable, which bears expanded implicational significance as well as it is own intrinsic power. An initiate knows the sandha terminology, the hidden or allusive meanings of the syllables themselves. *RAM* signifies fire or red, *AIM* the wife of Agni, *PHAT* is an explosive weapon, *HUM* is warrior, *EM* is the yoni or womb bija. Different mantras have different standard uses: "OM HUM PHAT is used in Buddhist tantra for banning and exorcism, for meditation on any of the dhyani-Buddhas, for the worship of the tantric goddess Kurukulla, and for preparing the mind to accept the truth of Voidness (sunyata); the Hindu mantra AM HUM PHAT is used when chopping off the head of the sacrificial goat during Kali and Durgapuja. . . ." (P. 121)

The guru must preside over the imparting of the information on mandala, mantra, and ritual. He must adapt the mantra and the techniques of indoctrination to the capacity and personality and physique of the candidate. Each relationship is unique and becomes itself an intense aesthetic experience leading to the goal of illumination.

In the West a much-talked-of phase of yogic indoctrination is the chakra or mandala system, the phantom companion spinal net reaching from the coiled, quiescent kundalini at the base of the spine up to the lotus center in the brain. The symbolism of yogic and tantric endeavor is to arouse the female element, the kundalini, and by stages of intense meditation to make it rise through the four (Buddhist) or six (Hindu) or twelve centers or "lotuses" located along the central duct.

The force that moves from the base to the top of the yogic body in the process of successful meditation is always visualized as female, and it is the microcosmic representation of the magna mater, whom the Hindus conceive of as Sakti, and the Buddhist Vajrayanis as wisdom (prajna, Tibetan ses rab). The brain centre is identified with the supreme cosmic principle, the *brahman* for the Hindus, and the Great Void, mahasunya (Tibetan stong pa chen), for the tantric

Buddhists. The merger or resorption of the dormant power conceived as female in the supreme principle is, of course, the esoteric pivot of all the erotic symbolism which pervades tantric thought and practice. The Buddhist tantras refer to the most complete nirvana as *mahasukha* (great bliss) and this is the term they use for enstasy reached through the three-fold control which is the keynote of tantric *sadhana*. . . . Now the practical axiom of the tantrics, formulated much more precisely in Buddhist Vajrayana than in Hindu Tantrism, is this: enstasy is reached when we learn to immobilize mind, breath and the seminal fluid. (Bharati, pp. 292, 293)

The simultaneous control of the three elements, the control of the mind being the most difficult, is the point of the final junction of kundalini force and the supreme chakra, the moment of ecstasy, the union of prajna and upaya in Vajrayana. For western seekers, it need not be stressed that the chakra system is an imaginary heuristic device to give a pattern to meditation, categorically similar but on a higher level than colored kasina or fancied Taras or the tip of one's nose.[11]

Union of Sensuous and Spiritual

Guenther would not agree with Bharati's statement on Vajrayana's concern for the triple immobilization[12] and his tendency is to move the physical statements of tantric lore into the aesthetic and symbolic as quickly as possible. He cites a many-leveled explication of this passage from Saraha:

> By eating and drinking and by enjoying copulation
> Forever and everywhere one fills the rounds.
> Thereby the world beyond is reached . . . (P. 59)

Karma Phrin-las-pa's interpretations of this passage touch first on the importance of the tactile sense in establishing man's connection with his inner and outer environment, the basis of the aesthetic cognition, which depends on "the warmth of closeness, not the coldness of distance."

Instead of disrupting the Unity of Being by separating and downgrading the instinctive side, as represented by the tactile experience, from the perceptual side which then becomes over-evaluated conceptually, the Tantric "Way" attempts to preserve this unity of sensuousness and spirituality. . . . (P. 60)

The Tibetan's first interpretation of Saraha is on the objective, physical level: the person eats the meat and drinks the beer, then unites with his partner, meanwhile conceiving of the body as a god, of speech as mantra, and of mind as absolute Being; "by such an experience he reaches a world-transcending Buddhahood experience." The second level likewise deals with the four chakras, "the four kinds of delight," in the process of unification of Mantrayoga; the third level is in terms of mystical experience: "by experiencing the ineffable, one forever and everywhere fills one's noetic being with original awareness . . ."; the fourth interpretation is from the viewpoint of ultimate Being:

> A follower of the Mahamudra teaching takes as his food the world of appearance rising incessantly in splendour, and has for his drink the open dimension (of Being) merging in the absoluteness of Being. By experiencing the unity and inseparability of appearance and openness of Being he is immediately aware with unsurpassable joy.[13]

To move from copulation to the joy of the unity of appearance and openness of Being requires some highly disciplined metaphysical indoctrination by a guru. Understood properly, says Guenther,

> sexuality is the dialectic of lived experience, in which I apprehend the other as subject, . . . which means to recognize the intrinsic value of the other, as indicated by the statement that in the realm of lived experience men and women are gods and goddesses. (P. 63)

In urging the transcendence of disciplined aesthetic experience, Guenther casts doubt on the validity of meditation as a means toward the unity of intrinsic awareness and openness (of Being). It is rather a restrictive, quiescent technique. Quoting Saraha, "By the swindle of meditation freedom is not found,"[14] Guenther declares that in seeking to escape samsara and gain nirvana, we demonstrate the bifurcation into mind and body, and the evaluation of mind as more valuable than body; "we unwittingly side with what seems to be more valuable and, by attending to the more valued pole, through what is commonly called 'meditation,' we merely perpetuate the bifurcation and the conflict" (p. 117). Later he compares ordinary perception ("fatiguing and frustrating because we abstract and therefore fail to perceive other aspects of the perceived object") and "perceiving intrinsically," which is "more alert, more astute and penetrating":

> Rather than detracting from action it makes action much more appropriate to the situation. Only when the mind is "fixed" on some aspect, commonly referred to as meditation or pure contemplation, action becomes inhibited and all feeling retrogressive. In such contemplation, all spontaneity and naturalness is lost. Intrinsic perception is both active and passive; it is passive in letting things be, in not forcing itself upon them, and it is active in being itself more alert. It is

a broadening of the perceptual field, as vast as the sky or space which is the whole world. (P. 134)

The Aesthetic Realization

Perhaps. Perhaps Guenther lets himself be carried away—unless all space is immediately, intrinsically perceptible. A generation ago D. W. Prall, this writer's teacher, approached the intrinsic, immediate aesthetic experience from the discipline of a naturalistic aesthetics and reached much the same fine conclusions as Guenther.

And the first and last steps in being human consist in being aesthetic, not being God or nature, but being limited to felt participation in the nature of the world in sensuous contemplation—tasting, smelling, hearing, seeing, feeling purely and innocently without ulterior purposes or desires of our own, since we have already—for the moment only, however—achieved Paradise.

He also agreed that what is perceived intrinsically and aesthetically depends on the quality and training of the perceiver:

the surface found depends for its character quite as much on the discriminating processes of perception and hence upon perceptual training as upon the external stimulus. What the surface is felt as, depends also upon the organism that feels it for all that it may amount to in an adequate response, a transaction in which the whole nervous system takes part to a degree depending upon its readiness for plastic adaptation to the external space-time object. Such readiness in response comes only of great gift or long training. . . . So that aesthetic experience is exciting and humanly and maturely satisfying just so far as the organism having such experience is adequately developed through its senses and their correlations and connections with deeper feeling processes to respond to what may, by virtue of this response, be objectively present to it.[15]

This convergence of western naturalism and Guenther's neo-Tantrism shows several points of contact. Aesthetic disinterestedness— "purely and innocently without ulterior purposes or desires of your own"—corresponds to the detachment of nondual, nonclinging Buddhist cognition; the dynamic aesthetic transaction is a long step toward the merging of subject and object in high Mahayana thought; the concern to apprehend the aesthetic object as it presents itself, not for its social, religious, or financial implications, suggests the cultivation of alert awareness in Zen.

Prall also presents in his own terms another basic theme in Zen and, indeed, in all Buddhism: the long-term growth of the mature human organism until a qualitatively new personality is born, responsive to things as they are, immediately and nondiscursively. Zen goes farther in this direction than Prall, who would require a many-sided social and political expression as well as the aesthetic; the objective of satori introduces a new personal ideal from a distant cultural base. Prall, less absolute than Tantra or Zen, points modestly to a way of health for western man not too dissimilar to theirs: a reduction of self-assertion and self-interest and complex confabulation:

> And if we wish to mark ourselves off as human and not merely natural, it is as aesthetic beings that we are best characterized, beings capable of enjoying the aesthetic aspect of the world, the world as we are directly acquainted with it. And this at all levels of experience, from bare conscious awareness of qualitative content as distinguishable external presentation, to the intelligent grasp of great works of art, where all the human faculties are exercised, where perceptual discrimination and the intellectual understanding of complex relational structures, are fused in the passionate realization of expressed feeling. (*Aesthetic Analysis*, p. 31)

Zen

Vimalakirti, who moved at ease in the red dust of earth, as a bodhisattva by rank was also a postgraduate arhant and therefore free of the defilements. Tantra and Zen, which judged between pure and impure only according to the attitude of the beholder, asked only: Did he cling to sense gratification, and did he have a false idea of Self? Vimalakirti did not, and therefore he was in a permanent state of grace.

Zen's ease in the world of sense and its legitimate derivation from Mahayana come clear in the earliest available statement by a Zen (or, in Chinese, Ch'an) master, the *Hsin-hsin Ming* (translated by Watts as "Treatise on Faith in the Mind" and by Waley as "On Trust in the Heart") by Seng-ts'an, the "Third Patriarch" in the dubious succession from the perhaps historical Bodhidharma. The poem marks the confluence of Tao and Mahayana:

> Let your nature blend with the Way and wander in it free from care. . . .
> If you want to follow the doctrine of the One, do not rage against the World of the Senses.
> Only by accepting the World of the Senses can you share in the True perception. . . .
> If the mind makes no distinctions all Dharmas become one. . . .
> Let the thought of the Dharmas as All-One bring you to the So-in-itself. . .

> To trust in the Heart is the Not Two, the Not Two is to trust in the Heart.
>
> (*BT,* pp. 297, 298)[16]

In Ch'an is the meeting of the hollow receptacle of Tao and the Void of Sunyata. Ch'an sees all dharmas as One in the Tathata, the So-in-itself; and trusting in the heart leads to the discovery of one's Buddha-nature by spontaneous action revealing the whole person no longer split by intellectualization. By a qualitatively new self-realization, called bodhi, wu, or satori, one steps outside the normal categories of sin and obligation.

Zen and the Sutras

Zen, like Buddhism, has undergone much change since its uncertain beginnings. Two main currents are discernible, sometimes in turbulent clash, sometimes, as at present, mingling peaceably. Bodhidharma is supposed to have arrived in China from India in 520 A.D., bearing an unexceptionable Mahayana message of Emptiness. His quirky refusal to explain the unexplainable in words to the eminently rational Chinese set him and his followers off from the Chinese Buddhist mainstream.[17] About 700 the doctrine and techniques that were attached to the name of the factitious "Sixth Patriarch" (Hui-neng; Eno in Japanese) split the followers of Bodhidharma, set the program for Ch'an for several centuries, and are still at work in Zen practice. The "abrupt realization" of the Buddha-mind within each person, by spontaneous reflex of the entire person rather than through painful study and debate, became a basic prescription. The school is symbolized by Liang K'ai's "Zen style" sketch of the Sixth Patriarch tearing up the sutras. The "abrupt" school gave Ch'an the tradition of dramatic, calculatedly absurd behavior, tricky koans or subtle word-play between masters testing each other, and beatings and violent behavior designed to jolt the novice into understanding.

But alongside the professed anti-intellectuality there has persisted the tradition of intense study of Tripitaka and Mahayana sutras and commentary. Before the student can be free of his mind he must bring it to a realization of the Void and the identity of nirvana and samsara. As the artist said, "Draw bamboos for ten years, then become a bamboo, then forget all about bamboos when you are painting." The school challenged by Hui-neng's followers was the "gradual enlightenment" school of Shen-hsiu, who followed the tradition of complete immersion in scriptures and commentary, and spiritual growth through understanding and the wiping away of obscurities and passions from the mirror of the pure original mind. Two centuries later a similar program of study and metaphysical training was that of the Ts'ao-Tung sect, which was called Soto when it was taken to Japan by the monk Dogen, who went to study in China in 1223. Dogen said, "To discard the sutras of the Buddha is to discard the mind of the Buddha . . . and when you have abandoned the teaching what will be left except a lot of bald-headed monks?"

Conze assumes the confluence of the two traditions today, and offers a warning:

Zen was designed to operate within emptiness. When coming West it is transferred into a vacuum. Let us just recollect what Zen took for granted, as its antecedents, basis and continuing background: a long and unbroken tradition of spiritual "know-how"; firm and unquestioned metaphysical beliefs, and not just a belief in everything; a superabundance of Scriptures and images; a definite discipline supervised by authoritative persons; insistence on right livelihood and an austere life for all exponents of the Dharma; and a strong Sangha, composed of thousands of mature and experienced persons housed in thousands of temples, who could keep deviations from Buddhist principles within narrow bounds. . . . When speaking of spontaneity he surely meant the spontaneity of Sages, and not that of overgrown schoolboys.[18]

The "Sixth Patriarch" Story

As with other Buddhist beliefs, we must separate the doctrine of Zen from the questionable tradition of its origin. The legendary first koan (the now-formalized test that is intended to tease the novice out of thought was posed by the Buddha himself when he held up a flower before his congregation and smiled. Only Mahakasyapa smiled in response. In Garma C. C. Chang's version, the Buddha then transferred to Mahakasyapa "the true form without form, the marvelous and subtle Dharma, beyond all words, the teachings to be given outside of the [regular Buddhist] doctrines." Suzuki lists the traditional twenty-eight Indian patriarchs, the last being Bodhidharma, who transmitted the Dharma "beyond all words." Bodhidharma is supposed to have come to China with this message:

> A special transmission outside the scriptures;
> No dependence upon words and letters;
> Direct pointing at the soul of man;
> Seeing into one's nature and the attainment of Buddhahood.[19]

These lines clearly represent the doctrine of the school of Hui-neng after it had established itself as the main line of Ch'an practice. But Hui-neng is not mentioned in the first authentic chronicle of Ch'an, discovered at Tun Huang and dating from about the time of Hui-neng's death in 713. The *Ch'uan fa pao chi* (described in detail in Philip Yampolsky's edition of the *Platform Sutra of the Sixth Patriarch*) lists the first five patriarchs as Bodhidharma, Hui-k'o, Seng-ts'an, Tao-hsin, and Hung-jan. The last died about 675, and transmitted the leadership of his many students to Fa Ju, about whom little is known. The seventh leader was another student of Hung-jan, the famous Shen-hsiu, according to this chronicle. (Pp. 5–18)

Hui-neng is first mentioned in a later chronicle, the *Leng-chia shih-tzu chi*, as one of ten famous students of Hung-jan, along with Shen-hsiu, who is listed as leader after Hung-jan, with Fa Ju omitted. P'u Chi was next, while Gunabhadra is inserted before Bodhidharma because he is identified with the translation of the Lankavatara sutra, the important Yogacara text that was stressed in Shen-hsiu's teaching.

This early tradition has been completely supplanted by the confections of Shen-hui, who was a student of Hui-neng. Suzuki, Watts, Dumoulin, and Chang repeat at face value the story of Hui-neng's victory over Shen-hsiu in the midnight poem contest, which earned Hui-neng the blessing of the Fifth Patriarch and the robe of succession. But the source of the incident which elevated Hui-neng is the book attributed to him, the Platform sutra, which, according to Hu Shih, the great modern scholar, is a fictionalized autobiography composed by an eighth-century monk on the basis of Shen-hui's polemics.

Shen-hui called a conference in 732 to attack the Ch'an of P'u Chi and especially the doctrine and reputation of the latter's teacher, Shen-hsiu. Shen-hui seems also to have been responsible for the elaborated myth of Bodhidharma, how he was surely to the Emperor Wu. Shen-hui seems to have made up also the myth of the transmission of Bodhidharma's robe as the symbol of succession, which Hung-jan secretly bestowed on the semiliterate Hui-neng after his poem showed true understanding.

The verse competition is reported in most books on Zen because it does indeed indicate a fundamental difference in doctrine between the traditional school of Shen-hsiu and the revolutionary "abrupt" sect of Shen-hui, which the latter attributed to Hui-neng. Shen-hsiu's gatha is a clear reference to the Lankavatara sutra and the Yogacara school:

> The body, a Bodhi tree;
> the mind, a bright mirror.
> Keep it wiped clean,
> allow no dust to collect.

The mirrorlike knowledge is the first of the five knowledges of Yogacara, which correspond in later Vajrayana parallels to the purified five personality aggregates, the skandhas. The poem refers to the meditative process of the Shen-hsiu school, which was in the Lankavatara tradition traced to the translator Gunabhadra.[20] Hui-neng, in the recalcitrant tradition of the nonresponsive Bodhidharma and the silent Vimalakirti, returned to Emptiness. He wrote (or, as the Platform Sutra tells it, had someone write for him) the verses:

> The Bodhi tree was not,
> nor the bright mirror anywhere;
> from the first, not one thing exists,
> so where can the dust collect?

Self-knowledge does not come by settling the mind to see itself in its pure state. A knife cannot cut itself, an eye cannot see itself, a thought cannot think of itself. The Buddha-nature is of itself pure, and one must contrive to let it come forth in unpremeditated acts, free from the discursiveness and duality of conscious thought. He cast doubt on the efficacy of meditation as the way to enlightenment. "To stop the working of mind and to sit quietly in meditation is a disease and not Zen, and there is no profit whatever to be gained from a long sitting," he said. Suzuki, after citing this passage (*Essentials*, p. 140), points out that Zen is not a system of dhyana as practiced in India and by other schools of Buddhism.[21] It is not a fixing of thought (as on Emptiness, in Mahayana), a sweeping clean of all forms of mental activity. The ecstasy or trance thus achieved is not Zen satori, which requires "a general mental upheaval which destroys the old accumulations of intellectuality and lays down a foundation for a new faith" (pp. 158–59). After satori nothing is changed, but everything is seen in a new light. There is the Zen saying, "A mountain is a mountain, water is water, when hungry I eat, when drowsy I sleep; I do not search for the Buddha, or look for Dharma, yet I always make my obeisance to the Buddha." Since there is awareness in every glance, every breath, every step, there too is the Buddha.[22]

Whatever we may think of Shen-hui's methods (he is supposed to have made a good thing of selling certificates to those professing the faith),[23] it is clear that he established Ch'an as a distinct way of enlightenment. The "abrupt" method, which does not rely on the long discipline of the dhyanas, requires the watchful eye of the master to guide, test, tease the novice into satori, and then to authenticate the achievement. The secret investiture of Hui-neng, however fictitious and forced by the practical need to unseat the Shen-hsiu line, signalizes the personal transmission of word and act. "Zen gradually became an *Art*—a unique art for transmitting the Prajna-Truth—refusing, as all great arts do, to follow any set form, pattern, or system in expressing itself." (Chang, p. 15) All serious books on Zen stress (a) the need for years of application to achieve the new way of experiencing; and (b) the indispensable teacher who transmits the truth "outside the scriptures."

Thought and Action

The role of the modern teacher, or roshi, comes through in such books as Herrigel's *Zen in the Art of Archery* and Wienpahl's *Zen Diary*. The silences, the answers that seem to be nonanswers, the spiritually intimate but unaffectionate relationship indicate the deep but unsentimental concern of the master for the progress of the pupil. Once, after years of frustration and one act of cheating, Herrigel finally had a proper shot loose itself. The Master made a deep bow. The student whooped with delight. The Master said,

What I have said was not praise, only a statement that ought not to touch you. Nor was my bow meant for you, for you are entirely innocent of this shot. You remained this time absolutely self-oblivious and without purpose in the highest tension, so that the shot fell from you like a ripe fruit. Now go on practicing as if nothing had happened. (P. 77)

Because of the Mahayana tradition that words can give only a part of the truth, Zen insists that the major teaching must be by action. The master shows, but more important he *is* and *acts* his message. Erich Fromm, indicating affinities between the psychoanalyst and the Zen master, discusses reserved relatedness as a condition of understanding:

It might be said that the Zen master loves his students. His love is one of realism and maturity, of making every effort to help the student in achieving his aim, and yet of knowing that nothing the master does can solve the problem *for* the student, can achieve the aim for him. This love of the Zen master is non-sentimental, realistic love, a love which accepts the reality of human fate in which none of us can save the other, and yet in which we must never cease to make every effort to give help so that another can save himself. (*Zen Buddhism and Psychoanalysis*, p. 125)

What, then, does the master help the student achieve? Enlightenment. The same experience or state that arhants and pratyekabuddhas sought? Evidently not. Ch'an used the word *wu* for enlightenment, defined by Chang as "to awaken to the fact," or to understand. He distinguishes two kinds of wu: "understanding-Wu" (Chinese, *chieh wu*) and "realization-Wu" (Chinese, *cheng wu*); the former, knowing the mind "through the teachings and words of the Buddhas and Patriarchs," may cause people to fall into conceptualization and intellection, so their minds remain discrete from outer objects (p. 116); while Zen wu is "the direct experience of beholding, unfolding, or realizing the Mind-essence in its fullness" (p. 162). Wu, the awakening to Prajna-truth, is different, Chang says, from samyaksambodhi (cheng-teng-chueh), "the final and perfect Enlightenment of Buddhahood." Wu, or satori, is not a complete and final fulfillment, the Nirvana of the arhant. For example, Wu Men remarked, "Even though Chao Chou became enlightened, he should still work for another thirty years to graduate." Chao Chou was the famous Joshu, one of the most imaginative of masters. Wu varied with the personality of the individual, his luck in finding a proper master at the right time in his development, and his perseverance. But always wu is an *affective* not a mental matter. Fromm relates "enlightenment" to *insight* in psychoanalysis.

Doubtlessly, in the first years of his psychoanalytic research Freud shared the conventional rationalistic belief that knowledge was intellectual, theoretical knowledge. . . . But soon Freud and other analysts had to discover the truth of Spinoza's statement that *intellectual* knowledge is conducive to change only inasmuch as it is also *affective* knowledge. . . . Discovering one's unconscious is, precisely, *not* an intellectual act, but an affective experience, which can hardly be put into words, if at all. This does not mean that thinking and speculation may not precede the act of discovery; but the act of discovery itself is always a *total* experience. It is total in the sense that the whole person experiences it; it is an experience which is characterized by its spontaneity and suddenness. (P. 110)

It is this spontaneity that Shen-hui or Hui-neng (who may have been little more than an inflated image to carry Shen-hui's message) impressed upon Ch'an. Here Madhyamika's despair of discursive thought emerges in a new expression, the letting go of the mind, which permits "seeing into one's own nature," in Hui-neng's phrase. "This is the most significant phrase ever coined in the development of Zen Buddhism," according to Suzuki (*Essentials*, p. 142). Buddha-nature, or prajna, is in each of us, and an adept can help us see through our normal confusion of thought. As distinct from the Old Wisdom discipline of achieving prajna after clearly directed striving through the various levels of dhyana, the new Ch'an stressed no-thought or no-mind as a condition of natural liberation. Instead of the carefully plotted subjects and order of meditation of Abhidharma, the new Buddhism proposed "awareness," observing thoughts and feeling come and go; holding or repressing a thought would be an exercise in duality, a clinging to desire or a distaste. Echoing the paradoxes of the Vajracchedika, the Diamond-Cutter Sutra, a favorite book of the Ch'an masters, Shen-hui wrote,

> If one has this knowledge, it is contemplation (*samadhi*) without contemplating, wisdom (*prajna*) without wisdom, practice without practicing. All cultivation of concentration is wrong-minded from the start. . . . If working with the mind is to discipline one's mind, how could this be called deliverance?

At this point Ch'an runs into its own paradox. Just as the old sravakas found themselves striving with might and main to achieve a state of no-desire, so Ch'an had to establish rigorous disciplines to insure that the freedom of no-thought would not be mere empty-headedness. How were the masters to bring their increasing numbers of followers to the personality change that betokened real insight? By the fifth generation after Hui-neng, the time of Lin-chi and Chao Chou (ca. 870), five major sects were forming, which settled down into the techniques named after Ts'ao Tung (Japanese, Soto) and Lin-chi (Rinzai). Soto to this day builds its discipline on meditation, zazen, while Rinzai has developed the koan, the question without a rational answer, into a complex psychological exercise. Lin-chi developed shouting and beating as techniques, having demonstrated his own enlightenment by striking his master, Huang-po. Two centuries after Lin-chi some followers brought the koan into full use. From the Chinese *kung-an,* "official document," or set procedure, the koan (or *hua tou,* "the essence of the sentence") became the distinctive device of the majority of Ch'an teachers and their Rinzai successors. The koan is supposed to drive the novice into a state of anxiety until he gives up trying to find a rational answer and comes up with a spontaneous, overwhelming resolution of the problem. The koan is descended from the non-answers or cryptic responses (*wen-ta, mondo*) that the old masters gave to silly, obvious, or pretentious questions. A monk asked Chao Chou to explain Ch'an. "If you've eaten, wash your bowl," was the answer, the point being that one learns by doing, not by words, and a simple act can manifest complete truth, if taken aright. Equally responsive is the common answer "a stick of dry dung" to questions concerning Buddha-nature or the Buddha himself—

since dung is as real as any other phenomenal or noumenal entity, and as pure. The "gateless gate" and "the sound of one hand clapping" are by now cliché examples of acts inconceivable in rational terms, and therefore proper Zen exercises. The Rinzai roshi observes the student's frustration and progress and moves him along until in exhaustion or in fever he breaks through into the quiet victory of satori.[24]

Soto, brought to Japan by the monk Dogen, harks back to the gradual-enlightenment school of Shen-hsiu, accepting meditation as the primary instrument of enlightenment. Dogen was reluctant to encourage sectarianism and factionalism in Buddhism, and refused to set himself up as a sect leader.[25] Although for political and economic reasons during the Tokugawa regime temples were categorized according to the various sects, today is little sectarian conflict in Japan, and adherence to one method or another is a matter of psychological difference.

Awareness

The deceptively obvious statement, "When I'm hungry, I eat; when drowsy, I sleep," sums up the two guides to daily Zen, spontaneity and awareness. It was a response to the heavy question, "How do you exercise yourself to get disciplined in the truth?" The answer is tricky because it is a real answer, but to understand it one must *hear*. When he is hungry he does the natural thing, and with full attention, full taste, full experiencing; every bite, every chewing, every swallowing is literally a vital sensation in each momentary moment. His mind does not wander discursively or in reverie. When he sleeps, it is as if he concentrates on sleep with the same fierce enjoyment. A poet, P'ang Chin-shih, wrote, "How wondrous, this, how mysterious: I carry fuel, I draw water." Each muscle sings of glory. Another poet saw a woman as she was, and sang,

> All is left to her natural beauty
> Her skin is intact,
> Her bones are as they are:
> There is no need for the paints, powders of any tint.
> She is as she is, no more, no less.
> How marvelous.

Basho is called a Zen poet for a number of reasons: the deceptive simplicity of his haiku, the occasional strangeness, but above all his *closeness* to the subject. "The Zen approach," says Suzuki, "is to enter right into the object itself and see it, as it were, from the inside." This suggests the Mahayana theme that all is one when discrimination is supervened. Suzuki writes on haiku in his *Zen and Japanese Culture,* and expands one passage in the opening essay of *Zen Buddhism and Psychoanalysis.* He cites Basho's poem,

> When I look carefully
> I see the nazuna blooming
> by the hedge!

Basho wonders at, feels at one with the insignificant wildflower. He does not conceptualize it; unlike Tennyson, who first plucks his flower from the crannied wall (*analysis,* indeed) and then strives mightily to understand it, root and all, all in all, and God and man. If Suzuki had known of Tennyson's boyhood samadhis, he might have rebuked him for failing to recognize that he had already been in the way of understanding all-in-all, since he had *been* all-in-all, in mystical parlance. But here Tennyson is concerned with himself as subject, and uses the flower as object of his mental quest; Basho sees the nazuna and the nazuna sees Basho, and neither is assertive.

Looking at Basho somewhat as he looks at the nazuna, respecting its uniqueness, one gains perspective for another of his haiku cited by Suzuki. After three days in a stable waiting for the rain to stop, the walker-viewer of Japan writes, "Fleas, lice, / The horse pissing / Near my pillow." He is not complaining. We cannot know whether Basho was doing anything more than aligning himself with the way things were, and they were there first. When we know a little about Basho, and a little about Zen, we see the poem in a Buddha-light.

In the arts, where personality, philosophy, tradition, talent, and training all come together, we have a test of Zen theory. We start, of course, with a contradiction, the one faced in the paragraph from Prall's *Aesthetic Analysis:* how spontaneous can the expression of a trained lifetime be? Here we need not depend on Parson Weems–style stories of the Sixth Patriarch tearing up the sutras or of a monk proving his liberation by running a barrow over Ma Tsu's extended leg. We have the actual poem, or better, the painting. Unlike the Sung scholar-painters who painted mountain landscapes recollected in tranquillity, the Zen artist goes literally to the mat with brush, ink, and paper and, no matter how much preliminary conceptualization, conscious or unconscious, has gone on, the actual working is an immediate transaction, a live setting down of an embodied feeling, made urgent by drying ink and absorbent paper. The esteemed product is the rough, perhaps caricatured momentary figure, implying sunyata not only in the contrast between ink-paint and white space, but also in the uneven inking of the stroke itself, swift, undiscriminated. Upon request Giotto proved his skill by drawing a perfect circle freehand. If he and his prospective client had been Zen, he would have let his chalk skip a couple of degrees, like Sengai's brush.

A haiku may not be so demonstrably spontaneous as a drawing, except perhaps the lines that Basho would compose around campfires with country folk met on his walkings. But the effect is almost as convincing. The poetess Chiyo of Kaga wrote,

> Ah! Morning Glory!
> The bucket taken captive!
> I begged for water.

The slightly un-Zen pathetic fallacy or personification is both playful and yet serious in its restraint of the normal human impulse, to tear the bucket free.

The ultimate in Zen spontaneity in the nondual merging of subject and object is the life-and-death contradiction of the swordsman: he who is most ready to lose his life (and therefore is free of clinging, intellection, and hesitation) is most likely to save it with lightning-fast intuitive readiness.

If a man makes one false movement he is doomed forever, and he has no time for conceptualization or calculated acts. Everything he does must come right out of his inner mechanism, which is not under the control of consciousness. He must act instinctually and not intellectually.... The moment of intense concentration is the moment when a perfect identification takes place between subject and object, the person and his behavior.[26]

Wu, Samadhi, Satori

As we read the stories of the Zen masters in Chang, we find examples of wu at different levels, distinct from *the* enlightenment of the old Buddhists. Now and then we run into a classical description of the zero-experience, as in this passage from Han Shan, age thirty in 1575:

One day, after having my gruel, I took a walk. Suddenly I stood still, filled with the realization that I had no body or mind. All I could see was one great illuminating Whole—omnipresent, perfect, lucid, and serene. It was like an all-embracing river from which the mountains and rivers of the earth were projected as reflections. When I awoke from this experience, I felt as "clear-and-transparent" as though my body and mind did not exist at all. (Pp. 130–31)

TANTRA AND ZEN: THE RESTORERS

Master Hsueh Yen relates that after being ordained at sixteen he started his travel-for-study visits. At one congregation he took the standard first koan, wu, for his subject of meditation.

> One day I suddenly turned my mind inward, seeking to discover where and how the thought first arose. Instantly I felt as if my mind had become frozen. It became clear, serene, and limpid, neither moving nor shaking. The whole day seemed like a passing second. I did not even hear the sounds of drum and bells, which occurred at regular intervals in the monastery. (P. 145)

But a friend called this only a small enlightenment, brought forth by a small "inquiry-doubt" (the stronger the doubt, the stronger the realization, Hakuin was to say centuries later).[27] Hsueh Yen changed his hua tou to the "dry dung," and became confused and weary. He was asked by the chief monk, "What is this you call the Tao?" and became more confused, but then the monk told him "Just open your eyes and see what it is!"

> As I was just going to sit down, something broke abruptly before my face as if the ground were sinking away. I wanted to tell how I felt, but I could not express it. Nothing in the world could be used as a simile to describe it.... As soon as Hsiu (the chief monk) saw me he said, "Congratulations! Congratulations!" Holding my hand, he led me out of the monastery. (P. 147)

But because he did not have an advanced Zen master to instruct him, he was held up in further progress for ten years.

Master Meng Shan, after a couple of preliminary advances, was shouted at by Master Wan Shan. Six months later, after a journey, he returned to the city:

> While climbing some stone steps I suddenly felt all the doubts and obstacles that were weighing me down melt away like thawing ice. I did not feel I was walking the road with a physical body. Immediately I went to see Master Shan. He asked me the same question he had put before. In answer I just turned his bed upside down onto the ground. Thus, one by one, I understood some of the most obscure and misleading koans. (P. 152)

Suzuki describes the continuing awakened states as one of heightened sensibility, in terms not far in import from Guenther's eulogy of aesthetic Vajrayana:

> All your mental activities will now be working in a different key which will be more satisfying, more peaceful, more full of joy than anything you ever experienced before. The tone of life will be alerted. There is something rejuvenating in the possession of Zen. The spring flower will look prettier, and the mountain stream runs cooler and more transparent. (*Essentials of Zen Buddhism*, p. 160)

But wu has its dangers, of the kind warned against by Bharati and serious Zen teachers who fear what the "Yoga Self-taught" manuals can do to psychically unprepared seekers, if any pursue it long enough. Han Shan, in 1574, met the renowned Master Fa Kuang. "I then realized that the speech and behavior of those who actually understood the Truth of Mind are quite different from the speech and behavior of ordinary people." But he also noticed the master's hands constantly waving and his mouth murmuring. Fa Kuang replied:

> This is my Zen-sickness. When the "Wu" experience came for the first time, automatically and instantaneously poems and stanzas poured from my mouth, like a gushing river flowing night and day without ceasing. I could not stop. . . . When this Zen-sickness first appears, one should notice it immediately. If he is not aware of it, a Zen Master should correct it for him at once by striking him severely and beating it out of him. Then the Master should put him to sleep. . . . I regret to say that my Master was not alert and severe enough to beat it out of me at that time.[28]

The lives of the Zen masters demonstrate that their quest was lifelong. Each success was an incentive to deeper probing. There was no final degree. Each moment was a challenge to the quality of their enlightenment. Chao Chou said, "For the past thirty years I have never diverted my mind except when eating or dressing."

Zen transplanted in the West has taken many forms: some centers maintain Soto zazen as the basic discipline; some present a combination of Zen and Vajrayana doctrine, with awareness meditation, mantra and mandala concentration, and movement intervals in group activity. The trend is toward new symbiotic and eclectic relationships between various eastern disciplines and western scientific psychology and social healing procedures.[29] Zennists who believe that their practice can be of use in a corrupt and collapsing western culture must face the question: What is the social content of so intensely personal a search for individual liberation? Fromm answers indirectly for both Zen and psychoanalysis:

> It might be said that both systems assume that the achievement of their aim brings with it an ethical transformation, the overcoming of greed and the capacity for love and compassion. . . . they expect that the evil desire will melt away and disappear under the light and warmth of enlarged consciousness. . . . it would be a fundamental error to believe that the goal of Zen can be separated from the goal of overcoming greed, self-glorification and folly, or that satori can be achieved without achieving humility, love, and compassion.

TANTRA AND ZEN: THE RESTORERS

Fromm's other works indicate that he is aware of the two-headed question that lies beneath any economic, social, and political discussion of ways and means toward a better society, whether capitalist or socialist: How can one hope for betterment of mankind without first removing the structural base of "greed, self-glorification, and folly"? and How can one hope for betterment of man's social relations under any kind of economic and political structure without improving individual character?

Clearly, Zen works, as Buddhism works, to reduce self-assertion and vanity, and extend love and compassion. But so do true Christianity and Judaism and Islam. Each belief has its saints and teachers. Many intellectuals and young people, turned away from established religion, are turning to the benefits of meditation and as-yet-unestablished rigorous disciplines, both Buddhist and Hindu. It is doubtful how soon the new practices will affect our beleaguered culture, and how deeply. In the next chapter we shall discuss how mystical disciplines can be understood in relation to each other, to scientific investigation, and to new social forms.

EIGHT

What Is Nirvana?

> The psychology of trance is indeed a characteristic feature of many Indian systems, not of Buddhism alone. It appears almost inevitably in that part of every Indian system which is called "the path" (marga) in which the means of a transition out of the phenomenal world into the Absolute are considered.
>
> —Theodore Stcherbatsky, *The Conception of Buddhist Nirvana* [1]

Nirvana is the term used primarily among the early Buddhists for the psychophysiological state that meant to the arhant liberation from samsara, the condition of flux and sorrow. Mahayana Buddhism depreciated nirvana as a haven sought by those not ready to engage themselves in the full struggle for salvation of all men. Because Mahayana metaphysic was moving from the Old Wisdom pluralism to various forms of Absolutism, it viewed the unitive-trance state not as ultimate consummation but as a mere signal of Enlightenment, as intuition of the identity of Samsara and Nirvana in Sunyata, or as the state of "undifferentiated cognition" that proves the unreality of all objects, according to the Yogacarins.[2] Tantra and Zen, we have seen, seek a holistic reorganization of one's response to the outside world, in which unitive trance, essential for the nirvana of the arhants, may be a merely incidental stage.

Although similar to traditional yoga in requiring strenuous disciplines to break free from the shortsighted preoccupations of daily life, the nirvana of the arhants goes beyond yoga in requiring a moral and intellectual change, a climactic aversion that leaves the aspirant permanently free of the taint of the phenomenal world. Like the jivanmukta yogin, he may live free of attachment for many years after the event, the outflows (asrava) extinct, as did the Buddha, Sariputra, and Kasyapa.[3] Before Enlightenment Gautama turned away from the accomplished yogins Arada and Udraka; his was a yoga responsive to the needs of all mankind. In his trance of enlightenment he gained complete and immediate knowledge of all dharmas, and therefore freedom from their inter-

WHAT IS NIRVANA?

play; his cognition of men's suffering and the path they must tread to deliverance was a synthesis of ontology and morality.

In discussing the Buddhist nirvana we must first place it alongside and then apart from other "mystical" (a confusing but unavoidable term) practices of yogins, Jains, Upanishadic seers, Christian ecstatics, Sufis, and Jewish mystics, as well as modern experimenters in "altered states of consciousness," with or without hallucinatory drugs.

Varieties of Mystical Experience

Various mystical traditions use different terms for the trance states they seek: nirvana, samadhi, kaivalya, beatific experience, devekut, fana, realization, the union of atman and Brahman. These terms represent varying metaphysical and theological expectations. Christians and Vedantists, defining the experience as an externalization of the spirit in quest of higher reality, God or Brahman, call it ecstatic. Classical yoga, achieving mastery of the self and penetration to pure, unconditioned consciousness, seeks enstasy (Mircea Eliade's now standard term). But there are certain similarities in all samadhic manifestations, whatever the personality or ideology of the aspirant.

The condition brings a unique quality of perception, in which the distinctions of daily survival, the duality of subject and object, are confounded (William Blake said, "If the doors of perception were cleansed, man would see everything as it is, infinite"). This impression of unity is often taken to indicate the presence of godhead, and the reported feeling-tone will be awe. Or the feeling may be triumphant, as in the Buddhist context. But if the cultural context makes no provision for mystic ecstasy, the sudden, unexpected experience of nonduality may bring disorientation and fear, as reported by individual Americans who fell into the trance state unaware. Among the distinctions wiped out are time and place.

> I saw Eternity the other night
> Like a great ring of pure and endless light,
> All calm as it was bright;
> And round beneath it, Time, in hours, days, years,
> Driven by the spheres
> Like a vast shadow moved . . .

wrote the poet Vaughan; and the Meister Eckhart said,

It [mystical union] ranks so high that it communes with God face to face as He is. . . . [It] is unconscious of yesterday or the day before and of tomorrow and the day after, for in eternity there is no yesterday nor any tomorrow but only NOW.[4]

William James, in his pioneer chapter on mysticism in *The Varieties of Religious Experience,* lists four qualities which would justify calling an experience mystical: _ineffability_ ("it defies expression, . . . no adequate report of its content can be given in words, . . . its quality must be directly experienced . . . like states of feeling"); _noetic quality_ ("states of insight into depths of truth unplumbed by the discursive intellect. They are illuminations, revelations . . . they carry with them a curious sense of authority for after-time");[5] _transiency_ ("Except in rare instances, half an hour, or at most an hour or two, seems to be the limit . . ."); _passivity_ ("Although the oncoming of mystical states may be facilitated by . . . ways which manuals of mysticism prescribe; yet . . . the mystic feels as if his own will were in abeyance, and indeed sometimes as if he were grasped and held by a superior power"). Indian authorities would question the last two qualities. Ramakrishna and Sri Anandamayi would be cited as mystics whose samadhi sometimes lasted days (or even months, the devout declare) rather than hours; and practical activity, with the yogin alert and in control all the way, is the distinguishing feature of Patanjali yoga.[6] James's impression of the passivity of mystical experience and the chanciness of its occurrence is due to the absence of a western yoga tradition, or any appreciation of mysticism outside the Catholic church or the extreme nonconformist Protestant sects. He cites Catholic mystics and the manuals of St. John of the Cross and St. Ignatius but takes his primary evidence from laymen, dilettante-amateurs one might say, such as Tennyson, Symonds, Whitman, and the coiner of the term "cosmic consciousness," the Canadian psychiatrist R. M. Bucke. Their witnessing of the ineffability and the noetic certainty of their visitations may be more convincing than that of professional yogins.

The impression of oneness with the universe, of the wiping-out of sense discrimination, subject–object duality, and discursive thought is at once the objective and the mark of triumph in both Theravada Buddhism and classical yoga. Curiously, it also turns out, as we shall see, to be the key to scientific analysis of the mystical experience in the psychology laboratory. Aldous Huxley, among the first to bring yoga into respectability in the West, said of this fresh way of seeing:

All yogas have a single purpose—to help the individual to by-pass his conditioning as the heir to a culture and the speaker of a language. Mental silence blessedly uncreates the universe superimposed upon immediate experience by

WHAT IS NIRVANA?

our memories of words and traditional notions. Mystics are persons who have become acutely aware of the necessity for this kind of de-conditioning.[7]

Deconditioning, dishabituation, and deautomatization are the operant words under which Abhidharma and the behavior laboratory, the testimony of the arhant and the electroencephalograph come together.

Samadhi, Prajna, Nirvana

What part does the trance state play in this deconditioning, what part the intellect? This question is important in a discussion of Buddhist nirvana. Stcherbatsky, discussing dharma, the subject of *The Central Conception of Buddhism,* states, "A thorough knowledge, a discrimination, of all elements of existence is essential for Salvation, since when they are known they can be singled out and gradually suppressed, one after the other."[8] Prajna, when developed beyond ordinary understanding into anasrava prajna, "understanding uninfluenced (by mundane considerations)," acts as an antidote against unfavorable elements; "they gradually disappear and cannot reappear in the same stream."

> The first thing to be realized in such a state is the theory of the elements (*dharmata*), the idea that there is no permanent personality (*pudgala, atma*), that the supposed personality really is a congeries of eighteen components (*dhatu*). When the wrong view of an existing personality (*satkaya-drsti*) is disposed of, the path that leads to Final Deliverance is entered. . . . But only the initial stages of saintliness can be reached through this so-called *drsti-marga,* i.e., through knowledge a certain amount of *dharmas* has its flashings stopped. The remainder are stopped by mystical concentration, they are *bhavana-heya,* i.e., to be suppressed by entering the realms of trance. (Pp. 42–43)

We can see that this special meaning of prajna, which gives the truth about Ego, is a necessary insertion in the ladder of disciplines to distinguish Buddhist yoga from the general practice of the time; but then the two styles come together. Stcherbatsky continues:

> In all Indian systems the ultimate instrument of salvation is Yoga. This can not only do away with the intellectual and moral elements that are "unfavorable" but can stop the existence or appearance of matter itself. We have seen that matter is reduced in this system to sense-data, which are conceived rather as forces, momentary flashings. Practical observation has shown to the philosopher that when a certain degree of intense concentration is reached the sensations of taste and smell disappear, hence, it is concluded, the objects, the sense data of odor and taste, have likewise vanished. (P. 43)

In continuing his discussion of Vasubandhu's *Abhidharma-kosha,* he points out that mere knowledge can suppress only three of the eighteen elements: those dealing with the false notion of a real personality. The other fifteen (the impure elements, sasrava; material elements; and sensuous consciousness) "can be suppressed only by ecstasy."[9] One can project a world of purely spiritual beings who, by analogy to our world, could

> have their consciousness and mental phenomena brought to a standstill at some very high planes of transic existence: the unconscious trance and cessation trance. But this is, nevertheless, not an eternal extinction. At last the absolute stoppage of all the pure *dharmas* of the highest spiritual beings is reached, an eternal blank is substituted for them. This is Nirvana, absolute annihilation of the *samskrta-dharmas.* . . . (P. 44)

Stcherbatsky's conclusion that nirvana is annihilation follows logically from the dharma theory. "Thus the ultimate goal of the world process, the final result of all purifying, spiritualizing agencies and efforts is complete extinction of consciousness and all mental processes." He disposes of the popular opinion that nirvana is bliss, the cessation of unrest, duhkha—an opinion which the Buddha, despite his distaste for speculation, could have permitted to develop for its encouragement of striving, and which received support from the blissful quality of achieved trance:

> Bliss is a feeling, and in the absolute there neither is a feeling, nor conception, nor volition, nor even consciousness. The theory is that consciousness cannot appear alone without its satellites, the phenomena of feeling, volition, etc. and the last moment in the life of a *bodhisattva,* before merging into the absolute, is also the last moment of consciousness in his continuity of many lives. (P. 45)

But the ultimate nirvana of the Sarvastivadin metaphysicians is not the achievable nirvana of the arhant or the samadhi of the jivanmukta yogin. In his later book, *The Conception of Buddhist Nirvana,* Stcherbatsky accepts the preliminary stage—vivid, joyous, indubitable:

> The Buddhist saint is supposed, in a moment of mystic illumination, suddenly to perceive the whole construction, with its gross and mystic worlds, as vividly as if it were a direct sense perception. . . . Beginning with this moment he is a saint, all his habits of thought are changed. He directly views the universe as an infinite continuity of single moments in gradual evolution towards final extinction. (P. 25)

> In Hinayana the process of illumination is described as a double moment, it consists in a moment of feeling and a moment of knowledge. The feeling is

satisfaction, after which in the next following moment comes intuition, the vision of the elements of existence. The intuition refers at first to the surrounding gross world, and then, as is always the case, it is transferred to the imagined worlds of trance. . . . The supreme moment of illumination is the central point of the teaching about the path to salvation. An enormous literature, especially in Mahayana, is devoted to this concept of mystic intuition. . . . (P. 27)

In Hinayana, where, as we have seen, both samsara and nirvana were considered realities, the mystic power of Yoga was called upon to achieve the transition out of the one into the other. Actual experience of trance in meditation suggested to the Buddhist philosophers that Yoga was capable of arresting some functions of the senses and of the intellect. And since the world was analyzed in bits of senses and sense data, it seemed only logical to admit that Yoga could achieve the task of arresting the life of the universe forever. (P. 55)

Buddhism and Yoga

"What the Buddha taught was Yoga," said Stcherbatsky. In one's quest for the intellectual parameters of nirvana (one can *understand* nirvana, of course, only by experiencing it after the full course of Buddhist gnosis and practice), one is well advised to plot out both the similarities and the differences between Buddhism and the classical yoga of Patanjali's *Yoga Sutras*, with a preliminary look at Samkhya, which provided both the intellectual basis of Yoga and the view of Self that the Buddha rejected.

Samkhya predicates the categorical distinction between purusha (spirit) and prakrti (matter). Spirit, overwhelmed by matter, does not know itself, and man is subjected to a nature in flux that he cannot understand. Freedom is achieved by an understanding of man's relation to nature ("desolidarization with the cosmos and profane life," says Eliade in *Patanjali and Yoga*), a reaction against suffering and a realization that the ephemeral world can be transcended.

This deliverance from suffering inflicted by nature and one's own organism can be accomplished by gnosis, intellectual activity overcoming the ignorance that makes one subject to suffering. In the Samkhya system the main ignorance is to confuse purusha, spirit that by nature is unconditioned, with mental activities or psychomental states that, no matter how subtle, are still phases of prakrti.

Between psychic states and inanimate objects or living beings the only differences are those of degree. But, between psychic states and the spirit, there is a difference of an ontological character: They belong to two distinct modes of being. "Deliverance" appears when this truth has been grasped and when the spirit regains its original freedom. (*Patanjali and Yoga*, p. 26)

The main difference between Samkhya and Yoga is that Yoga requires ascetic and meditative discipline to achieve full realization of the liberated spirit in samadhi; Samkhya depends on gnosis alone. The theistic element that is intruded in Patanjali's *Yoga Sutras,* the Ishvara who can help toward samadhi the aspirant who takes him as an object of contemplation, presents no functional distinction between Yoga and atheistic Samkhya; both strive for liberation of purusha from its material trappings. Buddhism differs from both in denying the existence of purusha as a permanent soul-element.

Although by definition mysticism is the way of getting beyond or behind phenomena to perceive reality in some form of trance state, various mysticisms differ in ideology and procedures. The minimum characteristics of mysticism, according to H. K. De Chaudhuri, are

a penetrating insight into the depths of Reality, i.e., a state of esoteric knowledge and revelation accompanied by some kind of feeling of joy and transport. The mystic tendency is rather an abnormal faculty for piercing phenomena seemingly inexplicable by physical and psychological sciences. . . .

The mystic is on the quest for the Transcendent One and this One is a living and personal object of love, the goal of his spiritual adventure and pilgrimage, his Divine Home. (Pp. 341, 340)

Christian mysticism and Hindu Bhakti are alike in this quest for union. But yoga's quest is different.

The main type of *yoga* is not a mysticism of union (*unio mystica*) with or absorption in the Divine. It is a mysticism of will aiming at the equalization or realization of the true nature of Atman *per se*, i.e., *kaivalya*. Certain forms of *yoga* aim at deification. The other types of Indian mysticism correspond, more or less, to contemplative, intellectual, and voluntary types of mysticism. (*Ibid,* p. 341)

Like Samkhya, Buddhism in its path to nirvana places knowledge as the solvent of the karma dust that obscures the elusive nature of phenomena. Knowledge dissolves the first of the twelve preconditions of the pratityasamutpada, avidya, the ultimate explanation of suffering. The final stage of Buddhist gnosis is prajna, the sixth and highest of the perfections, which Guenther translates as "discriminating awareness arising from wisdom,"[10] without which enlightenment cannot be attained. But this gnosis must be crowned and authenticated by mystical trance, whether it be called nirvana or sunyata:

WHAT IS NIRVANA?

Thus, to live only a single moment in the sphere of the ultimately real, Sunyata or Perfection of Awareness is of more worth and has more immeasurable merits than to listen to the Dharma, read it or practice liberality or the other virtues. . . .[11]

Likewise, of course, samadhic trance is both the climax and definition of yogic liberation. So, for Samkhya, gnosis is both necessary and sufficient for liberation; for Buddhism it is necessary but not sufficient. Conversely, trance is for Buddhism necessary but not sufficient (as in Gautama's trance incident in youth, or Arada's and Udraka's yoga, adept in trance but inadequate in gnosis).

In Yoga, as in Samkhya and Buddhism, the incentive toward freedom is, theoretically, the unsatisfactory quality of conditioned existence. But the emphasis is clearly on the techniques of achieving the euphoria of unconditioned trance. Even though the classical *Yoga Sutras* lists mental and spiritual obstacles to concentration, such as mental laziness, doubt, and clinging to sense enjoyments, and positive aids to pacifying the citta, such as friendship, mercy, gladness, and indifference (the four Brahmaviharas, indeed), the context is not spiritual and social healing but simply pragmatic procedures toward samadhi. Yoga, sutra 2 says, is the arresting of the turnings of the mind (yogascittavrttinirodhah). So one may say that samadhic trance is both necessary and sufficient to define yoga. This becomes apparent in some forms of yoga, such as hatha yoga, which is depreciated by some critics as without true mystical aspiration:

The mental states and phenomena which may be induced by voluntary efforts (e.g. Hatha-yoga) or by the administration of drugs and which may appear, at surface, to be somewhat identical with the mystic states and phenomena are not qualitatively comparable. . . . the experience . . . which is artificially inducible by Hatha-yoga is not comparable with the genuine mystic experience. (De Chaudhuri, p. 341)

Permanent deliverance, the reward of the true yogin or arhant, cannot be achieved by the mere yogic athlete or the drug-taker, according to Hindu and Buddhist expositors and some graduates of the drug culture. Jivanmukti, the permanent condition of freedom in life, is a necessary consequence of the complete spiritual change that is a precondition of success in breaking away from the wheel of karma. Eliade describes the jivanmukta:

He will continue to act because the potentials of earlier existences and also those of his own existence before "awakening" demand to be actualized and consummated in conformity with the law of karma. . . . But this activity is no longer *his own*; it is objective, mechanical, disinterested; in short, it is not undertaken with a view to its "fruit." When the "delivered man" acts, he is conscious not that "I act" but that "one acts"; in other words he does not draw the Self into a psychophysical process. The force of ignorance having lost its energy, new nuclei of karma are no longer created. . . . He has nothing to fear, for his acts no longer have any *consequences* for him and therefore they have no *limits*. (*Patanjali and Yoga*, p. 47)

Similarly, Conze describes the arhant:

With the attainment of Nirvana all effort and striving will cease because one "has done what had to be done." Whatever "action" there may still appear to take place is no longer the work of the "impulses" which make up the fourth skandha, and in consequence it is senseless to attribute it to desire, or an act of the will. Without disquiet the Arhat is wishlessly happy and contented, he no longer looks forward to a future which holds for him neither hope nor dread, and his supreme and irrevocable achievement leaves no room for wishes of any kind. (*Buddhist Thought in India*, p. 68)

Actions that have no consequences for the agent, and no limits, would be a natural occasion of concern in the West. In India, antinomian behavior is expected of holy men as a sign of their rejection of householders' ways; they are forgiven much, even when their holiness is suspect. Buddhist saints in any context are less likely to abuse their many-sided freedom because they are responsible to the sangha and also relate to lay society.

Both yogin and arhant undergo ascetic and moral training early on the path to freedom, but with different contexts and emphases. We have seen that the *Yoga Sutras* lists obstacles and aids to stilling the mind. The first two stages of Patanjali are yama and niyama, the "restraints" and the "disciplines," or "observances." The yama (almost identical with the Buddhist panch-sila) are nonkilling, truthfulness, nonstealing, continence, and nonreceiving (Vivekananda's translation). The niyama are internal and external physical purification, contentment, mortification (tapas), study and worship of God. These two categories of discipline have one objective: achievement of ekagrata, single-mindedness, which is necessary to control the flow of sensations and ideas. Only then can the yogin set about the business of arresting the mind-currents with the six yoga states proper: asana (posture—"Seat being conquered, the dualities do not obstruct," *Yoga Sutras*, II, 48); pranayama (breath control—"by reflecting on external or internal objects," *Y.S.*, II, 51); pratyahara (withdrawal of senses—"by their giving up their own objects and taking the form of the mind-stuff, as it were," *Y.S.*, II, 54); dharana

WHAT IS NIRVANA? 149

(concentration—"holding the mind on to some particular object," *Y.S.*, III, 1); dhyana (meditation—"an unbroken flow of knowledge in that object," *Y.S.*, III, 2); samadhi (super-consciousness—"when that, giving up all forms, reflects only the meaning," *Y.S.*, III, 3). Without his commentators from Vyasa (sixth century) to Eliade, Patanjali, a master of the Sanskritist game of condensation, would be unintelligible.

There are other formulations of the steps toward samadhi, as in the Yoga Upanishads and Buddhist Abhidharma manuals, but all present one essential progression: from uncontrolled momentariness of sense-perception and mind movement to the imposition of physical and then mental control by concentration and maintenance of attention, then to increasing abstraction of the object of attention until there is total absorption in self, in God, or in sunyata.

Samadhi in Yoga has several levels, comparable roughly (remember, we are dealing with indescribable states) to the four rupajhanas, the "jhanas-with-form." These are called samprajnata samadhi (enstasis with support, or differentiated, as Eliade calls them), achieved by concentrating thought on a point in space or on an idea. Corresponding to the Buddhist arupajhanas, the formless trances, of which the fourth is the "station of neither perception nor nonperception," is Yoga's asamprajnata samadhi, "undifferentiated" enstasis, "when one achieves a 'conjunction' in which there is no intervention of 'otherness,' but which is simply a full comprehension of being"—the final stage before kaivalya, Self-in-itself. "The self-revelation of the *purusha* is equivalent to a taking of possession of Being in all its amplitude. In *asamprajnata samadhi* the yogi is in effect the whole of Being." (Eliade, p. 115)

In Buddhism the road to nirvana begins with unremitting awareness of the three marks of conditioned things: impermanence, sorrowfulness or malaise, soullessness. Overcoming impermanence, the momentariness of the dharmas, is the objective and technique of Buddhist yoga.

No amount of study or reflection will bring about a full understanding of the three marks and their opposites. What is needed is a total transformation, a new birth of the personality. This cannot take place without the emergence of the five cardinal virtues, i.e. faith, vigour, mindfulness, concentration and wisdom. (Conze, *Buddhist Thought in India*, p. 47)

In this series, as in the threefold training of sila, prajna, and samadhi, and in the six perfections, of which the fifth is dhyana, the stage of concentration or meditation marks the readiness for final detachment from the world of sense. But in all the stages on the way there has been a remaking of the personality, with awareness or mindfulness as the instrument. Breathing exercises have more than the purpose of pranayama ("cadencing the breathing should become an automatic matter in order that the yogi may forget it," according to Eliade, p. 69). They force awareness of the waywardness of one's body activity, of skandhas in continuous interaction. One acts

in full presence of mind whatever he may do, in going out and coming in, in looking and watching, in bending in his arm or stretching it forth, in wearing his robes or carrying his bowl, in eating or drinking, in consuming or tasting, . . . in talking and in being silent. (Satipatthanasutta)

The difference between yogic and Buddhist discipline, then, is twofold: the interpretation of the trance experience, and the effect of the preliminary training. Since enstasies are indescribable and therefore incommensurable, one cannot judge how the two ideologies modify the actual event that is called liberation. One can only state that Yoga discovers the Soul in its own self, "the liberation of the *purusha* from the clutch of *prakrti*" (Eliade, p. 111); and that the arhant by gnosis and by enstasy frees himself from the ignorance of the nature of dharmas and resides in the realm of the unconditioned, the nondual.

The life of the yogin, or sramana, as the Buddha called him, is alienated, aloof from the society of all men except his disciples; his behavior is accountable to no one, and in the realized state crime loses its definition. But the Buddhist monk, whether aspirant or arhant, is accountable to the sangha, although he may wander lonely as a rhinoceros, as the Master urged; further, he is in contact with society via his begging bowl and attached laity. And even if he does not achieve the beatitude of nirvana, being perhaps deficient in prajna and samadhi, he will have the fulfillment of a good and useful sila. Friendliness, compassion, and sympathetic joy may be lesser than even-mindedness, but they have more warmth; failing arhanthood, he anticipates the bodhisattva.

Nirvana to Sunyata to Salvation

But to the bodhisattva, compassion, friendship, and joy were not less than wisdom: they were an expression of skill-in-means, the consort of wisdom, in the world of samsara. At first these feelings are directed toward *beings*; they are "unsullied by motives of sense desire, passion, or hope of a return."[12] Then, with the spiritual growth of the bodhisattva, it has dharmas for object. Then, for the bodhisattva who has attained the most advanced stage, "acceptance of dharmas which fail to be produced," it has no object at all; the bodhisattva has reached a paradoxical stage of complete disinterest, but his love "is an inward condition of the heart which is one of the manifestations of spiritual maturity." (Conze, *Buddhist Thought in India,* p. 218).

On the moral level this is sufficient explanation of the bodhisattva's (and Mahayana's) rejection of nirvana as a haven forever secluded from the ongoing world. But side by side with the spiritual and religious development of Mahayana, and indeed supporting it, was the metaphysical critique of the Old Wisdom. Nirvana lost its impelling appeal when it was deprived of its believability.

Nagarjuna's basic critique is that the dharmas, the fundamental factors of existence which were the main preoccupation of the Abhidharma, are *not* self-sufficient entities (svabhava); if they were, their phenomenal change could not be accounted for. (The first verse of the *Madhyamakakarikas* reads, "Never have any existing things been found to originate / From themselves, or from something else, or from both, or from no cause."[13]) His critique of nirvana follows the same line. He also implies that the seekers of nirvana have reified their goal; they have lost themselves so deeply in the discussion of what it might be and how to attain it that it has become an object of attachment, for "grasping":

9. "I will be released without any acquisition." "Nirvana will be mine." Those who understand thus hold too much to "a holding on" [i.e., both to the acquisition of karma, and to a viewpoint]. (Streng, p. 70)

In Nagarjuna's dialectic it does not matter whether nirvana is viewed as a conditioned or as an unconditioned (and therefore more "real") state. He has already denied the distinction between the two states. Both were pragmatic constructs devoid of self-established reality, both were understood as Emptiness. In the Old Wisdom, nirvana is the state of freedom from causality, from the operation of karma. But Nagarjuna denied that causal relations had any meaning except from the relative, practical point of view. Early Buddhist thought replaced the absolute Brahman of Upanishadic thought, ground of all existence and activity, with the notion of Dependent Co-origination, pratityasamutpada, which posited the simultaneous functioning of independent factors, dharmas. Man's craving gave shape to the phenomenal world and bound him to it in duhkha. Only by understanding desire and conquering it could man free himself from subjection to things. But if, on the higher rather than the conventional level of thought, causal relations have no self-sufficient reality, and causal process is itself "a mentally fabricated illusion" (Streng, p. 59), then both product and producer are dependent on each other, rather than the produced being dependent on the producer. The conclusion of the arguments against a causal relationship is that dependent co-origination is identical with emptiness:

19. Since there is no *dharma* whatever originating independently, no *dharma* whatever exists which is not empty. (xxiv, 19; Streng, p. 63)

The same argument is applied to nirvana. The reality of dharma and moksha is denied:

If there is no real product, then there also exists no path to heaven nor to ultimate release.
Thus it logically follows that all producing actions are without purpose.
(viii, 6; p. 70)

On the operational level, however, the individual does make a construction or projection of the defilements and obsessions (klesa and asrava) that keep one bound to the wheel; so there could be a release from such constructions upon attainment of proper understanding.

On account of the destruction of the pains (klesa) of action there is release; for pains of action exist for him who constructs them.
These [pains] result from phenomenal extension (prapanca); but this phenomenal extension comes to a stop by emptiness. (xviii, 5; p. 71)

In the Old Wisdom sutras the Buddha set the framework for Nagarjuna's later dialectic. To Malunkyaputta and Vacchagotta he refused to conjecture about permanence or impermanence, for such discussion tended not toward edification. Nagarjuna carried the tetralemma to the nature of the Tathagata himself. Since the state of tathagata is neither self-existing nor a product of dependent relationships, "from the perspective of the Ultimate Truth, it has no essential ontological status."

The self-existence of the "fully completed" [being] is the self-existence of the world.
The "fully completed" [being] is without self-existence, [and] the world is without self-existence. (xxii, 16)

Whatever name is used to designate the "ultimate reality," whether it is *nirvana*, *tathagata*, or *tattva*, it is declared to be without a self-established nature. . . . *nirvana* is not an existent entity (xxv, verses 4–6); it is not a *non*existent entity (verses 7–10); it is not *both* an existent and nonexistent entity at the same time (verses 11–14); and it is not *neither* an existent nor nonexistent entity at the same time (verses 15–16). (P. 74)

Such a treatment undercuts, or cuts around, the tight arguments of Stcherbatsky and de la Vallée Poussin that the arhant after death ends

WHAT IS NIRVANA?

up in annihilation;[14] nirvana, seen as a mental fabrication, cannot be differentiated from existence-in-flux, samsara, although it has a practical use in turning the mind away from ignorance.

Emptiness, having been used to steal reality from both existence and nirvana, must not be given reality in their place. It must not be regarded as an undifferentiated essence, an Ultimate Principle, self-sufficient like Brahman; "rather, emptiness is the dynamics which avoids making essential differentiations . . . *sunyata* is a means to realize ultimate release from every differentiated thing" (p. 78). It is a way of formulating the Kantian dead end, the impossibility of making any statement about the world that will not end up in contradiction.

> One may not say that there is "emptiness," nor that there is "non-emptiness." Nor that both exist simultaneously, nor that neither exists; the purpose for saying "emptiness" is only for the purpose of conveying knowledge.
>
> (xxii, 11; p. 78)

Thus Nagarjuna reminds us that the objective of thought is not logical validity, but Buddhist salvation. The way is to rise above attachment. In the Astasahasrika Prajnaparamita the Buddha tells Subhuti, "a Bodhisattva does not generate attachment to anything, from form to all-knowledge. For all-knowledge is unattached, it is neither bound nor freed, and there is nothing that has risen above it." (Streng, p. 79) We have seen that Nagarjuna protested the preoccupation of the Abhidharma thinkers with the nature of nirvana and their loss of disinterest. In contrast, the Bodhisattva is in a continuing state of change, a growth and a becoming that soon outgrows attachment, even to eventual Buddhahood. As Richard Robinson puts it, "Bodhisattva vows are usually binding until the end of the bodhisattva career, a matter of eons. Even when the great bodhisattva has passed beyond dualistic cognitions and intentions, he is motivated, as if on automatic pilot, by the force of his original vows." (*The Buddhist Religion,* p. 56)

The paradoxical nature of the bodhisattva reminds us that we are dealing with religion, to which philosophy is ancillary. The doctrine of both Hinayana and Mahayana, accepting sense perception for practical affairs, refuses to rest on it and on thought based on it as conveying true information about reality; but Mahayana went beyond. Stcherbatsky says:

> The Absolute, or Nirvana, is nothing but the world viewed *sub specie aeternitatis.* Nor can this aspect of the absolutely Real be cognized through the ordinary means of empirical cognition. The methods and results of discursive thought are therefore condemned as quite useless for the cognition of the Absolute. There-

fore all logic as well as all constructions of early Buddhism, its Buddhology, its Nirvana, its four truths etc. are unflinchingly condemned as spurious and contradictory constructions. The only source of true knowledge is the mystic intuition of the Saint and the revelation of the new Buddhist Scriptures, in which the monistic view of the universe is the unique subject. (*Buddhist Logic,* I, 10)

Mystical intuition, fostered by meditation, helped move the new Buddhism from the epistemological nihilism of Nagarjuna to the idealism of the Vijnanavadins. The physiological fact that visions in trance, projected from within because sense impression has been cut off, are far more vivid and, to the trained meditator, more stable than actual sights and sounds, gave support to the hypothesis of the store-consciousness (alaya-vijnana).[15] Later, the Vajrayana made full use of the panoply of Buddhas and bodhisattvas as projected objects of meditation for self-identification and realization, and the term *nirvana* as a permanent goal lost its meaning. But some of the definitive characteristics of the mystical state—vividness and bliss, indescribable otherness, freedom from the body—reassert themselves in the new levels of experience or states of consciousness sought in Tantra, or as a sign of Enlightenment in Zen. Buddhism in general requires more than samadhi as a mark of liberation; the permanently changed citta, purified and stable, of the arhants, has its counterparts in later belief. The deep meditative state itself may provide the incentive for entering the stream toward arhantship or taking the vow of the bodhisattva, but it is not itself enlightenment.

Mystics and Orthodoxy

It may be difficult for western believers—Christian, Jew, or Muslim—in a Creator God, revealer of moral commandments, to understand how merely "arresting some functions of the senses and of the intellect" can be a mark of holiness, how an intuitive feeling of nonduality certifies the yogin as a saint. The Christian mystic claims to have met God, thus authenticating both God and his own intuition. He has risen to a direct egotistic experience of God's love and majesty and so can affirm His commandments. But the yogin, Buddhist or non-Buddhist, can claim only to have transcended the norms of human life; on the social plane, after enlightenment the jivanmukta can ignore the sanctions of ordinary mortals since his actions, no longer subject to ignorance, accumulate no karma. The right treading of the eightfold path and the cultivation of the four Brahmaviharas (the "unlimited" virtues common to Buddhist, Jain, and Hindu), can minimize bad karma and ego-concern, but only samadhi, which erases duality, can bring deliverance. The moral dimensions of the realized yogin will be discussed at the end of this chapter.

The Christian mystics, like the Indian, asserted the intuitive certainty of their experience but explained it as an ecstatic breakthrough to direct apprehension of godhead, even a union with God. A precursor of the Christian mystical terminology, and perhaps a beneficiary of Indian thought, was Plotinus, who is described thus by his follower Proclus:

> It is thus that this divine man, whose thoughts were always turned on the Supreme God and the unseen world, merited the privilege of beholding several times the immediate presence of Godhead, who has neither sensible nor intelligible form, since he is exalted above intelligence and being itself. (Quoted in William R. Inge, *Mysticism and Religion*, p. 108)

In this vein Eckhart spoke of "something in the soul which is above the soul, divine, simple, superessential essence, the simple ground in which there is no distinction, neither Father, Son, nor Holy Ghost, the unity where no man dwelleth." Dean Inge remarks, "We have noted the remarkable unanimity in the testimony of the mystics, and their complete confidence that the revelation granted them was genuine" (p. 149), and he quotes Leuba, "Mysticism is 'an intuitive certainty of contact with the supersensible world.' " Then he expresses the traditional caution of the establishment Christian:

> Some of them have believed that in rare moments of ecstasy they have transcended all distinctions, and passed into a state where even the "I" and "Thou" of prayer no longer apply. We may perhaps doubt whether such an experience is what the visionary believes it to be. We cannot entirely leave behind the conditions which make us human beings. In any case, such strange visitations must not be desired or sought for. (P. 150)

He also quotes Karl Barth's logical statement from the premise of a transcendent God: "A God who is 'wholly other' can enter into no relations with man, for we cannot apprehend what is entirely alien to ourselves." This reticence to claim understanding of what passes human understanding ("the secret things belong to the Lord") and even to claim identity with God, is structural in Jewish mysticism. Gershom Scholem points out,

> *Devekut,* or "communion," is not "union" in the sense of the mystical union between God and man of which many mystics speak. But it leads to a state, or, rather, implies an action which in Hebrew is called *yihud,* which means unification, the realization of union. . . . [A man] does not become God, but he

becomes "united" with Him by the process in which the core of his own being is bound up with the core of all being. There is one saying of the Baal Shem—apparently the only one—stating that the process of *yihud*, which is accomplished through *devekut*, transforms the Ego, or *ani*, into the Naught, or *ain*.[16]

Although Islam stresses Allah's transcendence with like firmness, the Sufis had less of this reticence, and identification of man with God and with man is the central theme of Rumi's poetry. The orthodox ulema, however, resented any too forthright declaration of identity, such as the formula "Ana 'l-Haqq" (I am God, or the Truth, or the One Real) of Mansur (Hallaj), who was executed at Baghdad in 922 A.D.[17]

Eckhart was aware of the danger of the charge of heretical pantheism by an unsympathetic orthodoxy (Pope John XXII said, "He wanted to know more than is necessary"). Either through caution or because his doctrinal training forbade Buddhist-like annihilation of awareness, he declared he never let go completely his human component in even the deepest enstasy. Therefore his amused paraphrase of St. Augustine's "what a man loves a man is":

> If he loves a stone he is just that stone, if he loves a man he is that man, if he loves God—nay, I durst not say more; were I to say, he is God, ye might stone me.[18]

Proponents of mystical cognition as an independent and legitimate way to truth see the enemy in encrusted orthodoxy whether in religion or in science. Sisirkumar Ghose, in *Mystics and Society* (1968), quotes Gerald Heard on the attitude that was the source of Eckhart's troubles: "The mystical tradition of Christianity . . . not only has it been intuitive and esoteric, but almost an underground movement, always subject to the accusation of antinomianism and heresy." He also quotes the ascetic mystic Simone Weil: "Christ rejected the Devil's offer of the kingdom of this world. But the Church, His Bride, has succumbed to it." And Sri Aurobindo: "This false socialization of religion has always been the chief cause of the failure to regenerate mankind." In recent times the inimical orthodoxy is that of the scientific establishment. Ghose quotes Aldous Huxley:

> Reality as actually experienced contains intuitions of value and significance, contains love, beauty, mystical ecstasy, intimations of Godhead....
> Science did not and still does not possess intellectual instruments with which to deal with these aspects of reality. Consequently it ignored them. This has led to the error of identifying the world of science, the world from which all meaning and value have been deliberately excluded, with ultimate reality. (Pp. 91-92)

WHAT IS NIRVANA? 157

But the heirs of nineteenth-century positivism (always the villain to those who would stretch the boundaries of the knowable) have recently been shaken by unimpugnable researches into extrasensory perception and telepathy, and even—terrifying thought—psychokinesis (see below). In such researches the "far out" is being brought within the purview of scientific analysis and even, ironically, scientific technology. The modern thrust into the formerly unthinkable is properly summed up by Jung:

> The passionate interest in these [psychic] movements arises undoubtedly from psychic energy which can no longer be invested in obsolete forms of religion. . . . The modern man abhors dogmatic postulates taken on faith. He holds them valid only in so far as their knowledge-content seems in accord with his own experience.[19]

Mysticism Methodized

Analyzing the evidence for the existence of a distinct state called the mystical experience, W. T. Stace says, "We assume, at least as a methodological postulate, the universality of the reign of law in nature. This means that all macrocosmic existences and events occurring in the space–time world are explicable without exception by natural causes."(*Mysticism and Philosophy,* p. 22) And a bit later, "the genesis of mystical consciousness is explicable in terms of the psychological and physiological makeup of those who have it" (p. 27). Yet this cautious naturalism does not prevent Stace from following his own argument, based on the unique and paradoxical quality of the state, into an acceptance of what is usually called the supernatural.

> The naturalistic principle is not inconsistent with belief in an "ultimate reality," or Absolute, or God, outside of or beyond the space–time world—whatever the metaphors "outside of" and "beyond" may mean. (P. 25)

Stace takes a cue from the Buddha's refusal to locate nirvana in space–time terms.

Similarly, and in more specific terms, Conze reminds us that "the experience of immortality is won by physical means, for it is said that the sage 'touches the deathless element with his body' ":

> By European standards the frequent assertion that the yogin "touches Nirvana with his body," in other words the belief that the thoughtless or incognizant body is wiser than the wisest mind, must seem most extraordinary and nearly incredible. . . . In Buddhism physical and spiritual reality are co-terminous, all spiritual experiences have their physical basis and counterpart, and the body,

brought to full maturity by the practice of Yoga, is a cognitive organ of the highest order, more closely in touch with transcendental reality than the intellect can possibly be. (*Buddhist Thought in India,* pp. 72–73)

A proper conclusion would be that the mystic's strange path must be traced through the workings of the human brain and nervous system. Stace's *Mysticism and Philosophy* is an impressive exercise in method, both inductive (from reports of mystical experiences in various times and places from the Buddha to Arthur Koestler) and speculative, but it does not ground itself on psycho-physiological studies. Nor does the explication of Conze and other Buddhists, who quite properly feel no need to authenticate the Enlightenment in the laboratory. Yet some observations by Stace and Conze find support and explanation in recent technical investigations.

Because human bodies respond variously to external stimulation and their own demands, we should follow Stace's precaution in analyzing various incidents of what are generally called mystical experiences before accepting any archetype or norm for the state. We are already aware of two distinct conditions, both called "mystical": the spontaneous beatitude that enveloped variously the young Gautama, Tennyson, and Koestler; and the sought-after samadhi proper of the disciplined yogin, the later arhants following Abhidharma prescriptions, Saint John of the Cross, and modern Zazen practitioners. But once achieved, is there a functional difference between the two states? Yes and no; such is the conclusion to be derived from theoretical analysis, authentic practice, and laboratory investigation.

The non-adept, beset by sudden rapture, sees the sticks and stones of the world in a new, wondrous light—interrelated, one, alive, no longer separated from him in space and time. Ecstasy, a liberation from the separateness of the body bound by skin and space, is the accepted term for this beatific state.

The practicing yogin looks inward, follows the beaten path of meditation to achieve enstasy by stopping the movement of the senses and the mind.

Extrovertive and Introvertive

This distinction between the chance and the studied, the "amateur" and the "professional," and the varieties of experience they are likely to incur, is subject, of course, to human variability. Stace induces from his library of mystical literature two broad patterns and calls them "extrovertive" (or pantheistic) and "introvertive." He presents as "the model and pattern for the understanding" of the extrovertive group a statement by Eckhart (most of whose testimony leads in the other direction, "to flow full-flood into the unity of the divine nature" by *cessation* of sense-perception and imagination).

All that a man has here externally in multiplicity is intrinsically One. Here all blades of grass, wood, and stone, all things are One. This is the deepest depth. (P. 63)

And elsewhere he says, "When he sees all in all, then a man stands above mere understanding" (p. 64).

In complement, Stace cites a report by an acquaintance, called "N. M." The modern phrasing sheds light on Eckhart's perception:

The buildings were decrepit and ugly, the ground covered with boards, rags, and debris. Suddenly every object in my field of vision took on a curious and intense kind of existence of its own; that is, everything appeared to have an "inside"—to exist as I existed, having inwardness, a kind of individual life, and every object, seen under this aspect, appeared exceedingly beautiful. There was a cat out there, with its head lifted, effortlessly watching a wasp that moved without moving just above its head. Everything was *urgent* with life . . . which was the same in the cat, the wasp, the broken bottles, and merely manifested itself differently in these individuals (which did not therefore cease to be individuals however). All things seemed to glow with a light that came from within them. I experienced a complete certainty that at that moment I saw things as they really were. . . . I began to be aware of time again, and the impression of entering into time was as marked as though I had stepped from air into water, from a rarer into a thicker element. (Pp. 71–73)

A similar incident is related by Jacob Boehme, a more studied mystic. Evelyn Underhill relates:

there were three distinct onsets of illumination; all of the pantheistic and external type. . . . About the year 1600 occurred the second illumination, initiated by a trance-like state of consciousness, the result of gazing at a polished disc. . . . This experience brought with it that peculiar and lucid vision of the inner reality of the world in which, as he said, he looked into the deepest foundation of things. . . . He believed that it was only a fancy, and in order to banish it from his mind he went out upon the green. But here he remarked that he gazed into the very heart of things, the very herbs and grass, and that actual nature harmonized with what he had seen. (*Mysticism,* p. 255)

As a Christian, Boehme declared, "I recognized God in grass and plants." The *interpretation* (as distinct from the *report* of sensation) one makes of any occurrence depends on background and context.

Another Christian mystic, Jan van Ruysbroeck, is quoted by Stace to illustrate the introvertive experience.

The God-seeing man . . . can always enter, naked and unencumbered with images, into the inmost part of his spirit. There he finds revealed an Eternal Light. . . . [His spirit] is undifferentiated and without distinction, and therefore feels nothing but the unity. (P. 94)

One takes no great liberty in connecting this formulation with the arupajhanas of Pali Buddhism. Other reminders of Buddhist concern with transcending sense and duality are found in Plotinus:

Our self-seeing there is a communion with the self restored to its purity. No doubt we should not speak of seeing but, instead of seen and seer, speak boldy of a simple unity. For in this seeing we neither distinguish nor are there two. The man . . . is merged with the Supreme, one with it. Only in separation is there duality. This is why the vision baffles telling; for how can a man bring back tidings of the Supreme as detached when he has seen it as one with himself. . . . Beholder was one with beheld . . . he is become the unity, having no diversity either in relation to himself or anything else . . . reason is in abeyance and intellection, and even the very self, caught away, God-possessed, in perfect stillness, all the being calmed . . . (*Enneads* VI, IX, XI quoted in Stace, p. 104)

The quest for oneness is even more succinctly explained by Eckhart. The human spirit "presses on further into the vortex, the source in which the spirit originates."

There the spirit in knowing has no use for number, for numbers are of use only in time, in this defective world. No one can strike his roots into eternity without being rid of the concept of number. . . . God leads the human spirit into the desert, into his own unity which is pure One. (Stace, p. 99)

For self-conscious, modern terminology, that places at the center not Divinity but a Self that seems to correspond to the Upanishadic Atman, Stace turns to William James for this report by John Addington Symonds on several incidents:

I felt the approach of the mood. Irresistibly it took possession of my mind and will, lasted what seemed an eternity and disappeared in a series of rapid sensations which resembled the awakening from an anaesthetic influence. One reason why I disliked this kind of trance was that I could not describe it to myself. I cannot even now find words to render it intelligible. It consisted in a gradual

WHAT IS NIRVANA?

but swiftly progressive obliteration of space, time, sensation, and the multifarious factors of experience which seem to qualify what we are pleased to call our Self. In proportion as these conditions of ordinary consciousness were subtracted, the sense of an underlying or essential consciousness acquired intensity. At last nothing remained but a pure absolute, abstract Self. The universe became without form and void of content. But Self persisted, formidable in its vivid keenness. . . . This trance occurred with diminishing frequency until I reached the age of twenty-eight.[20]

From the words of Symonds and Tennyson, as from those of the Buddha and the Jains, one can conclude that Divinity is merely an imputed element in mystical consciousness. St. Teresa was not troubled by metaphysical distinctions in her "orisons" seeking requital of her yearning for union with God. But Eckhart, subtle thinker as well as an administrator of the Church and a practicing mystic, had to distinguish between God, member of the operational Trinity concerned with the affairs of mankind, and Godhead, the ineffable unmoving Absolute, in India called Brahman. Sankara, equally subtle Advaitist, had made a similar distinction between two levels of Brahman. Eckhart said,

In this way the soul enters into the unity of the Holy Trinity, but it may become even more blessed by going further, to the barren Godhead, of which Trinity is a revelation. In this barren Godhead activity has ceased and therefore the soul will be most perfect when it is thrown into the desert of the Godhead, where both activity and forms are no more, so that it is sunk and lost in this desert where its identity is destroyed. (Stace, p. 98)

It is not too great a presumption, given the common qualities of mystical consciousness and its commanding position in Eckhart's and Buddhist thought, to relate "barren" with sunya and "activity and forms" with samsara. At this point theological distinction enters: Eckhart does not bring the barren transcendent Godhead and activity-and-forms together, as the Mahayanists did with sunyata and samsara.

Evaluating the Ineffable

After his thorough inductive analysis, Stace asks, "What characteristics are common to all mystical states, extrovertive and introvertive alike?" (P. 131) He lists seven items for each type, and finds five identical on both lists. The five are: (3) Sense of objectivity or reality. (4) Blessedness, peace, etc. (5) Feeling of the holy, sacred, or divine. (6) Paradoxicality. (7) Testimony of ineffability. The differences are (1) For extrovertive: The Unifying Vision—all things are One; for introvertive: The Unitary Consciousness; the One, the Void; pure consciousness. (2)

For extrovertive: The more concrete apprehension of the One as an inner subjectivity, or life, in all things; for introvertive: Nonspatial, nontemporal.

Stace sets up an order of value. "These facts seem to suggest that the extrovertive experience . . . is actually on a lower level. . . . [It] shows a partly realized tendency to unity which the introvertive kind completely realizes. In the introvertive type the multiplicity has been wholly obliterated and therefore must be spaceless and timeless, since space and time are themselves principles of multiplicity." (P. 132) Then he introduces a question that makes sense only in Christian or Vedantist terms, not Buddhist:

> The mystics themselves take it for granted that the One which is disclosed in the introvertive experience is identical with the One which is disclosed in the extrovertive experience. There are not two Ones, but only one, which, in the mystic's interpretation, is God or the Universal Self of the whole universe. (P. 133)

The question anticipates his own conclusion that there is a Universal Consciousness, or Cosmic self, "in which the individuality of the mystic becomes merged at the time at least of his 'union' " (p. 161). Stace is as aware as the Buddha of the paradoxicality of the word "is" in discussing transcendence. "The onefold One has neither a manner nor properties" (Eckhart). He turns to Lao Tzu's image of "the empty vessel that may yet be drawn from" and Suzuki's statement, "Sunyata is not to be conceived statically but dynamically, or better, as at once static and dynamic." Stace is willing to use the word "God" for the Universal Self, or the One, in its character of being the creator of the world.

A modern Tibetan Buddhist teacher increasingly popular in the West presents an interesting version of two types of meditation that correspond roughly with Stace's two types of mystical experience. Chögyam Trungpa, Rinpoche, posits two different objectives. "The first stems from the teachings which are concerned with the discovery of the nature of existence; the second concerns communication with the external or universal concept of God. In either case meditation is the only way to put the teachings into practice." (*Meditation in Action,* p. 51) The first, it turns out, corresponds to Buddhist, more properly Zen, procedure; the second to Christian and yogic.

In the latter, the quest for a higher Being assumes a lower, an internal personality known as I or the Ego. It requires

> an inward, or introvert practice of meditation, which is well known in the Hindu teachings, where the emphasis is on going into the inward state of sama-

dhi, into the depths of the heart. One finds a similar technique practised in the Orthodox teachings of Christianity, where the prayer of the heart is used. . . . This is a means of identifying oneself with an external Being and necessitates purifying oneself. This approach makes use of emotions and devotional practices which are aimed at making contact with God or gods or some particular saint. These devotional practices may also include the recitation of the mantra. (Pp. 51–52)

The other principal form requires no belief in higher or lower, and there is no centralizing concept. The concern is to see what *is*, and the techniques are directed to opening oneself.

The achievement of this kind of meditation is not, therefore, the result of some long-term, arduous practise through which we build ourselves up into a "higher" state, nor does it necessitate going into any kind of inner trance state. It is rather what one might call "working" meditation or extrovert meditation, where skillful means and wisdom must be combined like the two wings of a bird. This is not a question of trying to retreat from the world. In fact without the external world, the world of apparent phenomena, meditation would be almost impossible to practise, for the individual and the external world are not separate, but merely co-exist together. Therefore the concept of trying to communicate and trying to become one with some higher Being does not arise.

In this kind of meditation practise the concept of *nowness* plays a very important part. In fact, it is the essence of meditation. . . . One has to become aware of the present moment through such means as concentrating on the breathing, a practise which has developed in the Buddhist tradition. This is based on developing the knowledge of nowness, for each respiration is unique, it is an expression of *now*. Each breath is separate from the next and is fully seen and fully felt, not in a visualized form, nor simply as an aid to concentration, but it should be fully and properly dealt with. (Pp. 52–53)

Concepts, as distinct from direct experience, can limit and veil clarity of consciousness; a critical mind, applied even to Buddhist philosophy, will establish a basis of intuitive knowledge that one should not try to verbalize, lest one limit one's scope. "Nevertheless, as this feeling grows and develops one finally attains direct knowledge, rather than achieving something which is separate from oneself. As in the analogy of the hungry man, you become one with the subject."

Trungpa does not rate one method as superior to the other. But he warns against ambition or "wantingness," which "acts as a veil and becomes an obstacle to the discovery of the moment of nowness, because the wanting is based either on the future or on trying to continue something which existed in the past, so the nowness is completely forgotten" (p. 54). This passage may be taken as a reminder of the Mahayana depreciation of the arhant's single-minded yearning for nirvana, as distinct from the bodhisattva's free-wheeling, no longer motivated love for mankind.

If one can let slide the need to segregate oneself from the external, and with it the protection of the Ego,

one doesn't have to deliberately destroy the Ego or deliberately condemn God. And when that barrier is removed one can expand and swim through straight away. But this can only be achieved through the practice of meditation, which must be approached in a very practical and simple way. Then the mystical experience of joy or Grace, or whatever it might be, can be found in every object. (P. 56)

We have met this cultivation of awareness, the joyous identification with every aspect of the outside world, in Zen and in Guenther's Vajrayana. "And the more one expands, the closer one gets to the realization of centreless existence," according to Trungpa. And so awareness meets its polar opposite, concentration.

We must now move from nirvana of the saints to the equally mysterious realm tapped by the wires of the electroencephalograph. We must ground the saint, blow the powder off his wings, see how they work, and then see whether he can fly again, his flight computerized.

Biofeedback, EEG, and Alpha

Recent theoretical and experimental investigations of the nature of animal and human consciousness throw light on the inductive conjectures of Stace and the practical observations of Trungpa Rinpoche. After testing the dogma of "involuntary" tissue with biofeedback procedures, investigators applied the EEG to various meditative techniques to test whether meditation is in fact different from hypnosis, the hypnagogic state, or deep sleep. Their work casts light on the two types of meditation distinguished by the philosophy professor and the practicing teacher.

Meditation, according to Robert Ornstein in a stimulating book, *The Psychology of Consciousness,* is a set of exercises "designed to produce an alteration in consciousness—a shift away from the active, outward-oriented, linear mode and toward the receptive and quiescent mode" (p. 107). The two modes are elaborated earlier in the book with reference to classical Yang–Yin polarity and studies of normal and surgically modified brain functioning: the left hemisphere, governing the right side of the body, controls analytic speech, linear activity, sequential thought-

or, in traditional imagery, the masculine, the active, the light of day; the right hemisphere controls the left side, the holistic, spatial, integrative—or the "sinister," the intuitive, the artistic, the twilight, where "the left hand is the dreamer."

Like Stace and Trungpa, but without theological overtones, Ornstein presents two approaches to meditation, the "concentrative" and the "opening-up." The first approach attempts to restrict awareness to a single, unchanging stimulus—visual, aural, or repetitive movement—for a definite period of time. Visual concentration has employed the kasina, the polished disc or gem, the mandala; aural, a continuous or repeated sound, a chant, a prayer, a mantra; kinesthetic, the whirling dance of the sufi, the thumb touching the fingers in order, the Eskimo achieving trance by rubbing a hard stone on a soft one in circular motion. The traditional Buddhist introductory exercise calls for concentration on the act of breathing; the Zen refinement is to count one's breaths from one to ten, then start over again until one loses track or runs over ten. Rinzai Zen imposes nonlogical concentration on the "meaningless" koan; the answer is complete realization of "emptiness" and thence enlightenment. The repeated mantra excludes all else from the mind; it may be *Om* or *Mu* or *Om mane padme hum* or "Christ have mercy" or the personalized mantra assigned the aspirant by his guru (which seems to be a leading procedure of franchised Transcendental Meditation, fittingly packaged and streamlined for Americans, but not ineffective). Mandala is the visual counterpart of the mantra, effecting complete absorption in its interplay of shapes and embodied meanings. The kasina, mentioned by early Buddhists, and probably much older than Gautama, is applied in hypnosis. Mudra, in a technical yogic sense, refers to repetitive motion. All these devices or techniques have in common the effect of preventing the ordinary impingement of impressions from the outside world and permitting an inward concentration.

Rehabituating the Vision Splendid

Experimentation has shown that when the retina is permitted to see only a single continuing stimulus (a "stabilized image") or the opposite, no image at all (the *ganzfeld,* obtained by facing the subject against a blank, whitewashed surface, or placing half ping-pong balls over his eyes), the result was the same: a blanking out of vision, the disappearance of images.[21] And during the period of blank-out, the electroencephalograph indicated an increase of alpha rhythm (see p. 170). Individuals with high alpha-wave activity were found to be more easily susceptible to blank-out.

In meditation there is a similar but self-induced inhibition of sense impression. And EEG studies showed similar results: meditation is a high-alpha state.

The "opening-up" approach described by Ornstein is similar to the "extrovertive" of Stace and the "awareness" of Trungpa. Although it does not cut out the reception of sense impressions, it does contrive to prevent an ordered *response* to them, a fitting together into a sequence or pattern. In Buddhist terms, one does not cling to the impressions, become attached to them, let them build a memory or a karma. A paradox develops. By not fitting each act or sensation into a pattern or a concept or a preparation for future action, one heightens present awareness of each discrete sensation. Ornstein quotes Rahula's restatement of the Buddha's words on mindfulness:

> Whether you walk, stand, sit, lie down, or sleep, whether you stretch or bend your limbs, whether you look around, whether you put on your clothes, whether you talk or keep silent, whether you eat or drink—even when you answer the calls of nature—in these and other activities you should be fully aware and mindful of the act you perform at the moment. (*What the Buddha Taught*, p. 71)

The way of Zen forwards this heightened awareness—"I hew wood, I draw water! How wonderful!" Satori manifests the realization of emptiness, the vanity of plotting and planning by discriminating means and subordinating one action to another, in attachment to ends. And then the paradox. Nonattachment permits intense involvement in the momentary, the immediate, the joy of each pulsation of light, each blade of grass, the leap of a puppy—the "isness" confounding existence and essence. That Zen awareness training brings distinct effects in meditation as well as in the "normal" state seems to have been demonstrated in EEG investigation, we shall see.

In recent discussion of what actually happens in meditation and the mystical experience, a key process is habituation and dishabituation, or deautomatization. The principle was brought to bear by Arthur J. Deikman in an article, "Deautomatization and the Mystic Experience" (1966), republished in the useful sourcebook edited by Charles Tart, *Altered States of Consciousness* (1969). Deikman started from Hartmann's discussion of the automatization of motor behavior, perception, and thought:

WHAT IS NIRVANA?

In well-established achievements they [motor apparatuses] function automatically: the integration of the somatic systems involved in the action is automatized, and so is the integration of the individual mental acts involved in it. With increasing exercise of the action its intermediate steps disappear from consciousness . . . not only motor behavior but perception and thinking, too, show automatization. . . . (P. 30)

The undoing of automatization, then, would reinvest actions and percepts with attention. Because automatization is a hierarchically organized developmental process, undoing it would "result in a shift toward a perceptual and cognitive organization characterized as 'primitive,' . . . preceding the analytic, abstract, intellectual mode typical of present-day adult thought." It has been found that eidetic imagery of children, when applied as an instrument of expression in abstract mental activity, changes structure. "This is why, of necessity, the sensuousness, fullness of detail, the color and vivacity of the image must fade."[22] The classical statement of this process is Wordsworth's "Ode," in which every common sight once had "the glory and the freshness of a dream," but as the child grew older, the "shades of the prison house begin to close / upon the growing Boy" and the "vision splendid" is seen by the Man to "fade into the light of common day."

Adult life, as we all know, is not simple. Deautomatization of the complex structure of maturity would lead to greater simplicity and ultimately, of course, to undifferentiated unity. The child, and perhaps even the baby, perceives its surroundings with an intensity that grown-up categories of memory cannot handle. Perhaps the vividness of the feeling of Unity in mystical transcendence is the counterpart of a similar feeling in early childhood, which cannot "discriminate." As James said, "This overcoming of all the usual barriers between the individual and the Absolute is the great mystic achievement. In mystic states we both become One with the Absolute and we become aware of our oneness." Deikman suggests that if the automatization underlying the mature organization of the perceptive and cognitive world, with its exclusion and subordination of some stimuli, were to be reversed, or temporarily suspended,

aspects of reality that were formerly unavailable might then enter awareness. Unity may in fact be a property of the real world that becomes perceptible via the techniques of meditation and renunciation, or under the special conditions, as yet unknown, that create the spontaneous, brief mystic experience of untrained persons. (Pp. 39–40)

Whether this perception of Unity, "the idea and the experience that we are one with the world and with God," is more than the electrochemical activity that constitutes perception and thinking, and in fact does express a truth about the external world, requires an elaborate exercise in definition and epistemology that must be avoided here. Deikman concludes,

> The available scientific evidence tends to support the view that the mystic experience is one of internal perception, an experience that can be ecstatic, profound, or therapeutic for purely internal reasons. Yet for psychological science, the problem of understanding such internal processes is hardly less complex than the theological problem of understanding God. (P. 43)

A model of such internal processes is proposed by Ronald Fischer.[23] The "I" of the normal perceptive state can move in either of two directions: toward increased arousal and activity (the continuum of increased *ergotropic* arousal) or toward tranquillity and relaxation (the *trophotropic* continuum). In the active direction normal arousal is marked by sensitivity, creativity, and then anxiety; hyperarousal is marked by acute schizophrenic states and catatonia; at the end of the continuum is the ecstatic stage, represented by mystical rapture, in which the only perception is "Self." ("The talented mystic, of course, does not need to go through every intermediate step to attain ecstasy.") In the trophotropic direction, from relaxation one moves to tranquillity as in Zazen meditation; the state of hypoarousal leads to yoga samadhi, and also to contact with "Self." "The 'Self' of ecstasy and samadhi are one and the same," according to Fischer:

> During the "I" state of daily routine, the outside world is experienced as separate from oneself, and this may be a reflection of the greater freedom (that is, separateness or independence) of cortical interpretation from subcortical activity. With increasing ergotropic and trophotropic arousal, however, this separateness gradually disappears, apparently because in the "Self"-state of ecstasy and samadhi, cortical and subcortical activity are indistinguishably integrated. This unity is reflected in the experience of Oneness with everything, a Oneness with the universe that is oneself. (P. 902)

The article translates into terms of modern brain research the major characteristics of mystical experience: Oneness, depersonalization, merging of subject and object, euphoria, absolute certainty, transcendence of the categories of space and time. But does the psychologist contribute anything more than a new vocabulary to describe what yogins have known for millennia? For example, can the inhibition of cortical interpretation, the integration of cortical and subcortical activity be demonstrated to prove the explanation of nonduality and nondiscrimination in the samadhic state? Fischer does refer to increased saccadic eye movement along the ergotropic line, and decreased movement along the trophotropic; and the complete arrest of saccadic movement ("by optical immobilization of the retinal image"—as in the ganzfeld phenomenon, one can assume) "results in periodic fading, disintegration, and fragmented reconstruction of the image" and thus "may be linked with the Yogi's comment that, at the peak of a meditative experience, he can still see 'objects,' but they have no predicative properties." Also, in the other direction, "increasing stereotypy (loss of freedom) with increasing ergotropic arousal can be observed . . . as a decrease in the variability of the EEG amplitude." Several observations of the effects of hallucinogenic and tranquilizing drugs, leading to hyper- and hypoarousal states similar to ecstatic and samadhic conditions, must be regarded here as merely suggestive and without cogent reference to mystical states.

One can relate Fischer's ergotropic ecstatic state to the extrovertive pattern of Stace, in which separate objects lose their identity, and become One. But he places both Zen and yogic samadhi at the other end of his spectrum, the difference being only of degree: "the Yoga samadhi apparently represents a more intense state of trophotropic arousal than Zazen does and must also express a greater inability to function in physical space-time than Zazen does." The experimental basis for this conclusion will appear below.

Biofeedback and Alpha

Much of the scientific study of internal perception has been made possible by the electroencephalograph. Along with the electrocardiograph (dealing with "autonomous" functions such as heartbeat and blood pressure) and the electromyograph (dealing with muscle tension affecting anxiety and headache, for example), the EEG has been applied in biofeedback-control studies, especially those dealing with the anomalous states of consciousness, meditation, and extrasensory perception. The intricate connections that have been discovered between heartbeat, metabolism, blood pressure, meditation success, and ESP sensitivity can be indicated only sketchily here but must be taken into account in any discussion of the nature of mystical experience. The problem of "mind" in relation to body posed by the Buddha still remains a mystery, having receded behind an array of new physical data.

The EEG has demarcated thus far four types of brain waves.[24] Alpha waves have been found to indicate states of relaxed awareness and pleasurable reverie. The alpha patterns characteristic of meditation have been demonstrated to be clearly different from alpha that may appear in states of sleep, the hypnagogic state (pre-sleep), and hypnosis.

Biofeedback mechanisms, especially the EEG, provide new means of testing what has been hitherto the main source of data in human psychology, the introspective report. The EEG detects, amplifies, and records minute bio-potentials, the voltages that originate in the brain cells, pass through cerebral fluids, and are picked up by electrodes, which are attached to the scalp by resistance-reducing jelly.

It has also shed light on the various types of meditation itself, and has shown differences between Yoga and Zen in surprising corroboration of the two general types described by Stace, Trungpa, and Ornstein. And along with other instruments, the EEG has helped test the traditional claims of supernormal powers made by and for yogins and fakirs, such as insensibility to pain, suspension of heartbeat, and reduced metabolism.

Before turning to such investigations of actual meditative processes, professional or amateur, let us look at one of the earliest alpha-wave studies, which was designed to test the possibilities of biofeedback as a check of introspective report. Kamiya asked, "Can we get individuals to say 'A' when the alpha rhythm is present and to say 'B' when it is absent?" When the subject heard a bell, he was to say whether he was in brain wave state A, or in state B; and he was told immediately whether he was correct. Within three hours, some subjects were 75 or 80 percent correct, some even 100 percent. All found it difficult to describe the states they were in and to say how they distinguished between them.

The next step was to produce the alpha and nonalpha states. In a later series of tests Kamiya found he could train subjects to control their brain waves without this prior discrimination training; they could produce alpha at will or *suppress it*.[25]

All the Buddhist injunctions against involvement in things, injunctions to seek nonduality and nondiscrimination in physical perceptions, and the universal practices of meditation suddenly assume specific relevance to the trial-and-error techniques worked up by Kamiya's subjects in suppressing alpha. They focused attention; they *discriminated*. "All they would have to do was to conjure up an image of a person's face, hold it, and look at it very *carefully*, so much so that they could actually see the features of a person's face . . . or if he fixated the spots that float around in the visual field, the visual phosphenes, or if he engaged in other kinds of visual imagery activity, it seemed to be effective in turning alpha off" (p. 510). When taught the trick, less successful subjects improved their suppression scores.

Another test corroborated introspection reports on the pleasant quality of the alpha state. After a series of trials on keeping alpha on, subjects were told to rest "while we tuned the machine." Even though the tone of the feedback instrument was switched off, the subject kept alpha running during the rest period, until the next test, which was to suppress alpha. Verbal reports describing the frame of mind that is likely to produce alpha also coincide with old Buddhist abhaya, the conquest of anxiety: "it seems to have to do with some kind of *relaxation* of the mental apparatus, . . . a general calming-down of the mind . . . you stop being *critical* about anything, including the experiment." Kamiya concluded that high alpha people were likely to engage in "what I shall loosely call 'meditation' . . . If the individual has had a long history of introspection on his own, he seems to be especially good at enhancing the alpha rhythm. Also he is likely to be an individual who uses words like *images, dreams, wants,* and *feelings.* . . . People who look you in the eye and feel at ease in close interpersonal relationships, who are good at intuitively sensing the way you feel, are also good at this." And, of course, actual practitioners of meditation were good subjects, he found, and continued to improve their skills during the experiments.

In later experiments Kamiya found that subjects could learn to vary the frequency of alpha rhythm.[26] Recent investigators believe that mere occurrence and duration of alpha is of less importance than the specifications: its amplitude and frequency, the amount of shift from baseline test conditions, and the portion of brain in which the waves originate.[27]

Yoga in the Laboratory

The much-debated powers of Indian yogins to survive burial alive by suspending animation and to bear pain and not to feel it would seem to cry for scrutiny by means of objective instruments, including the new biofeedback techniques. Their supernormal powers or siddhi—clairvoyance, levitation, being in two places at once—call for a separate treatment in this chapter. Here we shall report certain well-known biofeedback studies of adept yogins.

A classic experiment was reported in 1961,[28] testing some yogins' claim that "during samadhi (meditation) they are oblivious to 'external' and 'internal' environmental stimuli although their higher nervous activity remains in a state of 'ecstasy' (mahanand)." Four subjects had their EEG recordings taken before and during meditation. During the resting periods they showed prominent alpha activity, and during meditation showed "persistent alpha activity with well-marked increased amplitude modulation." An important phase of the test proved the imperviousness of yogins in meditation to external stimulus: light, noise, and touch stimuli failed to cause blockage of alpha rhythms and thus indicate interference with their concentration. During rest, these stimuli blocked alpha and changed it to a low-voltage, fast activity, but "did not show any adaptation to repetition of the same stimuli"—a response quite different from that of ordinary subjects.

In a parallel study, "two Yogis, who had developed increased pain threshold to cold water, . . . were able to keep their hand in water at 4°C for 45–55 minutes respectively without experiencing any discomfort. . . . also showed persistent alpha activity both before and during this practice."

Another observation by Anand, Chhina, and Singh was that among beginners in meditation, "Those who had a well-marked alpha activity in their normal resting records showed greater aptitude and zeal for maintaining the practice of yoga." This bears out the general conclusions of Kamiya on "high alpha" people.

Elmer Green of the Menninger Clinic in Topeka, Kansas, reported briefly on a visit of Swami Rama to his laboratory. In one run the yogin seems to have employed the old "blue sky" ganzfeld technique of sGam.po.pa;[29] in another five-minute period he produced theta waves 70 percent of the time and described the experience as unpleasant, "very noisy." His description seems to be consistent with other descriptions of theta as indicating mental states of uncertainty, problem solving, and future planning. "The things he had wanted to do but didn't do, the things he should have done but did not do, and associated images and memories of people who wanted him to do things, came up in a rush and began shouting at him." Some manuals on meditation refer to a certain stage in which the learner is beset with doubt, unpleasant and shameful feelings. It would be interesting to know whether an EEG would run theta at that stage. And, during the conflict with the hosts of Mara, would Gautama's chart have shown theta, in support of the interpretation of the myth that the assailants, including Mara's daughters, represented internal states and Gautama's own psyche in its last throes of clinging and fear? This application of theta may or may not conflict with the opinion of Fischer and others that theta occurs in deep samadhi.

WHAT IS NIRVANA? 173

Another of the Swami Rama's feats in the Topeka laboratory was to induce, by means of what he called solar plexus lock, atrial flutter and to not pump blood for seventeen seconds.

What actually happens in such displays is still uncertain. In India in 1961 a series of systematic autonomic recordings of over fifty yogins was made by Wenger, Bagchi, and Anand.[30] Three men claimed to be able to stop their hearts. The study showed "(a) absence of radial pulse, (b) absence of most heart sounds, (c) blood pressure radically increased, but (d) no stoppage of the heart and, in fact, (e) very little slowing in heart rate." The conclusion was that they were utilizing thoracic muscle interference with venous return which led to a radical decrease in blood flow. Another yogin could reduce his heart rate from sixty beats per minute to thirty, by blocking the action of the sinoatrial node. Recently, the yogic exercise "shavasan" has been applied with apparently salubrious effects to hypertensive patients.[31]

Increased blood flow is one of the phenomena found in students of transcendental meditation. This was explained by an effect on the autonomic nervous system, the reduction of norepinephrin, a secretion which ordinarily constricts blood vessels and increases blood lactate. Other effects are sharply reduced blood lactate, marked increase in skin resistance, reduced blood pressure, slowing of heart rate, reduced metabolic rate, and reduction of oxygen consumption and carbon-dioxide elimination and rate and volume of respiration.[32]

Zen meditation turns out to be different from yoga in EEG charts as well as in theory. In 1966 Kasamatsu and Hirai made an EEG study of Zazen (sitting meditation) in the eye-open state, with forty-eight subjects of both Soto and Rinzai sects.[33] A typical EEG pattern of a Zen master shows, in the normal premeditation alert state, normal low-voltage, fast activity. Within fifty seconds after meditation starts, well-organized alpha appears in all regions of the scalp. In about one half hour rhythmical theta trains may appear. After meditation, alpha continues for over two minutes.[34] In the untrained control subjects, normal eye-open activating pattern continues, with no EEG changes during their "sitting."

The same investigation showed distinct differences betweeen meditation and hypnosis and drowsiness and sleep. In hypnotic trance, the EEG showed few alpha waves, a more prominent activating pattern, and a lack of the EEG changes customary in meditation.[35]

A Zen master evaluated twenty-three subjects according to their meditative aptitude; this evaluation was found to correlate closely with the subjects' EEG data. Years of experience in Zazen also correlated with EEG findings.

The special nature of the "awareness" or "mindfulness" meditation favored in Zen, as opposed to the introvertive or concentrative technique of yoga, received a degree of corroboration from the EEG. The "habituation" or adaptive theory of normal attention posits that repeated stimuli will soon be ignored if they have no significance as a warning or indicator of a change in situation; we block out the ticking of a clock (but not of a bomb!) or bland background music. But Buddhist awareness training, especially Zen, teaches openness to stimuli, without any attempt to fit them into a differentiated hierarchy of significance such as would subordinate some of the stimuli or eliminate them from attention.

A Zen master during meditation responded to click stimulation with the same two-second blocking of alpha for each of twenty clicks, showing continuing awareness during open-eye meditation.[36] In the Indian yoga experiment, stimuli of sight, sound, and touch did not produce blocking of alpha; the subjects cut out the stimuli in their concentration. But in the waking state, surprisingly, they showed no habituation, as alpha, apparent during resting periods, was blocked by stimuli. The Zen meditators, on the other hand, reported that they had more clearly perceived each stimulus than in their ordinary waking state (in which, one presumes, a certain amount of habituation is necessary for sheer survival, or continued sanity). One might conclude that a trained EEG technician, given certain instructions, would be able to separate the charts of a Zen meditator from those of a yogin.

The distinct relationship to samsara and physical sensation (awareness without concern) that is fostered in Buddhist and especially Zen doctrine carries over into meditation, in which, according to Kasamatsu and Hirai,

> one cannot be affected by either external or internal stimulus, nevertheless he is able to respond to it. He perceives the object, responds to it, and yet is never disturbed by it. Each stimulus is accepted as stimulus itself and treated as such. One Zen master described such a state of mind as that of noticing every person one sees on the street but of not looking back with emotional curiosity. (P. 499)

It appears then that the electroencephalograph supports both Deikman's deautomatization hypothesis and the Buddha's prescription for nirvana: in meditation and samadhi there is no duality, no craving that requires choice and hierarchizing and discrimination, but simply an equal brightness of each dharma in its own being, appareled, if not in a celestial light, at least in its own.

We now have double evidence, physiological as well as scriptural, for postmeditation glow. One can say, with Kasamatsu and Hirai, that meditation induces "a special state of consciousness, in which the cortical excitatory level becomes lower than in ordinary wakefulness, but is not lowered as in sleep, and yet outer or inner stimulus is precisely perceived with steady responsiveness." (P. 500) And, like Kamiya's subjects "at rest," Sariputra was probably keeping his alpha waves running when the Buddha remarked on how calm and clear he looked after meditation—or during it, because Sariputra, arhant and jivanmukta, replied, "Sir, I am now completely absorbed in the state of emptiness." (Majjhima Nikaya III, 293)[37]

The Buddha knew indeed what caused his disciple's euphoria: he too was in "the state of emptiness," and more, as guru of the sangha, he was sensitive to the psyche and mind of each of his followers (quite apart, of course, from the omniscience of a Tathagata). The tradition of the guru in India is explained by Lannoy:

> The oracular authority of the guru partly rests on the mysterious ability which is recognized by most civilizations as the mark of saintly wisdom: an almost uncannily penetrating insight into human nature. His gift is not arrived at with artificial stimulants but through disinterestedness, he is not caught in the net of contradictory pressures, selfishness, irrationality, and contesting emotions. (*The Speaking Tree*, p. 351)

ESP, Psychical Research, and Meditation

We have edged over into the subject of "extrasensory perception" because its relation to meditation is ancient and because the two altered states of consciousness shed light on each other. Parsimony in this treatment of ESP has been exercised for economy of overall design; supportive material can be found in the Notes.

Abhinna (including the superknowledges and siddhi—see Chapter 3) are the ancient versions of "psi" (the term-of-art for paranormal capabilities, which include, in descending order of contemporary acceptance, telepathy, clairvoyance, psychokinesis, and precognition.[38] False claims of the superknowledges were grounds for dismissal from the sangha, and the Buddha scorned showing-off of siddhi, such as walking on water ("Why not pay the boatman his penny!"). We shall discuss two links observable today between psi and meditation, taken for its own virtue or as a preliminary to transcendent mystical experience. These links are the guru-sensitive and the laboratory investigator.

Until the last decade or so, it was easy for the positivistic–scientific westerner and the westernizing Indian to shrug off as coincidence or fakery the kinds of incidents reported in Yogananda's *Autobiography of a Yogi* and *Be Here Now* by Baba Ram Dass (Dr. Richard Alpert). In one we have several instances of bilocality ("producing a phantasm or apparition of himself which manifests itself at a distance")[39] and precognition; in the other we are told of the guru who penetrated a new visitor's thoughts of his recently deceased mother. But now such psi activity, taken for granted by the great mass of Indians and accepted with awe by the growing number of Hindu converts from the West, and long the subject of sporadic reports in parapsychological journals, is being subjected to more formal scrutiny.

The need for recognition of their studies as legitimate science (achieved by acceptance in 1969, after several rejections, of the Parapsychological Association as an affiliated society of The American Association for the Advancement of Science) has intensified discussion of what more is needed than an accumulation of authenticated incidents and formal experiments in ESP and psychokinesis. First, obviously, is an answer to the question, How is it done? Is it the application of forms of energy already known—like "bat's radar," the emission and reception of high-pitched sounds inaudible to man—respectable and measurable when one knows where to look?[40] Or should one look for a new, anomalous form of energy, called psi-force or psi-field, not yet located, just as radioactivity and radio waves were not even suspected in the mid-nineteenth century.[41]

Whatever the explanation, the ultimate need is to fit psi *facts* into a conceptual system. Gardner Murphy cites the demand of Henry Margenau, professor of physics and philosophy at Yale, "that the real business of psychical research should not be with disconnected facts, but with facts which are scientifically coherent and meaningful."[42] But parapsychologists, like mystics, run into some peculiar problems in attempting to establish order and intellectual relatedness in their data. They cannot use the known categories of physics, which cannot yet be made to apply;[43] and to hypothesize "psi-fields" is an ad hoc construction that will raise reminders of "phlogiston" or "ether." Arthur Koestler warns them with Whitehead's phrase "misplaced concreteness," and with Heisenberg's opinion that the complementarity of particles and waves is a very pretty parallel to mind–body complementarity (the implication being that at a certain fundamental level one simply must accept paradox).[44] And Niels Bohr, whom Einstein affectionately referred to as The Mystic,[45] has put his finger, according to Rosalind Heywood, "on a very real difficulty which faces the experient who tries to be articulate: that the part of the self which is, so to speak, in focus during an ESP-type experiment is not the part which later tries to analyse it."[46]

Whatever the eventual acceptable scientific explanation of psi (or explanations—for surely psychokinesis is of a different order of energy transfer than telepathy), queries into the "how" of psi now ask, What makes an ESP-sensitive, and what makes a sensitive more sensitive? Here the relation to meditation develops, with the EEG as one means of contact between the two states of consciousness.

ESP-Sensitivity, Creativity, and Meditation

An early experimenter in ESP (Brugmans in Gröningen, 1922) pronounced three principles on the mental and physical conditions which facilitated telepathic response: (1) relaxation; (2) splitting of mind, or dissociation, with one part open for telepathic contact; (3) motivation for paranormal success, but not tenseness. More recently, similar conditions were phrased differently: From self-report, subjects performed more effectively when they felt (1) a lowering of barriers, a closeness to others, and openness; (2) a stillness, "a state in which the mind is not active with thoughts and images"; (3) a buoyant mood; (4) a dimension of meaningfulness.[47] More recently, the EEG was applied to see whether the alpha state had any effect on ESP sensitivity. The observation, "Alpha rhythm activity was associated with verbal reports of relaxation, passivity, narrowing of perceptual awareness, and pleasant feeling state,"[48] could also apply to meditation. Other experiments on states of sleep most conducive to ESP sensitivity, actual reception of ESP messages in deep sleep, states of sensory deprivation, and other psychophysical conditions seem to point to the anticipated conclusion: ESP, like meditation, is a passive, nondiscursive or nondiscriminatory activity, a "left-hand / right-brain" intuitive activity. One study concluded tentatively, "Changed states of consciousness induced by meditation also seem to be ideal for ESP. . . . Persons who appear to have had frequent ESP experiences also indicated a relationship between ESP and peak experiences induced by meditation." The article also referred to Ramakrishna's use of ESP to interact with his disciples. "He 'saw' his chief disciple, Vivekananda, by ESP long before they first met."[49]

A related theme is introduced by Green: the conditions of creativity. Developing the well-known phenomenon of the spontaneous solution of complex intellectual problems, he writes, "Creativity in the mental domain involves the emergence of new and valid ideas, or a new and valid *synthesis of ideas*, not by deduction, but springing by 'intuition' from unconscious sources.[50] He suggests a cultivation of reverie, with an approach by means of theta brainwave training in which the gap between conscious and unconscious processes is voluntarily narrowed, and temporarily eliminated when useful. "When that self-regulated reverie is established, the body can apparently be programmed at will and the instructions given will be carried out." Green also offers the hypothesis that useful parapsychological talents can perhaps be developed by the use of the reverie-generating processes of yoga and feedback.[51]

The flow of Tao is heard in reports of ESP-sensitives trying to explain their processes. Eileen J. Garrett, a foremost American subject, described how she withdrew her consciousness from the outside world: "better results [in paranormal functioning] were achieved when I projected myself into a detached, yet highly accelerated state of breathing and rhythm. In this state I was able to function without recourse either to my mental powers or to my subconscious [physical senses]." Rosalind Heywood said, "Clues as to why I pick up one thing and not another are hard to find. To me quiet and a more or less inactive brain are important—and *no expectation* on the part of my conscious mind."[52]

The parallel between ESP and meditation seems close. Abstracted from the active pattern of hodiernal outer-directedness, with its striving and cogitated decisions, ESP and meditation are indeed alike in their unfocused receptivity. LeShan points to three similarities: nonsensory access to information, a pervasive sense of unity, and the feeling of the unreality of time.[53]

But the evidence is still inconclusive. After studies conducted in 1970 and replicated in 1971, Rex Stanford urged caution: "The actual experimental work has so far failed to support, with any consistency, the so-called alpha-ESP hypothesis."[54] One reason for discrepancy is suggested by the conclusion of an article by Osis and Bokert:

On the basis of our own model, we assumed that ESP would be facilitated by a holistic state which produced increased interaction—even fusing—between conscious and subconscious processes. However, our ESP tests often required thought and judgment—what Freud called secondary processes—and these somehow seemed to disrupt the conscious-subconscious unity of the changed state.[55]

The descriptions by Garrett, Heywood, and other sensitives of their *preparatory* state meet the holistic description, the nondiscriminative quality of meditation. But in their active stages ESP and meditation diverge categorically. Yoga, seeking undifferentiated enstasy first by control then by elimination of sense perception and mental activity, and Buddhist mindfulness meditation, letting internal vrtti flit by without curiosity and without grasping, mark their success by dissolving duality, the subject–object distinction. ESP marks success by "hits," active reproductions of external stimuli, clearly perceived and specifically described in linear verbal terms or reproduced by drawing, requiring "pursuit tracking" of the pencil. A methodical comparison of the two anomalous states of consciousness is presented by D. Scott Rogo, using Stace's list of seven characteristics of the mystical experience.[56] Even though the sensitives describe their states of feeling (apart from the routine of daily life) in terms pretty close to Stace's (unitary, nontemporal, elevated, ineffable, etc.), their actual ESP functioning is on a different level of concentration.

Research continues into ways of finding and increasing ESP sensitivity.[57] If techniques of improving ESP capability and developing it where it is not now apparent (*some* success will bring more "sheep" into the fold) can be demonstrated, such operational control will go far toward convincing the scientific world that ESP should be taken seriously, and toward providing the coherent conceptual system desiderated by Margenau.

Meditation for Therapy

But meditation alone, apart from any genetic relation to ESP, has already provided knowledge useful for therapy in psychic and psychosomatic ills. The direction of such study was guided by demonstrated yogic control of both voluntary and autonomic functions. When biofeedback tests proved that ordinary individuals (as well as Neal Miller's rats!) could "learn" (without knowing how) to reproduce yogic feats such as raising the temperature of one part of the body or achieving complete muscle relaxation, a new demesne of therapy was opened for exploration. For example, it is known that "muscle tension chronically inhibits the flood of painful memories which return if the individual relaxes, . . . and anxiety cannot exist in the presence of deep muscle relaxation . . . and that one empirical treatment of anxiety consists of simply reducing muscle tension. This appears to be a stable cornerstone upon which important neurophysiological and therapeutic structures can be built."[58] The EMG was used in the 1950's to teach patients muscle relaxation; it can now be used to help make memories accessible to consciousness in preparation for therapeutic psychological reorganization. Because alpha waves indicate relaxed awareness, and because meditation is the relaxed state par excellence, and thus encourages (at least in its Buddhist ways, based on millennia of psychological experience) the undismayed airing of unpleasant memories, the way is clear for future collaboration between EMG, EKG, and EEG feedback techniques in therapy. And in normal personal and professional functioning, the new knowledge will improve competence.[59]

Scientific confirmation is gratifying to those who had taken to meditation, parapsychology, and other manifestations of the counterculture, and it provides another ironic instance of a manifestation of alienation being shunted back, like long hair or "organic foods," into the mainstream and taken over by the Establishment. But to the individual who is attracted to meditation and mystical practice, whether as part of or apart from Buddhist discipline, science and therapy are all very well, but irrelevant. He has a more immediate question to ask: How will meditation help me personally? And there is another, not so immediate: What would a spread of meditative practice do for the world?

"You know what a good loser is? It's somebody who hates to lose." President Nixon, the paradigm of the American ethos, was quoting his football coach. Long before the Watergate affair (the first crescendo of the overture to the Götterdämmerung of the strive-up and put-down ethic), long before the Cambodian bombing in 1970 and the shootings at Kent State and Jackson State, an alternative culture had appeared that no longer needed the cardiologist's warning, "Slow down, you can't win them all." "Sitting" had become a badge of the counterculture (along with marijuana) just as jogging and jargon and the over-the-shoulder-check-up reflex had become the mark of the inmates of the Executive Office Building. How does meditation immunize against the Watergate syndrome?

Would it be useful first to distinguish between meditation, an exercise open to all, and its extreme, the unitive mystical experience? Certainly kaivalya or satori or the beatific state would seem to provide a fortiori all the benefits of meditation, since ecstasy traditionally degrades as dross the vanities of samsara, the emptiness of Koheleth.

When a man comes out of Samadhi, they [the Vedantists] assure us that he remains "enlightened, a sage, a prophet, a saint, his whole character changed, his life changed, illumined."[60]

WHAT IS NIRVANA?

But just as a television executive might buy an alpha-biofeedback machine to place next to his sun lamp, and put in some creative-relaxation time before a big presentation, so we must accept the possibility of a yoga adept, or a tantrist without the spiritual involvement of a Milarepa, making out with psychophysiological enstasy for kicks. Yet taking LSD would be much easier, with comparable temporary results. Mystical experience is either too difficult or too chancy to attempt for assured personal effect or broad social effect.

Meditation, however, which is available to all, has received this accolade from Edward Maupin:

> It is a powerful way to learn to be quiet and pay attention. The special combination of suspended action and waking attention make it possible to become aware of small cues. Calm, greater ability to cope with tense situations, and improved sleep are frequently reported. ("On Meditation," in *Altered States of Consciousness*, p. 179)

The usual psychosomatic benefits of relaxation can be added. In the context of interpersonal relations, meditation brings some dissolution of ego-boundaries and the subject–object distinction, and makes it easier to "relate."[61] Freud pointed out that a great deal of the neurotic's energy is expended in the service of the ego, with defense mechanisms applied to avoid exposure to thoughts and feelings perceived as unacceptable. Buddhist meditation encourages glancing at such thoughts and feelings.

By fostering detachment and, in Zen style, observation without attachment, meditation lessens the grip of envy. It bestows the epicurean gift of sensitivity to small joys, and the stoic inurement to deprivation or loss. It puts things in their place. It stills the flutter of a small soul, and helps it grow in unashamed self-knowledge. It asks, "Who is this thinker?" and takes an objective look.

NINE

Toward the Unified World

The odds are long against survival of our complex and inefficient[1] way of life, in which economic individualism asserts itself in earth-rape, class exploitation, and war. In such a world, desperately in need of a breakdown of barriers, the religions of love and compassion and the ego-softening accomplished by meditation have made only a slight step toward the brotherhood of man. Only as elements in a new combination of salutary disciplines can the traditional teachings and eastern sadhana help minimize imminent disaster and salvage some of its leavings.

The earliest evidence of primitive man indicates that an apt slogan might have been, "What's good for the group (or clan, or tribe) is good for the individual." We need the slogan on a helically higher level, the tribe of man, for society to survive. Mo Tzu, about 400 B.C., tried to break the distinction between the brother and the other.[2] "Partiality is to be replaced by universality. . . . When everyone regards the states of others as he regards his own, who would attack the other's state? One would regard others as one's self." The world was not ready for Mo Tzu, nor perhaps are we, although many since Mo have preached love of one's neighbor and the universal brotherhood of man. Under the banner of free enterprise, can No. 1 trust he can climb the economic ladder more securely side by side with No. 2 than by kicking him down?[3]

Meditation and Buddhist discipline are adduced as one solution of the age-old debate on how to improve man's condition: change man's soul or change society? The obvious solution of such dichotomies is the dialectic "Not either; both." V. R. Dhiravamsa voices the essential involution of Theravada Buddhism:

Who creates society, and who will put it right? Individuals. Each one of us. We cannot separate ourselves from society, from the network of human relations and institutions here on earth. If we want an Alternative Society we have to look to ourselves; change our ways of thinking, feeling, acting, and then the structures in society will spontaneously be saved.

You may say that much harm is done by present social structures, institutions and systems, and this may be true, but if they are forced away by external pressures, such as revolution, they will re-emerge in different guise as long as the source of individual egoism remains to sustain them. This permeates the entire fabric of society, and individuals tend to escape from changing themselves by directing all their attention towards changing society.[4]

The old Buddhists taught of a world in change, but not evolution. They taught the transformation of the individual inspired by the Buddha to find the Buddha in himself. The bodhisattvas lingered to help until their vow would be fulfilled many kotis of aeons in the future. But we do not have aeons. We have, it appears to one no longer young, just about one generation to reverse an accelerating downward spiral, in which unsolvable internal stresses are relieved by unstable alliances and foreign war; we have one generation to stop stifling the air, rivers, and oceans with the products of greed and self-indulgence. Pollution ignores national boundaries, as does depletion of earth's resources, fossil and live. Out of the struggle for dwindling oil and fisheries, as well as the humane shame at the destruction of whales, wolves, and poor peoples, there *may* come Teilhard's "planetization" of spaceship earth; and one nation, with six per cent of the world's population, will no longer consume forty per cent of the world's annual production of energy. But this can come instead of holocaustic war only if the Buddha's teaching, that Ego is false obsession, is added to that of Jesus and Hillel, that one cannot be for oneself alone. Self-assertion is a disease when it makes a politician keep killing "with honor" rather than be deemed the first to have lost a war.

We seek desperately for a way of life that will not build ego barriers of fear and suspicion against one's neighbor, where each is not against all. Our counterculture folk are groping for ways of communion, sometimes with meditation at the center of their activities, in urban or rural communities, where their ideal is to live on little and do so according to "nature." But sooner or later they must cope with the rent, the taxation, and the commodity prices of a greed-motivated society. Our time sees Watergate as an inevitable expression of an economic way of life that assumes slashing self-interest, expressed in limited production to raise prices, in strikes, and in "public relations" (the half-truth) as the normal conditions of an adversary system. Many still accept the teaching that such conflict and alienation are "human nature." Others see human nature as adaptable to more salutary relationships.

Two Cambridge scholars have found Ta T'ung, the Great Togetherness, in the land of Mo Tzu, engendered by economic necessity and age-old social ideals. The unmystical, pragmatic, humorous, and cheerful Chinese are building the Kingdom of God in the hearts of men, according to Joseph Needham, author of the monumental *Science and Civilisation in China*, who lived in China during the Second World War and returned in 1952, 1958, 1964, and 1972.[5] Needham speaks not of the maneuvering for power of Chinese leaders, nor of the making of Party policy, nor of intellectual expression. He speaks of the "simple people with humanistic values, mastering more and more high technology, with unquestionably great enthusiasm for the new society." They have problems, but not ours: "they have no exploitation of sado-masochism or sex or violence for financial profit, . . . and no problem of youth alienation, since all the young people are enthusiastic about the job they are doing . . . being a peasant farmer or a bare-foot doctor." They realize that the revolution was only the first step toward a classless society; new administrators can turn their jobs into new privilege and can become new class enemies. So they express basic human principles (*religious* principles, Needham calls them) in slogans: "Fight self-interest, repudiate privilege." "In everything you do, do it for others." This spirit Needham calls *gesta Dei per Sinenses*, "under the banner of implacable hostility to organized religion." He hears in the oft-repeated "Chairman Mao teaches us . . . ," an echo of Orthodox liturgy. The title of a painting of Yenan is properly translated "Holy place of the Revolution," "and if there isn't a numinous tinge about that, I wouldn't know how to express it otherwise in Chinese." He concludes that China is "a society which is actually practising Christ's teachings in so many ways under the aegis of a highly conscientious atheism. . . . I might paradoxically say that I think China is the only truly Christian country in the world at the present day."

Joan Robinson, Professor Emeritus of Economics of the University of Cambridge, provides factual data of a different kind that support Needham's impressions of a people producing and sharing. In a pamphlet, *Economic Management, China 1972*,[6] she shows how the cooperative, humanist morality of the Chinese people is supported by their system of pay and prices. Rejecting the "capitalist road of putting profits in command," the system does not give design initiative, pricing decisions, and economic power to the producer, but takes account of the consumer's needs and tastes. "The workers and the management of an enterprise are concerned with efficiency and quality of production, but have nothing to do with sales."

Certainly, it is a necessary condition for such a system that individuals have no pecuniary interest in production, for as long as income or bonuses depend on sales, there is an irresistible temptation for the producer and the retailer to fix up schemes to exploit the public and share the swag. The Chinese system depends upon a high level of morality (or "political consciousness") in every sphere from top to bottom. If this has been lost in Eastern Europe, it cannot be recovered merely by changing the relations between commerce and industry. But the Chinese communists are not at all sentimental; they do not rely on morality alone. They rely on the fact that the mass of the workers, who in the nature of the case have nothing to gain from corruption, can see what is going on and, especially since the cultural revolution, are alerted to their rights and their duty to keep it clean. (P. 7)

Within the productive team, similarly, self-interest is made dependent on public interest. Each member is allotted a certain number of work points for his task, usually by general team agreement and evaluation of the job and the worker.

The fact that the income received for a work point depends on the produce that a team gets from its own particular area of land prevents a negative response of work forthcoming to rising income. Most people, if they are free to choose, prefer to do less work as earnings per unit of effort rise. With the work-point system, slacking by any individual is doing wrong to his neighbors by checking the rise in the value of the work points that all will get. The individual is not free to please himself: he is kept up to the mark by his neighbours. This is another way in which Chinese institutions have been devised to support political motivation instead of pulling against it. Peasants are taught to feel that they are working for the nation, for the Revolution and for all the oppressed people of the world, but they are clearly and obviously doing good for themselves at the same time. (P. 8)

What happens to "human nature" under a system whereby selfishness is seen and rejected as "unpolitical," instead of being accepted as an "inevitable" condition of man's existence, and the base of economic activity? Robinson says, in a passage headed "The New Man":

The success of the Chinese economy in reducing the appeal of the money motive is connected with its success in economic development. When everyone has enough to eat today and hope of improvement tomorrow, when there is complete social security at the prevailing level of the standard of life and employment for all, then it is possible to appeal to the people *to combat egoism and eschew privilege.* It would not make much sense to the workers and peasants, say, in Mexico or Pakistan.

No doubt there are individuals in China with the temperamental itch for money, just as there are some people in the West who do not care about it.

Individual temperaments are moulded by the setting in which they find themselves. The enormous pressure to commercialize every aspect of life in our society is substituted in China by an even stronger pressure the other way. "Human nature" seems to fit it just as well, indeed, a good deal better, for the people whom one meets in China always seem much less nervous and ill-tempered than we are. (P. 13)

"Combat egoism and eschew privilege." The italics are Robinson's. *Gesta Buddhae per Sinenses.*

Not merely in ideal but in practice the Chinese socialist productive system seems to meet Buddhist requirements. Schumacher, in his chapter "Buddhist Economics" says,

The Buddhist point of view takes the function of work to be at least threefold: to give a man a chance to utilize and develop his faculties; to enable him to overcome his ego-centredness by joining with other people in a common task; and to bring forth the goods and services needed for a becoming existence. (P. 51)

The validity of Needham's and Robinson's judgments will be tested by time and by nonacademic observers less sympathetic toward socialism and the Chinese, such as Joseph Alsop and *Fortune.*[7] This excursus into the future of man will assume that somewhere in the socialist countries, including China, there already exists a humane way of life that gives daily expression to maitri and mudita. This is the way of life that has freed itself from one artificial barrier between man and man, the habit of private greed and exploitation that breeds competition for individual survival, and inhibits man's natural tendency toward communion, whereby, as Mencius said, "the people make friends on their way to the fields and back again, they help one another in keeping watch and ward, assist and support one another in times of sickness, and so everyone becomes intimate and friendly."[8] Then, alerted by our ventures unto the far shores of yoga and parapsychology, we shall be tempted to inquire whether such lowering of barriers in the land of Tao may not enhance and in turn benefit from ancient ways of nonconceptual communion, ESP, meditation, and mystical experience.

It was not Buddhism that brought maitri and mudita into practice among the Chinese workers and peasants. It was bitter revolution, first against Kuomintang landlords and then, in the Cultural Revolution, against remnants of their presence. It was revolution that brought the Chinese people over the razor's edge to a precarious security that makes humane community possible. The revolution, perhaps less bitter and violent from now on, will continue through many setbacks and mistakes, Mao tells his people, until the revolutionaries become Socialist Man—mature in selflessness but still in danger until the rest of the world finds or rediscovers the socialist path. Dhiravamsa and Krishnamurti are only partly right in warning that pushing aside an establishment changes nothing, and that physical revolutions end up in bureaucracy or tyranny as long as individual egoism remains.[9] The Chinese revolution has not escaped bureaucracy and tyranny, but one most potent source of individual egoism, private greed, is on the way to drying up because the revolution has changed property relationships and encouraged moral change.[10] Economic cooperation on the levels of the team (not too different from Mencius' eight families), the brigade, and the commune, fostered by a system of mutual benefit and profitable idealism, functions with little interference from the central bureaucracy, which by theory and hard necessity encourages local autonomy and self-sufficiency.

Even with its economic and social community, China is still a long way from surfeit in samsaric success, of the kind that turned the Buddha and some western middle-class youth to adopt voluntary poverty. The "normal" loss of a million peasants by starvation due to drought or flood in one province or another, year after year, is still within the memory of the older half of all living Chinese. The fiscal ability and the will to purchase grain abroad to make up shortages are still remarkable achievements of a central bureaucracy. There is still self-assertion and ambition among political leaders struggling for internal dominance and wielding or seeking power in the dangerous international arena, where national assertion is deemed a necessary deterrent to aggression. But if international diplomacy, threat, and bluff can provide some years of peace for *t'ien hsia ta t'ung*, "the great togetherness under heaven," to flourish, then what will be the next stage for the secure and benevolent Chinese masses?

The time will come for a pause before the next leap, a time when even the glorious example of Tachai[11] will exercise less inspiration to heroic labor, and even cadres will broaden their work rhythms to meet new goals. Then, will duhkha, ever lurking in man's psyche, again come to the fore, when people will find material security not enough? The Chinese masses have found spiritual fulfillment in the social community that alone could have killed the flies, cleansed the rivers of schistosomiasis-bearing snails, and greened the eroded hills with trees. Will such fulfillment meet the need for internal order that individual men have found in Buddhist enlightenment or the rhythm of Tao? In the past, Dharma and Tao tempered the age-old conflict of private greed and showed a few the way to self-mastery in detachment and a remade personality. For the mass, there was solace in prayer to the compassionate Amito Fo and Kwan Yin, the example of the sangha, guidance toward friendliness and compassion, and a promise of an improved lot (despaired of by most laymen) in the future incarnations. In *t'ien hsia ta t'ung*, Socialist Man, with a remade personality (already "much less nervous and ill-tempered than we are" according to Joan Robinson) will not require admonitions to maitri and mudita,[12] although as man his aspiration, disappointment, and mortality will always need solace, even that of a Kwan Yin. But a classless society will not mean a mentally conformist society. The May 7 schools may succeed in draining from the minds of teachers, managers, and intellectuals their traditional disdain of the peasants, backbone of the new nation. The brotherhood of socialist man may so utterly refashion the human psyche that it will no longer be defined by Kierkegaardian alienation and the core of loneliness. But in the land of Lao Tzu and Chuang Chou and the Ch'an masters will there be no men, however loyal to society and loving of their fellow men, who will not hear the rhythm of Tao and seek quietness at the center? In the past meditation was a suspension of samsara, and mystical experience was the only way to complete oneness. Dharma and Tao were accepted by society as the way to individual liberation— the only kind of liberation conceivable.

> To know harmony is to be in accord with the eternal
> To be in accord with the eternal means to be enlightened.
> (*Tao Te Ching*, 55)

> He who has achieved this state
> Is unconcerned with friends and enemies,
> With good and harm, with honor and disgrace.
> This therefore is the highest state of man. (56)

As a philosophy of change Tao anticipates historical materialism, which predicates change and defines freedom as the recognition of necessity. A Taoist poet wrote, "For riding on Change he entered into Freedom."[13] But high Tao fostered quietism and ignorance among the people, and low Tao fed on superstition. Tao offered the wealthy and educated a traditional escape from corrupt and conflictive regimes, but Marxist leaders rightly condemn its quietism as desertion in time of positive achievement. The question in the new China is, Will the philosophy of change, having achieved sufficiency by cooperation and healthy social relationships, close in upon itself and set up new tensions?

When the five grains are abundant, will the hundred flowers bloom again? Will the people, creative and self-sufficient by theory and necessity, freely communicate their proposals for continued growth and personal fulfillment? In 1957 the hundred schools of thought spoke in a Babel, the Party decided, because intellectuals were not identified with the masses in class and self-interest. Now, after the victory of the Great Proletarian Cultural Revolution and the rehabilitation of mandarin-minded leaders at the May 7 schools, where self-criticism and physical work bring mind and body closer to the conditioning of Mao Tse-tung's thought, will the barriers between mind and mind, which were felled by strenuous common enterprise, remain down? Or will they be erected once again by the tension of imposed conformity? Teilhard de Chardin, eloquently urgent of human cohesion, said in *The Future of Man*, "Achieved with sympathy, union does not restrict but exalts the possibility of our being. . . . where it is a matter of unanimity realised from *within* the effect is to personalise our activities, and, I will add, to make them unerring." But, he reminds us in another essay, this kind of synthesis remains fragile "because elements brought together under the compulsion of necessity or fear cohere only outwardly and on the surface. When the wave of fear or common interest has passed, the union dissolves without having given birth to a soul. Not through external pressure but only from an inward impulse can the unity of Mankind endure and grow." (Pp. 183–90)

In the continuing revolution which requires a rejection of Ego almost as drastic as that of the old arhant, conformity has been for most Chinese a light price to pay for victory over the fear of starvation. Now that socialist sufficiency has been won, will Marxism-Leninism-Maoism, the philosophy of dynamic change, encourage broad discussion of the direction of change? Mao has said it must. Poets and artists have done their duty with homilies and poster art and served the people by raising their hearts and inspiring them to work better. As surplus grows, will poets and artists, whose imaginings so often legislate the future, be allowed freer play? Will the authorized ballets, such as *The White-Haired Girl*, depicting heroic victories over a bitter past, be joined by less agitational subjects and styles depicting more individual conflicts, or even by the traditional themes of the colorful and elaborately costumed old Peking opera, in which property and sex relations are indeed fraught with revolutionary implications.

In modern China all men must earn their keep, and there is little official patience with full-time Buddhist monks. State policy has refrained from official persecution; premature efforts to abolish superstition, said Mao, would play into the hands of counter-revolutionaries. "Our policy is, to quote an ancient saying, 'to inspire, but let the people jump by themselves.' Let the peasants destroy their own gods, smash their ancestors' tablets, and tear down the temples or arches of chastity by themselves and of their own accord."[14] The state has used the Chinese Buddhist Association as a means of contact with minorities and as a showcase of goodwill to visitors from neighboring Buddhist countries. Local treatment has fluctuated over the years. Immediately after liberation local peasants and cadres beat and on occasion killed Buddhist abbots as exploiting landlords; monastery lands were requisitioned and distributed, and older monks and nuns, unable or unwilling to turn to farming or light industrial production, starved; many young monks and nuns disrobed on entering industry or even the army, during the Korean conflict. Most of the smaller Buddhist establishments were secularized and their dwindling complements moved to larger and more famous temples and monasteries, which have been preserved as public museums. During the Cultural Revolution there was some slight destruction, but usually the firm admonition of a caretaker or an army man sent the rampaging Red Guards away.

Holmes Welch, in *Buddhism Under Mao*, cites a Japanese Zen master who was impressed by the ubiquitous slogan, "Put the public welfare before one's own" (*hsien-kung hou-ssu*). To him this exemplified the Buddha-mind; so that to the extent that Maoism prospered, Buddhism prospered, and little matter that institutional Buddhism may disappear if the secular society is producing its own bodhisattvas. (P. 374) Many Buddhists doing their civilian jobs remark (prudently) on the coincidence of the regime's and the sangha's social ideals. Some expect the sangha to die out in China in "the era of the extinction of faith" predicted by the Buddha, but they hope for its survival elsewhere and its eventual return to China in Buddhist time.[15] Welch is reminded of the Jataka tale in which the Buddha gave first his blood and then his body to revive the starving tigress and her cubs.

The sangha started as the body of the Buddha's followers, but it soon separated into monks and laity. Sooner or later religious organizations break their spirit on the masses they hope to soften to salvation, usually with a call to brotherhood. Generations pass, and the work goes slowly. The Buddha expected the dharma to fade in one thousand years. Like other faiths, the sangha has not escaped falling into rigidity and superstition, but better than most has resisted the tendency to seek power through violence. The way of religious teaching is first to seek individual liberation or inspiration and then to return to samsara and share hard-won victory with all suffering ones, by example and word. But all over the world mass man, secular and superstitious at once, can receive only part of the message. If his church speaks the words of brotherhood and beatitude where there is no peace, he hears a comfortable buzz, but he sees violence and approves it. Others, more open to spiritual guidance and appalled by the secular world, seek a faith, but cannot wait for bodhisattvas or Vishnu or the Messiah, who are on a different time scale; so they turn to instant saviors. For a time the certitude of faith flows in milk and honey; then there is a new fad.

The other way to the good life is the materialist way of social change. We have taken China as the example; we have seen the first steps forward, and some steps backward, but clearly some progress in subsistence and social cohesion. Mao expects more upheaval and declares his trust in the masses to feel their tortuous way between extremism and revisionism, between the "overthrow all" and the "restore all" slogans of the last upheaval, between putting the dunce cap on all teachers and letting them grow their mandarin fingernails. Mao's gamble with history is that Tachai will prove to be a landmark in the movement of masses into individuality: by common decision, after open debate, to assume responsibility for one's own work and reward, to decide on objectives and techniques, and then gladly to share their experience with all who ask.

If the Chinese secular society continues to thrive, surviving Buddhists and curious folk abroad will ask: "One's work points earned, will one be free to sit in meditation instead of attending a political discussion, or even after it?" Will the great quietness of Lao Tzu and the Buddha survive the great togetherness of Mao Tse-tung? Will the individual spiritual component make its way back into Chinese life? Not the old gods and ancestral tablets and fortune-telling slips, but simply the private sense of wonder?

Unlike Needham, who perceives a "numinous tinge" in the people's reverence for Yenan as a "holy place of the Revolution," Welch fears that secular devotion and patriotic holidays cannot fill the need of any people for expression of "their ancient feeling that they are part of a universe in which everything is connected and makes sense" (p. 382). He believes that the Communist party has upset the "behavioral ecology" of the people, and that "subtle pressures will build up to burst the Party's holistic grip on human life and goals." He quotes Jung:

> Modern man does not understand how much his "rationalism" (which has destroyed his capacity to respond to numinous symbols and ideas) has put him

at the mercy of the psychic "underworld." He has freed himself from "superstition" (or so he believes), but in the process he has lost his spiritual values to a positively dangerous degree. (*Man and His Symbols*, p. 93)

Are China's ideals transcendent? Michael Polanyi says, "A society refusing to be dedicated to transcendent ideals chooses to be subjected to servitude. Intolerance comes back full cycle. For sceptical empiricism which had once broken the fetters of medieval priestly authority, goes on now to destroy the authority of conscience." (*Science, Faith, and Society*, quoted in *Manas*, Jan. 23, 1974, which points out the danger of reason becoming the handmaiden of empiricism.)

Farther along the socialist road, when work points and material incentives will no longer be needed, and the withering state apparatus will be no more than a liaison among many independent enterprises, then will the lotus, Communist Man, blossom out of common humanity—in fewer aeons, it is hoped, than for fulfillment of the bodhisattva's vow? External sanctions for correct individual behavior will then have less authority than internal; the model of humanity will not be Lenin or Stalin or even Mao, but the extreme anarchist Spinoza, who taught that the good man does right because it gives him pleasure, or even the Buddha, who taught individual development to the point of utter spontaneity. But spontaneous right action will please others too, and all will know together what is right and pleasing. So for individuality there must be communion.

Lenin's notion of the withering away of the state, and its inspiration, the Marx-Engels dream of Communist Man who will give what he can and take what he needs, have been absurd enough to "realistic" people. How much more absurd, to Lenin, Marx, and Engels themselves, would be the suggestion that the community they were setting up as a distant magnet to draw men's dreams would be brought closer by such strange side-practices of the religious superstructure as thought transference, meditation, and mystical experience! These practices are encouraged by community, and in turn enhance it. This post-positivistic age now can accept without shame the evidence of as yet unexplainable phenomena (such as gravity!)[16] and the evidence is strong that certain relaxed states of mind do encourage telepathic reception, that lovers do send and receive messages better than haters, that community breeds communion. Real gurus are (almost by definition) empathetic, and good classroom teachers know what their students are thinking. Intelligent political leaders, intent on the welfare and growth of their people, will eschew dogma (which is of less value than cow dung, according to Mao

Tse-tung), and perhaps accept the growing evidence that quiet inwardness can contribute to *t'ien hsia ta t'ung*.

Perhaps we can dare to think of the next step, the step suggested by Father Teilhard de Chardin and Sri Aurobindo. We can accept their hypothesis of a coming intensification of large-scale communication but stop short of their prophetic explanations—Omega Point or Supermind.[17] Their generative schema, that of the succession of integrative levels leading to ever higher development, has been independently developed in western scientific thought.[18] Teilhard moves from inanimate matter to life to man and thought and the planetization and involution of man on earth, so that the next step is the noosphere, because man has no other place to go but sidewise or inward.

Needham, who first referred to the concept in the *Modern Quarterly* in 1938 (using the term "mesoforms"—"matter at the point of transition from one level of organization to the next"), returned to it in his Cambridge Divinity Faculty talk:

And then of course you find that the wholes on the lower levels become parts on the new—like protein crystals in cells, or cells in metazoan organisms. . . . I believe there are grounds for seeing in collectivism, of the kind of which we could approve, a form of organization as much above the outlook of middle-class nations as their form of order is superior to that of primitive tribes. . . . The transition from economic individualism to the common ownership of the world's productive resources by humanity will be a step similar in nature to the transition from lifeless proteins to the living cell, or from primitive savagery to the first community, so clear is the continuity between inorganic, biological, and social order.

Speaking first as a scientist, then as a speculative philosopher, then as a *religieux*, Teilhard de Chardin traces in *The Future of Man* the development of our planet to the present day, then to the near future, then to the time of man's full potential. Until now evolution has worked by blind natural selection. From now on man's mind takes a hand, so to speak; and all men's minds coiled in on themselves form a planet-wide entity. "Like a heavenly body that heats as it contracts, such . . . is the Noosphere." One result of man's achieving his new potentiality is a break in "the infernal circle of egocentrism, meaning the isolation, in some sort ontological, which prohibits our escape from self to share the point of view even of those we love best"—a state which the Buddha deplored in similar terms. Man's new mind-communion will have more than spiritual implications:

The iron laws binding economic factors, the irrepressible recurrence of nationalisms, the apparent inevitability of war, the insoluble Hegelian conflicts "of master and slave"; what are these supposedly unalterable necessities of the human condition, except, finally, the diverse expression and outcome of exteriority and a mutual antagonism between the individual seeds of thought which we are?[19]

But despair not, says Teilhard; "the tide of evolutionary totalisation sweeping us along" is working toward unity.

We must assume that under the rapidly mounting pressures forcing them upon one another the human molecules will ultimately succeed in finding their way through the critical barrier of mutual repulsion to enter the inner zone of attraction. (*Ibid.*)

In a later essay he is more specific on one way in which men will work together after "the power of invention . . . begins to grasp the evolutionary reins"—"the prospect afforded to a growing number of individuals of being joined together and ever more closely unanimised in the inextinguishable fire of research pursued in common" (p. 293). This was written after Manhattan District, which spawned the atomic bomb, a demonstration of his point which perhaps the author was loathe to mention, but before the Soviet and the American space programs and before the *international* cooperation in space research now under way.

Perhaps this chapter's vision of the emergence of materialist man, *species sinensis*, into socialized man is no less utopian than Teilhard de Chardin's vision of *mega-synthesis*, "the 'super-arrangement' to which all thinking elements of the earth find themselves today individually and collectively subject," or Sri Aurobindo's vision of the Supermind descending, which will "make it possible for the human being . . . to grow out of his still animal humanity into a diviner race." But unlike the inspirational projections of Teilhard and Aurobindo, at least the data in this chapter are falsifiable, and the projection is a short one; it begins with man as he already seems to be. Their visions begin in divine faith and extrapolate from it to an unrecognizable aspiration. Teilhard declared that "faith in Man can and indeed must cast us at the feet and into the arms of One who is greater than ourselves" (p. 188), and that we can banish the specter of Death from our horizon "by the idea (a corollary, as we have seen, of the mechanization of planetization) that ahead of, or rather in the heart of, a universe prolonged along its axis of complexity, there exists a divine centre of convergence" (p. 122)—the Omega point—whence "constantly emanate radiations hitherto only perceptible to those persons whom we call 'mystics.' " And according to

Aurobindo, Man now is "a mental being whose mentality works here involved, obscure and degraded in a physical brain. . . . But divine superman will be a gnostic spirit." We who are engrossed by wondrous body and brain and their immediate survival are impatient with such literal abstractions.

We remain earthbound, but even our short focus into the next generation requires a degree of faith in man that few in the anxious West will confess. The Chinese masses illustrate the leap that can be made in one generation from despair to confidence. They are sure they have broken through "the iron laws binding economic factors, . . . the insoluble Hegelian conflicts of 'master and slave'" that Teilhard observes to be the expression of antagonism between individuals. They work in self-won harmony. We hope Teilhard is right in declaring irreversible each step forward. We hope that even if the present step forward, observed in amazement by delegations from all over the world,[20] should be halted by conflict, ideological and personal, among the successors of Mao Tse-tung and Chou En-lai, or by weariness of unending labor and slogans that will become empty if leadership fails, or by war—then we hope that perhaps not all will be lost, that in time the march will begin again. Not only the memory of the glorious age of Tachai will remain, but its techniques—which are nothing more than the old practices of creative man: cooperative self-reliance, democratic responsibility and decision, and the loving interchange of labor, information, and research. If any nation can survive a holocaust, it is decentralized, frugal, machine-poor, man-rich, ingenious China, which has never used up more energy to produce its food than the food itself provides. And if the thoughts of Chairman Mao have borne fruit among his loyal followers, already there are millions of leaders on the lower echelons of command, learning to govern, growing in responsibility and decision.

So let us project beyond the possible interruption, by civil strife or international conflict, the progress of the Chinese toward becoming socialized man. Let us look farther along the road from alienation to maitri. Nearer than we think, the road that materialism is building into the future will converge with another road. The road of individual self-fulfillment by love, too narrowly assigned as the spiritual or religious way, expressing itself in private and social action, will run parallel to and then merge with the road of cadres and good workers. Young Chinese are honored to be chosen by their team-mates to become barefoot doctors—at no extra pay. The slogan on the banners of both hosts will be "Combat egoism and eschew privilege."

And, if research into the ways of thought transfer is extended by national research institutes, then surely the techniques of spiritual communion—meditation, ESP, faith healing—will become rationalized (like hypnotism) and lose much of their numinous–mystical aura. They will be used matter-of-factly in spiritual-productive communes in the Rockies and productive-spiritual communes in Sinkiang, both of which have already cut away so many barriers between man and man. Perhaps that is the answer to the question, Will workers be permitted to meditate after work? May they not be *encouraged* by pragmatic, undogmatic cadres to do so, for their own mental well-being, for productive avocation, for improving communion between comrades?[21] And since every society, even the most materialistic, needs its spiritual leaders, its shamans interpreting the people's needs and exorcising their fears, its poets pointing to the future, will not the ESP-sensitive be sought out and commissioned? Even the mystical experience itself, once freed by the EEG lab from its implications of divinity, will not be relegated to the condition of a psychic curiosity or the ultimate nonchemical intoxicant. It will still mean what it meant to the Buddha and William Blake, a cleansing of the doors of perception, a furlough from samsaric particulars, a reacquaintance with the wonders of one's undifferentiated own-being. In a truly rational society, mystics will work together with poets and artists and political leaders to find the way to the community's higher development.

But such participation and acceptance of the mystic will exact a price. The alienation of the mystic from society will have lost much of its rationale. Milarepa sang, "For sons and nephews I have no appetite; . . . for women, the primary source of suffering, I have no appetite; . . . I renounce pleasant and sociable friends; for kinsmen and neighbors, I have no appetite." In a socially mature community, such rejection will have less excuse; it will fall back on the *absolute* unsatisfactoriness of samsaric existence. Even the most advanced individuals in the most advanced commune will fall short of the Mahayana ideal. "Non-self necessarily leads to detachment and renunciation, which then leads to altruism in its highest form," says Luis Gomez. The man on the commune will shrug off the Buddhist metaphysics of the following statement, even though his practical ideal of social behavior points in that direction:

No true goodness exists as long as there is the idea of a self, and as long as there is the idea of goodness. Merit and demerit belong to the sphere of personal transactions, but here there is no perfection as long as egotism of one kind or another is the primary motive: goodness appears only when there is no notion of a person or of a transaction.[22]

The prescription is exclusive and self-fulfilling. A community in which there is no notion of a person or of a transaction must be projected as far into an abstract future as Omega Point or Supermind. This Buddhist ideal, whether of the arhant or the bodhisattva, remains a metaphysical game of follow-the-absolute, or at best an ideal of solitary liberation. A more likely guide to future liberation on earth will be the middle way between the denial of goodness by the dog-eat-dog hamburger man because people are no damn good, and the denial of the *idea* of goodness by the Buddhist expositor because he believes it preserves the idea of self. The this-worldly middle way will not be concerned with the metaphysics of ego, but will lead the ego to fulfill itself in the traditional ways of maitri, karuna, and mudita, and thus perhaps wither itself away. For the saints and mystics among us, upeksha will follow, but without canonical renunciation of sons, women, and sociable friends.

But before we can close, we must consider one remaining alternative, one not lighted by maitri or Omega. Up to the level of man, evolution is involuntary, unless we accept a teleological Will. But man's will is a function of his being. Teilhard reminds us:

> There can be no natural selection, still less reflective invention, if the individual is not inwardly intent upon "super-living," or at least upon survival. No evolutionary mechanism can have any power over a cosmic matter if it is entirely passive, less still if it is opposed to it. But the possibility has to be faced of Mankind falling suddenly out of love with its own destiny. (*The Future of Man*, p. 296)

"Brennt Paris?" was one expression of this death of spirit. "Bomb them back to the stone age," uttered by a Vice-Presidential candidate, and Air Force commander, is another; that this was not simply the exasperated expression of a limited human being, but official Pentagon and White House policy, is clear from the deliberate, long-term program of defoliation, dike-bombing, saturation bombing of civilians, and My Lai—"destroy in order to save," in fact.

So the future must come fast, or maybe not at all. There is small comfort in the hope that some men somewhere will recover from Armageddon, and relive Tachai, and go on again from there. Better to start now. Already dim shapes of the near future can be discerned. Many young men and women have gone through despair to cynicism to new involvement; from beat to drugs to Zen to a commune. Some have moved from the sterile plethoric city to country life founded on spare self-sufficiency, with the compost heap as a working symbol of devotion to wounded earth. But these foci of spiritual health in a diseased body politic and economic can accomplish little to change their total environment. To make their good prevail they must move back into contact with other forces moving in the same direction. Along with tools (and necessary store-bought food) Thoreau took Homer with him to Walden Pond, and then he went back to the lecture circuit. The grave defect of student drop-outs is that they were not students, and so must reinvent the Buddha's wheel every day instead of falling in step with others who combat egoism, revere the earth, and help the farm workers, the most immediate human victims of earth-ravishing agribusiness. The alienated intuition that rejects destructive authority is vulnerable to new authority promising immediate salvation in Jesus or Krishna or maha-millionaires. The counterculture that is putting down healthy roots will need the informed skeptical intelligence that is the other voice of Thoreau, the voice that speaks in Veblen, Mumford, Martin Luther King, Jr., and Ralph Nader, all revolutionary in implication in putting public before private interest, if not in intent. Together, appalled by Watergate, where little lies pullulate to protect the big lie, they will combat the big lie, that the greed-society's leaders represent human nature. There may be enough of such, led by voices first raised on Vietnam, to win us time.

What is called the spirituality of the East—now pretty well discarded by the East—is being applied to the effort toward communion. The new activism includes the inactive disciplines, Buddhism and yoga. Meditation, whether Buddhist or Hindu or Zen or Tantra (often eclectic), is almost a badge of the new culture, bringing some self-knowledge and a reordering of tension. As altered states of consciousness (infra and supra) become more widely sought and better understood, in personal practice and in the test laboratory, there will be growing receptivity to new ways of communication. Mystical experience, having lost some of its mystery, will for some retain its numinous power; for others, as for many a Hindu or tantrist saddhu, it will be sought just for kicks. The words and example of the Buddha will continue to inspire men to social revolution even while declaring its inadequacy. Selflessness, an idea derived from sere Buddhist ontology, is an Omega point drawing man to a future abounding with grace. "The selflessness thus attained appears as the only basis for ethical action: 'If the self is dear to you, do not love yourself. If you want to protect yourself, you should not protect yourself.' "[23] Of such words are revolutions made, political as well as spiritual, as that *lamedvovnik*, the Foolish Old Man of the Mountain, knew.

NOTES

Chapter 1: The Legend and the Life

1. Was Suddhodana the father? Accepted legend has it that he was not, to enhance the miraculous quality of the event. At the festival Queen Maya took vows of abstinence, according to later "lives."
2. And thus the Buddha was unsoiled by the ordinary impurities of the womb.
3. But not the ushnisha, the "bump of wisdom," which in later centuries was an adventitious iconographic mark of the Buddha.
4. Already tribal structures had developed sufficiently in the direction of territorial states to find themselves engaged in aggressive–defensive wars; whence the notion of a broad-scale conqueror, a chakravartin.
5. "When the festival was at its climax, the nurses stole away from the Prince's presence to catch a glimpse of the wonderful spectacle. The thoughtful child, mature in intellect though young in age, seeing none by him, sat cross-legged, and intently concentrating on inhalation and exhalation, gained one-pointedness of the mind and developed the First Ecstasy (Jhana)." Narada Thera, *A Manual of Buddhism* (Columbo, Ceylon, 1953). A footnote explains Jhana as "a developed state of consciousness gained by concentration."
6. "And the king built three palaces for the Future Buddha, suited to the three seasons. . . . And he provided him with forty thousand dancing girls. . . . And the mother of Rahula was his principal queen," the introduction to the collection of Jataka stories (previous incarnations of the Buddha) tells us.
7. Some books on the Buddha simply repeat the story of the Four Omens without comment. Sangharakshita asks, sensibly, "Is it really credible that until his twenty-ninth year Siddhartha knew nothing of old age, disease and death?" or had never "set eyes on a wandering mendicant, when saffron robes and begging bowls were to be encountered at every street corner?" As the source of the passage he suggests Anguttara Nikaya I, 145, in which the Buddha declares it not fitting to be troubled, ashamed, and disgusted at the sight of old age, sickness, and death—"As thus I reflected on it, all the elation in youth utterly disappeared." *The Three Jewels,* p. 30.
8. Alfred Foucher suggests that Rahula was also the occasion of the father's *freedom.* Having produced a son, Gautama had performed his primary social duty as a householder and could enter the vanaprastha (forest-dwelling) stage, even if earlier than most. But the Code of Manu, compiled after the Buddha's

time but perhaps containing material dating back to his time, says, "When the householder observes wrinkles on his skin and white hair on his head, and sees also *a son to his son,* then he should take refuge in a forest" (VI, 2).

9. "The new eastern teachers rose above all ritual and broke the strongest tabu by eating cooked food from the hands of another caste however low, or even left-overs of soiled food. What the last means is difficult to explain to anyone who does not know that most Indians would rather go hungry, and many have preferred death by starvation to eating soiled food or that prepared by a person of lower caste." D. D. Kosambi, *Ancient India: A History of Its Culture and Civilization,* p. 103.

10. Arada (or Alara in Pali) is supposed to have mastered in yoga the superconscious state of the "Sphere of No-thing-ness," or the third attainment, or the seventh dhyana; and Udraka (Uddaka in Pali) had reached the "Sphere of Neither-Perception-nor-Non-Perception," or the fourth attainment, or eighth dhyana. Both seem to have taught the Samkhya philosophy as well.

11. Buddhist thinkers regard Mara not as a counterpart of Satan but as an objectification of a man's psychological experience. Useful discussions of the various Maras are found in Edward Conze's *Buddhist Thought in India,* p. 72, and James Boyd's "Symbols of Evil in Buddhism," *Journal of Asian Studies,* 30 (November 1971), 63 ff.

12. The Mahavagga I, 1, places the grasp of Dependent Origination after seven days of enjoying the bliss of emancipation. The Jataka introduction places it in the last watch of the night of the Enlightenment. See Henry Clarke Warren, *Buddhism in Translations,* pp. 82–84.

13. The Five Nikayas (Digha, Majjhima, Samyutta, Anguttara, Khuddaka) present the *doctrine* of the Buddha, usually in the form of conversations between him and followers or opponents. The Vinaya (in two parts, the Sutta-vibhanga and the Khandhakas, and a supplement, the Parivara) contains the *rules* of the Sangha, the Order. Later in compilation is the third "basket" of the Tripitaka, the Abhidhamma, the *commentary,* much of it arranged in lists for memorizing and for guidance in meditation. The most complete scriptures form the Pali canon, preserved in Ceylon by the Theravada school. The scriptures of other schools, preserved in Sanskrit, Chinese, and Tibetan, have been available in western languages only in part. See Chapter 2 for a discussion of similarities and differences among the various canons. The Khandaka (Sanskrit, Skandhaka) section of the Vinaya Pitaka is in two parts: the Mahavagga (Great Series) and the Cullavagga (Small Series).

14. The *Mahavastu* is an avadana, an account of the heroic deeds of the Master, in Sanskrit. It comes from a Mahasanghika school. The *Lalitavistara,* a Mahayana Sanskrit work, is based on an avadana of the Sarvastivadin school.

15. Gautama (Gotama in Pali) is the name of a brahmin clan; it is surmised that the name was applied to the kshatriya Sakyas as a reference to the priest who introduced brahmin rites among them. See Edward J. Thomas, *The History of Buddhist Thought,* p. 151.

16. The Jataka introduction says, "And whereas a womb that has been occupied by a Future Buddha is like the shrine of a temple, and can never be occupied or used again, therefore it was that the mother of the Future Buddha died when he was seven days old, and was reborn in the Tusita heaven." Warren, p. 45.

17. "Four Great Brahmas received him in a golden net [from Maya's side]. . . . Standing on the ground he faced the east, advanced seven steps, and said, 'I am the chief in the world.' " Thomas, p. 135.

Chapter 2: What Can We Know About What the Buddha Really Said?

1. The matter of the toothpicks is cited here, not irreverently, as an example of probable authenticity because of the very homeliness of the detail, the hodiernal quality of problems brought to the Master for decision, and his good-humored patience. In Cullavagga 5, 31, a complaint was presented that certain monks were using dangerously long food-sticks. The Master decided to allow food-sticks because neglect of them causes bad odor, is bad for the eyes, makes passages by which flavors pass become impure, lets phlegm and bile get into the blood, and makes food not taste well; but the sticks must be less than eight finger-breadths long. A too-short stick had stuck in the throat of a monk, so the Buddha ordered sticks to be at least four finger-breadths.

Another time he sneezed, and the monks said, "God bless you" ("Long life to your reverence."). But he asked, "Can a man live or die on such a wish?" So when the monks sneezed and lay folk said "Long life," the monks made no reply, and the lay folk were hurt. So the Buddha allowed the monks to reply to laymen after sneezing, "May you live long."

Onions also were forbidden, for obvious reasons, after a complaint. But Sariputra got rid of wind on the stomach by eating onions. So onions were permitted on account of disease.

2. See note 2, Chapter 3, for a discussion of the oral style.

3. Rhys Davids' translation of the passage in Sutta 16, the Mahaparinibbana, reads, "I used to become in colour like unto their colour, and in voice like unto their voice. . . . Then, . . . I would vanish away." The word for "sort" and "color" is *varna,* the traditional word for "caste"; and *saro* is the word for both "voice" and "language." The reliability of the passage as an indication of the Buddha's practical flexibility is weakened by the context: he uses the same phrase in narrating to Ananda how he used to approach "an assembly of many hundred kshatriya (nobles)" but also similar assemblies of "brahmins, householders and wanderers, the angel hosts of the Guardian Kings, of the great Thirty-three (High Gods), of the Maras, of the Brahmas." There is a magical,

mythological quality in the passage that makes us look elsewhere for actual descriptions of the Buddha's methods.

4. The phrase "sakaya nirutti" is not uniformly translated. G. C. Pande says, "Buddha permitted his teachings to be put down in 'one's own speech.' . . . It appears that Buddha did not want his teachings to be fixed in any learned language but wished them to circulate in different local dialects. One may recall that Asoka followed a similar policy." *Studies in the Origins of Buddhism,* p. 11, n. 50. But E. J. Thomas interprets the passage otherwise. " 'I order you monks, to master the word of Buddha (Buddhavacanam) in its own grammar.' . . . It is not grammatically possible to make *sakkaya niruttiya,* 'in its own grammar,' mean 'each in his own dialect,' nor did Buddhaghosa so understand it. According to him it meant that the primitive Magadhi language, the own grammar or dialect of the texts, was to be preserved. He expressly says 'the language of the Magadhas spoken by the All-enlightened.' " *The Life of Buddha as Legend and History,* p. 254.

5. The fifth Nikaya, the Khuddaka, composed of small books, is supposed to have been a gradual accumulation of smaller collections and to have taken its status as a Nikaya late. But it contains much material that is considered early, such as the Sutta Nipata, itself a collection of early and late pieces, and the Therigatha and Theragatha, autobiographical verses and hymns by nuns and monks.

6. See Conze, "Recent Progress," in *Thirty Years,* p. 9, for an example: "the senseless *dhammam kayena passati,* 'he sees dharma with his body.' " The proper word, *phusati,* "touches," is unmetrical.

7. See Chapter 3, notes 3 and 11 below, and related text. In some analyses, the first two Nidanas, or links, i.e., avijja (ignorance) and samkhara (aggregates), "the conative factors making for rebirth and persisting into another life" (Pande, pp. 437–38), really pertain to the *previous* existence. Alfred Foucher, the explorer-archaeologist who discovered many traditional Buddhist sites, sees the series referring to three lives: "les numéros 1 et 2 representent la vie passée, les numéros 3 à 10 se rapportent à la vie présente, les numéros 11–12 introduisent la future revenance." *La Vie du Bouddha.*

8. Pande, p. 85. He also says of vinnana: "originally the 'More-than-Body' which in its *patitthita* state was the mutable transmigrant; later it came to mean almost exclusively 'sense-perception' (this latter meaning has its beginnings in the latest Upanisadic texts) which is its status in the full-fledged five khandha theory" (p. 43). "According to some texts, what survives a man's death is his citta or vinnana. The doctrine is almost certainly pre-Buddhist. Buddha seems to have modified rather than rejected it. Vinnana doubtless fares on but it must not be regarded as an identically permanent entity. It is in fact extremely changeable. Its fate beyond death is determined by the act of the man during his life" (pp. 493–94). Cf. Chapter 5 below, in which Mara cannot find Godhika's "birth-consciousness."

9. Rhys Davids, in the Pali Text Society version, translates, "Decay is inherent in all component things! Work out your salvation with diligence."

Chapter 3: What Buddhists Have Believed

1. "The Buddha was not only a human being; he claimed no inspiration from any god or external power either. He attributed all his realization, attainments and achievements to human endeavour and human intelligence. A man and only a man can become a Buddha. Every man has within himself the potentiality of becoming a Buddha, if he so wills it and endeavours. We can call the Buddha a man par excellence. He was so perfect in his 'human-ness' that he came to be regarded later in popular religion almost as 'super-human.'

"Man's position, according to Buddha, is supreme. Man is his own master, and there is no higher being or power that sits in judgment over his destiny." Walpola Rahula, *What the Buddha Taught,* p. 1.

2. "Every reader will be struck at once with the constant repetitions. These repetitions are not essential, and are merely designed to facilitate the learning of the Suttas by heart. . . . It would follow that the Buddhist Scriptures were handed down by word of mouth only; and no one who is acquainted with the wonderful powers of memory possessed by Indian priests, who can devote their whole lives to the task of acquiring and repeating their sacred books by heart, will doubt. . . . the possibility of this having been the case." T. W. Rhys Davids, General Introduction, *Buddhist Suttas,* pp. xxii–xxiii, Vol. XI of *Sacred Books of the East* (1881).

But in 1942, the widow and collaborator of the leading spirit of the Pali Text Society, Mrs. C. A. F. Rhys Davids, wrote: "Both [Jain Angas and Pali Pitakas] should be read, not as the actual sayings of the early teachers alleged to be speaking, but as much later compilations, made up from very brief memoranda handed down orally, and much glossed over by speakers and then writers, holding later monastic views." *Wayfarer's Words,* III, 770.

3. Each school defined and redefined the boundaries of the skandhas. Sangharakshita, in his excellent introduction to modern Buddhism, *The Three Jewels,* emphasizes that "each of the skandhas represents not an unchanging 'thing' but rather a congeries of related processes" (p. 98). He goes on to explain that rupa consists of the four elementary qualities (earth, water, fire, and air) with their attributes of cohesion, undulation, radiation, and vibration, and varying numbers of secondary qualities. "The fact that such items as masculinity, femininity and gesture are listed among the secondary qualities should cause us to beware of thinking of this term as 'matter' in either the popular or philosophic usage of the term." *Vedana* is "the affective colouring which saturates a particular content of consciousness. . . . It covers, thus, not only sensation, or hedonic feeling, but also emotion, which can be not only hedonic but also ethical and even

spiritual." Thus upeksha, neutral feeling, "can mean not only hedonic indifference, both sensational and emotional, but also that positive state of spiritual balance or equanimity in respect of worldly things which plays so vital a part in the attainment of Supreme Enlightenment." (It is the last of the four Unlimiteds, the Brahmaviharas, benign steps toward depersonalization.) Samjna is of six kinds, one for each of the five senses and one for the mind. Samskarah are "not conditioned things in general, nor the formative psychological factors, but all mental phenomena whatsoever, with the exception of *vedana, samjna* and *vijnana.*" Vijnana is the discriminating consciousness, functioning in dependence on the contact of the six sense organs. Sangharakshita concludes, "there exists no unchanging substantial entity but only an ever-changing stream of physical and psychical (including mental and spiritual) events outside which no such entity can be discerned. Hence there can be no such thing, either, as human nature in the sense of a fixed and determinate quality or condition holding good of such an entity at all times and places. . . . Human nature is in reality a no-nature. . . . Man is in fact indefinable. This is the very conclusion reached from similar premises by the French existentialist Jean-Paul Sartre."

Herbert Guenther uses the terms corporeality, feeling, concept-formation, motivated action, and perceptual judgments (*The Tantric View of Life,* p. 105). Conze says The Body, Feelings, Perceptions, Impulses and Emotions, Acts of Consciousness (*Buddhism: Its Essence and Development,* p. 14). Stcherbatsky's "five groups of elements" are matter, feelings, ideas, volitions and other faculties, and pure sensation or general consciousness (*The Central Conception of Buddhism and the Meaning of the Word "Dharma,"* p. 5).

4. *A Treatise of Human Understanding,* Book I, Part IV, Section 6, "Of Personal Identity," p. 300. The preceding sentences suggest the Buddhist "momentariness": "Pain and pleasure, grief and joy, passions and sensations succeed each other, and never all exist at the same time. It cannot, therefore, be from any of these impressions, or from any other, that the idea of self is derived; and consequently there is no such idea." And a sentence or two later he sounds like an *uccheda-vadin:* "And were all my perceptions remov'd by death, and cou'd I never think, nor feel, nor see, nor love, nor hate after the dissolution of my body, I should be entirely annihilated. . . ." But Coleridge, the master of synthesis, stands Hume's argument on its head: "How opposite to nature and the fact to talk of the one *moment* of Hume; of our whole being as an aggregate of successive single sensations. Who ever *felt* a *single* sensation? Is not every one at the same moment conscious that there co-exist a thousand others in a darker shade, or less light . . . ?" Quoted in a review of Richard Haven, *Patterns of Consciousness,* in the March 14, 1973, issue of *Manas,* that humane leader in the search for wholeness.

5. Rahula states and answers the question: "If there is no permanent, unchanging entity or substance like Self or Soul (atman), what is it that can re-exist or be reborn after death? . . . If we can understand that in this life we can continue without a permanent, unchanging substance like Self or Soul, why

can't we understand that those forces themselves can continue without a Self or a Soul behind them after the nonfunctioning of the body?

"When this physical body is no more capable of functioning, energies do not die with it, but continue to take some other shape or form, which we call another life. . . .

"As there is no permanent, unchanging substance, nothing passes from one moment to the next. So quite obviously, nothing permanent or unchanging can pass or transmigrate from one life to the next. It is a series that continues unbroken, but changes every moment. . . . Certainly the man of sixty is not the same as the child of sixty years ago, nor is he another person. Similarly, a person who dies here and is reborn elsewhere is neither the same person, nor another. . . . It is the continuity of the same series." *What the Buddha Taught,* pp. 33–34.

6. Immediately after the Enlightenment, he met the mendicant-recluse Upaka who remarked, "Your features shine with intellectual power, you have become a master over your senses," and asked who was his teacher. The new Buddha replied, "No teacher have I. None need I venerate, and none must I despise. Nirvana have I now obtained, and I am not the same as others are. Quite by myself, you see, have I the Dharma won." From Ashvaghosha, *Buddha-carita,* in *Buddhist Scriptures,* selected and translated by Conze, p. 53.

7. "According to the doctrine of the Old Wisdom School, wisdom alone is able to chase the illusion of individuality from our thoughts, where it has persisted from age-old habit. Not action, not trance, but only thought can kill the illusion which resides in thought." Conze, *Buddhism: Its Essence and Development,* p. 110.

8. "Dependent Origination" is the term used by Warren in his *Buddhism in Translations* in 1896 and by Stcherbatsky. Rhys Davids used "Chain of Causation," which is generally condemned as implying a sequence rather than interaction. Conze says "Conditioned Co-production" and "Conditioned Genesis." Richard Robinson says "Dependent Arising" or the "Preconditions."

9. In Edward J. Thomas, *The History of Buddhist Thought,* p. 59. Another, probably earlier version occurs in Vinaya Pitaka I, 1: "Conditioned by ignorance are the karma formations (volitional activity); conditioned by the karma foundations is consciousness; . . . by consciousness is mind-and-body; . . . the six sense-fields; . . . impression; . . . feeling; . . . craving; . . . grasping; . . . becoming; . . . birth; conditioned by birth there come into being aging and dying, grief, sorrow, suffering, lamentation and despair." *BT,* p. 66.

10. Foucher suggests that "ignorance" is too abstract a concept for so concrete a series. He suggests "unseen" or "unknowableness" as more in line with the Buddha's unwillingness to deal with ultimate metaphysical questions. And he holds no great awe for the intellectual achievement of the Twelve Links. *La Vie du Bouddha.*

11. From Samyutta Nikaya, Part 5, 421 ff.; also indicated as Chap. LVI, Book 12, Chap. 2, Para. 1, the first version of the Pali Text Society (henceforth

PTS). See also the more recent translation by K. Woodward, *Kindred Sayings,* PTS.

12. In Warren, p. 151, Samyutta Nikaya, Part I, Chap. XII, Para. 61; "priests" is a curious misrendering of *bhikkhu.*

13. *What the Buddha Taught;* see note 5 above on the argument against an unchanging soul-substance.

14. The *Lalitavistara* reports various practices, supplementing those reported in Digha Nikaya I, Sutta 8, Kassapa-Sihanada, and Majjhima Nikaya Sutta 12: some devotees sit in one spot and keep perpetual silence; some sleep in wet clothes or on ashes, gravel, boards, thorny grass, or spikes; some smear themselves with ashes, dust, or clay; some inhale smoke and fire; some gaze at the sun, or sit surrounded by "the five fires," the fifth being the sun, or rest on one foot, or keep one arm perpetually uplifted, or move about on their knees; some observe various types of fasting. In his introduction to Digha Sutta 8, T. W. Rhys Davids wrote, "The distinction seems to have been that it was rather power, worldly success, wealth, children, and heaven that were attained by sacrifice; and mystic, extraordinary, superhuman facilities that were attained by tapas." *Dialogues of the Buddha, Sacred Books of the Buddhists,* I, 210.

15. Kenneth J. Saunders wrote, "From the ordinary Yogi this great one differed in that his experience was profound and ethical and that he established the practice on a rational basis. From the seers of the Upanishads he differed in bringing into daily life some of the glamour of the Ineffable and in insisting more strongly that the way of Salvation is a Way of Purity." "The Quest of the Historic Sakya-muni," in *Buddhistic Studies,* ed. Bimala Churn Law (Calcutta, 1931). But Saunders, insisting that mystic ecstasy is at the center of the teaching, points to a difference in the Buddha's attitudes toward the monks and the laity: "Whatsoever householder desires to be reborn in a heaven let him attach himself to me with faith and devotion, but whatsoever monks would realize Nirvana let him tread the noble Eightfold Path." Majjhima Nikaya 184.

Mrs. Rhys Davids deplored some of the ideals with which Buddhism grew. "One of these was that the right aspiration of all men should be, sooner or later, to become monks, else the perfect, saintly life could not be led. The lay life was inferior, worthy chiefly as a vehicle for maintaining the saint." "Why India Is Poor in History," *Wayfarer's Words,* III, 1056.

16. Cf. upeksha in note 3.

17. "What is there, Vakkali, in seeing this vile body? Who sees Dhamma sees me; whoso sees me sees Dhamma. Seeing Dhamma, Vakkali, he sees me; seeing me, he sees Dhamma." Samyutta Nikaya, III, 120, in *BT,* p. 103.

18. Digha Nikaya Sutta 26, Cakkavatti-Sihanada Suttanta, "The Lion-Roar in the Turning of the Wheel." Perhaps the Metteyya reference should not be taken as serious doctrine. The theme is a glimpse into the future by the Buddha, when political and social morality will prevail, and kings will be just. T. W. Rhys Davids said, in his introduction to the sutta, "The whole is a fairy tale. . . . The point of the moral—and in this fairy tale the moral is the thing—is the

Reign of Law. Never before in the history of the world had this principle been proclaimed in so thorough-going and uncompromising a way."

19. *The Conception of Buddhist Nirvana,* p. 36.

20. Majjhima Nikaya I, 485–86, Aggi-Vacchagotta Sutta, No. 72, translated by Chalmers, modified by Murti, p. 47; also in Warren, pp. 124–25.

21. "*Jnana* or Knowledge stands for the subtlest type of *prajna,* that which sees not only the non-duality of the conditioned and the Unconditioned but also that this non-duality does not stand in the way of the one being the spontaneous outpouring of the other." Sangharakshita, *The Three Jewels,* p. 173.

22. In a review of Murti's book in *Journal of Asian Studies,* 16 (1956), 161, Donald Ingalls found too great emphasis on the rational in Murti's approach, too little on the emotional aspects of the Buddha's teaching.

23. H. Oldenberg, *Buddha, sein Leben, seine Lehre, seine Gemeinde* (1881; translated into English 1882), quoted in Thomas, p. 127. G. R. Welbon, in *The Buddhist Nirvana and Its Western Interpreters,* makes it clear that Oldenberg did not himself believe that the Buddha thought Nirvana was annihilation.

24. Krishnamurti makes sense on monkish celibacy. He quotes a sannyasi: "I have spent more time on resisting, and wasted more energy on it, than I have ever wasted on sex itself. . . . Conflict and struggle are far more deadening than the seeing of a woman's face, or even perhaps than sex itself." *The Only Revolution,* p. 81. Later K. says, "What is important is not to come to any conclusion, or any decision for or against sex, not to get caught in conceptual ideologies. . . . The monk has taken a vow of celibacy because he thinks that to gain his heaven he has to shun contact with a woman; but for the rest of his life he is struggling against his own physical demands: he is in conflict with heaven and with earth. . . ." (P. 102)

25. Quoted in Saunders (see note 15 above), who also quotes L. Poussin, "Buddhism, which does appeal to reason and which will later reason freely, places intuition Jnana, above all. It is in ecstasy that one sees things truly." *Nirvana,* p. 15.

But there are those who find the notion of an ecstatic Buddha distasteful. George Grimm, in the same volume of essays (ed. Law), declares: "The Buddha's doctrine contains not a trace of mysticism. To be sure, it brings unusual knowledge and teaches also how to set up the conditions for unusual powers, but all this in the normal human cognitive faculties, even if in the state of their highest possible development; and the whole thing in the form of the Law of Causation." "Christian Mysticism in the Light of the Buddha's Doctrine," p. 769. Mrs. Rhys Davids preferred the word "musing" as the true meaning of *jhana.* In *Buddhism in England* (1940), reprinted in *Wayfarer's Words* (1940), Chap. 18, "The Meaning of Jhana."

26. The trance in childhood was experienced by Tennyson. He is quoted in the chapter on Mysticism in William James's *Varieties of Religious Experience:* "I have never had any revelations through aesthetics, but a kind of waking trance—this for lack of a better word—I have frequently had, quite up from

boyhood, when I have been all alone. This has come upon me through repeating my own name to myself silently, till all at once, as it were out of the intensity of the consciousness of individuality, individuality itself seems to dissolve and fade away into boundless being, and this not a confused state but the clearest, the surest of the surest, utterly beyond words—where death was an almost laughable impossibility—the loss of personality (if so it were) seeming no extinction, but the only true life. I am ashamed of my feeble description. Have I not said the state is utterly beyond words?" It is interesting that in this almost classical description of the mystic state ("dissolve into boundless being," "beyond words," "individuality dissolves") the famed sound poet uses an aural key rather than the visual "kasina" of Buddhist mediation discipline.

In "The Light at the Center" (forthcoming) Agehananda Bharati, author of *The Ochre Robe* and *The Tantric Tradition,* describes his first mystical experience at the age of twelve. Also see below, p. 83, on Anandamayi. And, perhaps relevant is the Commentary on *Theragata* and *Therigata,* which refers to a boy of seven and a girl of six reaching enlightenment.

James's personal statement on these matters applies also to the present author: "Whether my treatment of mystical states will shed more light or darkness, I do not know, for my own constitution shuts me out from their enjoyment almost entirely, and I can speak of them only at second hand. But though forced to look upon the subject so externally, I will be as objective and receptive as I can; and I think I shall at least succeed in convincing you of the reality of the states in question, and of the paramount importance of their function."

Chapter 4: Background—Orthodoxy, Heterodoxy, and Buddhism

1. According to Kosambi in *Ancient India,* the new duties that the Buddha or some anonymous early disciple set for the king went to the root of social evil, poverty, and unemployment. The king should provide seed and food when necessary. "New wealth would thus be generated, the *janapadas* liberated from robbers and cheats. . . . The new philosophy gave man control over himself" (p. 113).

2. S. Yamaguchi, "Development of Mahayana Buddhist Beliefs," in *The Path of the Buddha,* ed. Kenneth Morgan: "It is an open question as to whether or not primitive Buddhism believed in rebirth" (p. 153).

3. The term "heresy" is improper, of course, because with its fellow "heresy," Jainism, Buddhism had never been within the fold of Brahmanism. The two doctrines had deep roots in pre-Aryan times. "The ascetic thought of the Buddha has been traced to the *Yoga* practices of pre-Vedic India which are attested by ascetic sculptures of the Indus Valley civilization through the non-Vedic

ascetics *(munis, yatis)* occasionally mentioned in the Vedic Samhitas and the Brahmana texts." L. M. Joshi, "Historical Introduction," *Buddhism,* p. 2.

4. Joshi quotes A. B. Keith: "It is wholly impossible to make out any case for dating the oldest, even, of the extant *Upanisads* beyond the sixth century B.C. and the acceptance of an earlier date must rest merely on individual fancy" *(ibid.,* p. 2). And Joshi reports that R. E. Hume and Stcherbatsky have shown that "evidences of Buddhist influences are not wanting" in the older Upanishads; there is wide disagreement on the subject.

5. Paul Deussen, *The Philosophy of the Upanishads,* p. 15.

6. See Kosambi: "Celibacy and abstinence from holding property made the new teachers much more economic than greedy fire priests in an acquisitive society" (p. 104).

7. Jayatilleke, *Early Buddhist Theory of Knowledge,* states that the theories of Yajnavalkya, Prajapati, and Uddalaka were probably known to the Buddhists (pp. 39, 372–73).

8. In the Pratimoksha, false boasting of such powers was a Parijika offense—the most serious.

9. See *Altered States of Consciousness,* ed. Charles T. Tart, and discussion in Chapter 8 below.

10. Jayatilleke, p. 106. He quotes Gunaratna, that there were some yogins who were nastikas (disbelievers in Veda), where the content shows reference to the Materialist schools.

11. "Liberated energy experienced as light may be the core sensory experience of mysticism," suggests Arthur Deikman in "Deautomatization and the Mystic Experience," in *Altered States of Consciousness,* p. 38.

12. This may be an anachronism. It is doubtful that Mahavira lived until Ajatasatru's reign, in the last years of the Buddha's life.

13. Helmut von Glasenapp, *Buddhism, a Non-Theistic Religion,* p. 31. It is doubtful that Nagarjuna is here mounting a specific campaign against the gods; nothing else has "concrete being" either.

14. U Thittila, "The Fundamental Principles of Theravada Buddhism," in *The Path of the Buddha,* ed. Morgan, p. 76.

Chapter 5: Lamps Unto Themselves

1. Edward Conze, *Buddhism: Its Essence and Development* (p. 93): "An Arhat is normally depicted as dignified, bald, and with a certain severity."

2. Mahaparinibbanasutta, VI, 19. At this point Anuruddha exhorted the brethren not to weep, because "whatever born, brought into being, and organized, contains within itself the inherent necessity of dissolution." Later, when Maha Kassapa and others are informed of the decease, a similar passage occurs, and Kassapa makes the same speech. The same passage occurs also in Cullavag-

ga 11, 1, 1. Frauwallner might say that the Skandhaka-Mahaparinibbana author is giving Kassapa a place of prominence, perhaps for sectarian reasons. *Arahat, arhat, arhant, arahant* are various acceptable transcriptions of the original term.

3. Samyutta Nikaya III, 83, in *BT,* p. 42. The "outflows" are the asravas (Pali, asava): sense desire, desire for life process, ignorance of higher knowledge, wrong views (of self).

4. Cullavagga 11, 1, 6. The footnote in the PTS edition states: "In other words, he became an Arahat. Some MSS omit the clause about the feet."

5. We have met this formula in Chapter 3, note 6, in Ashvaghosha's version of the Enlightenment, in which the recluse Upaka meets the new Buddha, remarks on his shining countenance, hears the message, says "How interesting," and moves on.

6. Harley C. Shands, *The War with Words: Structure and Transcendence,* pp. 17, 18.

7. "The neurologist Alajouanine, in a paper dealing with Dostoevsky's epilepsy, quotes from a passage in which the author describes the conviction carried to him in the aura, 'God exists, He exists—the air was filled with a big noise and I tried to move. I felt the heaven was going down on the earth and that it had engulfed me. I have really touched God. . . . You all, healthy people . . . cannot imagine the happiness epileptics feel the second before our fit.' " Shands, p. 92 n.

8. The astrology that tells all Aquarians to refrain from acquisitive activity on Thursday is, of course, nonsense, or simple venality. But astrology that seeks to study the environmental effects of planetary positions is another thing. Sunspots affect the earth in known ways (radio and atmospheric), and the position of a planet affects sunspot activity. There may well be other influences that can as yet be demonstrated only statistically, such as comparative numbers of scientists born in certain months. The matter is treated thoughtfully in Lyall Watson's *Supernature,* pp. 54–76.

9. *What the Buddha Taught,* p. 32. Note the avoidance of the term "soul" in the narrative and the Buddha's refusal to imply that the "consciousness" fixes itself in nirvana.

10. "The ecstatic feeling involved in the transcendent state is a conviction of a safe loss of personal identity, usually rationalized as a sense of continuity into the divine presence. When we examine the history of such feelings, we find that they generally follow a protracted relation of intense quality with a preceptor or master. It is very suggestive that the ultimate 'liberation' is a metamorphosis of what in psychiatric terms we would call a 'transference' feeling. In the process, the particular relation is generalized and depersonalized—and it would seem that intense non-sexual communication involving two persons is only possible when the relation can be so depersonalized." Shands, p. 17.

Lannoy presents an acute analysis of the guru-shishya relationship in modern India (pp. 351–53). Lizelle Reymond is less analytical: "Pandityi [her host] explained. 'That man acts as guru for many souls. Through his austerities, he has unravelled one of the mysteries of Divine Knowledge. He knows one of the direct paths of the Way. . . . All that he transmits is the reverberation of certain *bijas* (holy syllables) which he has gleaned from the *Mantra-Shastras,* and he communicates this reverberation to those prepared to receive it. . . . That man, through the power of his mantras, could cause a tree to germinate or die, for all the elements of nature are revealed to him, as well as the Law that establishes the forces relating them one to another.' " *My Life with a Brahmin Family,* pp. 148–49.

Agehananda Bharati, a mystic qualified by experience and theory, is less rhapsodic about the saintly accruals of samadhi. "The full-time mystic, i.e. the person who does not have to do anything else in the world but talk about the zero-experience, and orients his life toward it and toward nothing else, is a fool when out in the market place. But he is surrounded by a wall of devotees, of monastic institutes, of ecclesiastic functionaries and ashramites. . . . I want readers to disabuse themselves of this traditional, uncritical, ancient notion, that there is something beyond the experience itself to be sought after or hoped for, something that will change the man and the world. There isn't. . . . The zero-experience is a peak experience, in one category perhaps with totally consummated erotic experiences, or with artistic and similar peak sensations. . . . Their value is intrinsic, it is not teleological. . . . The modern mystic must learn what some very few mystics through the ages knew: *that the zero-experience does not and cannot confer existential status on its content.* . . . The mystic who was a stinker before he had the zero-experience remains a stinker, socially speaking, after the experience." *Passim* in ms., "The Light at the Centre."

11. *BT,* pp. 119, 134. The need for "spiritual friends" is stressed by sGam.po.pa: "In general, the Buddhas of the past, present and future make it clear why friends are necessary, while the Pratyekabuddhas illustrate the fact that without friends the ultimately real remains unattainable." *The Jewel Ornament of Liberation,* translated and annotated by Herbert V. Guenther, p. 30. The Tibetan teacher Chögyam Trungpa says, "I am afraid the word 'guru' is overused in the West. It would be better to speak of one's 'spiritual friend,' because the teachings emphasize a mutual meeting of two minds. It is a matter of mutual communication, rather than a master–servant relationship between a highly evolved being and a miserable, confused one." *Cutting Through Spiritual Materialism,* pp. 39–40.

12. H. Saddhatissa, *Buddhist Ethics,* p. 84. "There are four pairs of saints who realize the paths *(magga)* and fruitions *(phala)* of the following stages: (i) Stream-winning *(Sotapatti)* (ii) Once-return *(Sakadagami)* (iii) Never-return *(Anagami)* (iv) Perfection *(Arahatta)*" (p. 55, n. 2).

13. Guenther lists "four great philosophical schools, all of which are still (or were) studied in Tibet. They are the Vaibhasikas representing a naive realism, the Sautrantikas with a critical realism, the Vijnanavadins who are very similar to the idealistic-mentalistic thinkers in Western philosophy, and the Madhyamikas. The latter divide into two groups, the Svatantrikas who still upheld the idea

of an essence, and the Prasangikas who instead advocated a philosophy which superficially looks like nominalism." *Treasures on the Tibetan Middle Way*, p. 9.

14. "For the Vaibhasikas, mind and mental events were different substances existing simultaneous with each other, the one being a function of the other; for the Sautrantikas, they were one substance; hence any total noetic situation was anteceded or followed by another noetic situation, which implies temporal sequence and not co-existence. Here again we note the pre-eminent interest in psychological and cognitive processes, which, in turn, had a moral-ethical reference. . . . Human morality remained bound up with the phenomena of non-human nature. After all, man is part of the universe. It is he who as 'causal agent' creates his world which, in turn, is a 'causal agent' creating him. This is so, because 'causality' in Buddhism is . . . an interlocking system and not a linear sequence of cause and effect." Guenther, *Buddhist Philosophy in Theory and Practice*, p. 76.

15. Murti, *The Central Philosophy of Buddhism*, p. 80, n. 2; quoting Kimura, *Hinayana and Mahayana*, pp. 86–87.

16. *The Jewel Ornament of Liberation*, p. 142. "An 'enlightened attitude' is qualified as 'supreme.' This is to emphasize the Mahayanist conception of enlightenment as an active and dynamic way of being, and not the static ideal of the Sravakas and Pratyekabuddhas who each have their own idea of what enlightenment may mean, namely the expulsion of all that obstructs integration and the attainment of all that furthers it. In a very restricted sense, to develop an enlightened attitude means to become and remain goal-conscious." Guenther, *Treasures on the Tibetan Middle Way*, p. 11.

Chapter 6: The Paradoxes of Mahayana

1. Edward Conze, *Buddhism*, p. 217. A footnote to this passage states, "This opposition was probably alien to the original Buddhism, in which the Abhidharmic *prajna* did not even form one of the stages of the eightfold path, much less the highest one."

2. Guenther stresses the importance of compassion in Tantra, a highly developed Mahayana. Quoting a Tibetan source, he says, "Compassion, and especially 'Great Compassion,' . . . has 'as its special cause and antecedent the practice of loving-kindness throughout many aeons, as its actuality,—(in other words) one feels the plight of any sentient being as acutely as if one's leg were hit by a sharp weapon. As its effect it has the capacity of developing the noble intention of always being ready (to help) others.' " *Treasures on the Tibetan Middle Way*, p. 37.

3. Is the reference here to Suddhodana's continued rejection of his son's antisocietal teaching? One is reminded here of the dirty trick played on Nanda,

who "had no zest for Brahma-faring" because when he had left home with the other youths, "a Sakyan girl, the fairest in the land, with hair half combed, looked back" at him and said, "Come back soon." The Buddha lifted Nanda up to deva-heaven, where five hundred nymphs were in attendance. Compared to them, Nanda had to admit, the Sakyan girl was "like a monkey with ears and nose cut off." Sangharakshita, in *The Three Jewels*, sees the story as allegorical for the ascent of the devout from conditioned existence to higher planes. Still, only the extremely devout can refrain from sympathy with the young Nanda and others charmed into premature celibacy.

4. Kosambi, p. 176, quotes Hsuan Tsang on the luxuries of Nalanda, to which he was welcomed in 630 A.D.: "The king gave them the revenues of more than 100 villages to support them, and each of the villages had 200 families who daily offered several hundred *tan* of rice, butter, and milk. Thus the students could have the four requisites (clothing, food, shelter, and medicine) sufficient for their needs without going to beg for them. It was because of this support that they had achieved so much in their learning." Meanwhile they were losing the support of the people.

5. An important contribution is that of Jacques Gernet, *Les Aspects économiques du Bouddhisme dans la société chinoise du Ve au Xe siècle* (1956). The monasteries in China put out their wealth at interest, introducing the notion and the technique of the productive use of capital. The justification was that expiatory gifts were productive of spiritual benefits.

6. Anguttara Nikaya 4, 8, 7, 64, in von Glasenapp, *Buddhism, a Non-Theistic Religion*, p. 140.

7. Conze, "Mahayana Buddhism," in *Thirty Years of Buddhist Studies*, p. 65.

8. Candrakirti, *Prasannapada*, in *BT*, pp. 168–69. Similarly the Tibetan sage sGam.po.pa says, "Thus, Nirvana is not something which can be found (as an ens) by inventing, destroying, rejecting or accepting (some tenet), but it can be described as stopping all intellectualistic processes." In *The Jewel Ornament of Liberation*, p. 215.

9. Similarly, "The Bodhisattva-Mahasattva should also bestow alms, uninfluenced by any preconceived thoughts as to self and other selves and for the sole purpose of benefiting sentient beings, always remembering that both the phenomena and sentient beings are to be considered as mere expressions." And, "Should there be any sentient beings to be delivered by the Tathagata, it would mean that the Tathagata was cherishing within his mind arbitrary conceptions of phenomena such as one's own self, other selves, living beings, and a universal self. Even when the Tathagata refers to himself, he is not holding in his mind any such arbitrary thought." In *A Buddhist Bible*, edited by Dwight Goddard, pp. 90–92.

10. Majjhima Nikaya 3, 104–9, in Berry, *Religions of India*, p. 171.

11. In Conze's translation of Chap. V, "On Plants," in *Thirty Years*, pp. 119–22.

12. In Conze's translation of the first part of "The Perfection of Wisdom in 700 Lines," in *Thirty Years,* p. 192.
13. Daisetz Teitaro Suzuki, *Outlines of Mahayana Buddhism,* p. 95.
14. Conze, "Mahayana Buddhism," in *Thirty Years,* pp. 64, 66.
15. *The Vimalakirti Nirdesa Sutra,* translated and edited by Charles Luk, pp. 25–26, 30, 37–38.
16. "Hate, Love and Perfect Wisdom," in *Thirty Years,* pp. 186–87. Conze goes on to say, "The Prajnaparamita to some extent destroys hate by refining it into universal compassion, which is the reverse of cruelty. . . . the Gnosis of perfect wisdom further helps to sublimate hatred. It is the aim and purpose of hatred to smash that which offends. While 'nihilism' is by no means the last word of the Prajnaparamita, the thorough annihilation of the world, emotional and intellectual, is an important step on the way towards winning her."

Wayman points out that the five Buddhas are regularly explained as the nature of the five knowledges and associated with the five eyes: Amitabha, discriminative (knowledge) and insight (eye); Amoghasiddhi, procedure-of-duty and fleshly; Ratnasambhava, equality and divine; Akshobya, mirror-like and Buddha; Vairocana, dharmadhatu and dharma. "The five Buddhas appear to be personifications of five knowledge-vision aspects of deity." *Historia Religionum,* Vol. II, Religions of the Present, p. 417.

17. Thomas has a useful discussion of the meaning of the name in *The History of Buddhist Thought,* p. 189. He rejects "looking down at" the world. In later times Avalokitesvara assumed even the forms of the Hindu gods, especially Siva, Mahesvara, to preach the Dharma. The Hindus won the battle of assimilation in the end.

18. "Such are Tsongkhapa, the father of the Gelukpa School, who on account of his wisdom and kindred virtues is regarded as a manifestation of Manjusri, and a number of other personages prominent in the history of Tibetan Buddhism" (p. 193). And Nichiren identified himself with the bodhisattva Visistacaritra of the Lotus Sutra.

Chapter 7: Tantra and Zen—The Restorers

1. King Ajatasattu in the Samannaphala sutta says he would not return to slavery a man who had run off and become a monk.
2. The Yogacara inheritance asserts itself here. Just as Mara's daughters—Desire, Pleasure, and Delight—took the forms they thought might appeal to a man, whatever his tastes, so the Bodhisattva could make his own thought projections.
3. *The Hundred Thousand Songs of Milarepa,* translated and annotated by Garma C. Chang, abridged edition, p. 191.

NOTES TO PAGES 109-139

4. Chintarahan Chakravarty, *Tantras: Studies on Their Religion and Literature*. A more extreme statement of the same attitude: "If at any time in the history of India the mind of the nation as a whole has been diseased, it was in the Tantric age, or the period immediately preceding the Muhammedan conquest of India. . . . The Hindu population of India as a whole is even today in the grip of this very Tantrism in its daily life, customs and usage, and is suffering from the same disease which originated 1300 years ago and consumed the vitality slowly but surely during these long centuries." Benoytosh Bhattacharya, *An Introduction to Buddhist Esotericism*, Preface.

5. Agehananda Bharati, *The Tantric Tradition*, pp. 20–21. Bharati, Viennese by birth, is an ordained member of the Dasanami order of the Shankaracarya tradition. He is at this writing chairman of the Department of Anthropology at Syracuse University. His years in India are reported in *The Ochre Robe*.

6. *The Tantric View of Life*, p. 2. The passage continues, "Dominance or power has a strong appeal to the ego, as it enables the ego to think that it is master of its world. . . . a person who feels insecure and is afraid of becoming himself may turn to anything that seems to promise him the attainment or power. Because of this slanted view and because the word *sakti*, 'creative energy,' frequently used in Hinduist Tantra, but never in Buddhist Tantra, could be understood as 'power,' the word Tantrism has almost exclusively become synonymous with Hinduist 'Tantra,' and more is known about it than about Buddhist 'Tantra' which stresses individual growth and tries to realize the uniqueness of being human." A later passage (p. 64) reads: "Inasmuch as Hindu Tantrism has been deeply influenced by the dominance psychology of the Samkhya system, professing a dualism of *purusa* who is male, and of *prakrti* who is female and who dances or stops dancing at the bidding of the Lord or *purusa*, this purely Hinduistic power mentality, so similar to the Western dominance psychology, was generalized and applied to all forms of Tantrism by writers who did not see or, due to their being steeped so much in dominance psychology, could not understand that the desire to realize Being is not the same as the craving for power. Hence Tantrism was equated with 'power.' And since *purusa* and *prakrti* involved a sexual symbolism, which was concretized in the sense that the sexual act was the proof of one's masculinity, the paranoid Western conception about Tantrism resulted. . . ."

7. Saraha was "one of the chiefs of the 84 Perfect Ones (Siddhas), to whom the beginnings of the Tantras are traditionally ascribed." Introduction to *BT*, p. 14.

8. *BT*, pp. 232–33. the first line of this passage is translated less vividly by Guenther, "Although he enjoys the objective world he is not taken in by the objects." In *Yuganaddha: The Tantric View of Life,* p. 162; the preface is by Bharati, who attended Guenther's ordination.

9. For a non-entity, Nairatmya (the early Buddhist term for "soullessness") plays a positive role in the *Hevajra* Tantra, as the consort of Hevajra. "In her the yogin is consubstantiated, for it is her bliss that he enjoys. With her that

perfection is found that bestows the bliss of the Great Symbol. Form and sound, smell, taste, touch and sphere of thought are all enjoyed in this *Prajna*. She is the Innate itself, the divine yogini of great bliss. She is the whole *mandala* and comprehends the fine Wisdom. . . . "

10. *Mudra* to left-hand tantrists means woman, not fried grain as stated by Chakravarty (note 4 above.)

11. Snellgrove points out that between literal belief in the chakra column and the figurative view that the sophisticated West holds, there is a middle ground of as-if pragmatic conviction held by those practitioners to whom the exercise is no more than a mere device.

12. "In certain texts, *Sekoddesatika*, p. 25, for instance, it is stated that in the union between man and woman 'the *bodhicitta* must not be discharged.' The use of the term *bodhicitta*, rich in symbolical content, is ample evidence that it is not primarily a matter of avoiding an ejaculation. It rather serves as an advice not to allow the pulsatory movement that unites the different aspects of man's personality (i.e., love and sex) to be disrupted. Moreover, the conscious attempt at preventing an ejaculation introduces conceptual (inhibitory) operations which in this specific case are known to result in erective impotence and which are characteristic of the schizoid person and his obsession with sex as a means of establishing contact with others. . . ." *The Tantric View of Life*, p. 154.

13. *The Tantric View of Life*, pp. 61–62. See also a similar treatment, p. 99: "Coition is the union with the Karmamudra; the awareness in self-validating intrinsic perception, symbolized by the vision of the birth of bliss supreme. 'Symbol' means openness of Being and 'enacting the commitment' means to have absolute compassionateness. Therefore the yogi who is aware of the unity of appropriate action and appreciative awareness understands the self-sameness of intrinsic awareness and openness; intrinsic awareness being a symbol for Samsara and openness for Nirvana. Since this understanding is Mahamudra they temper everything into the self-sameness of intrinsic awareness and openness."

In a different context Chögyam Trungpa writes, "While the basic teaching of Mahayana Buddhism is concerned with developing prajna, transcendental knowledge, the basic teaching of Tantra is connected with working with energy. . . . At this point whatever is experienced in everyday life through sense perception is a naked experience, because it is direct. There is no veil between him and 'that.' When we speak of transcendence in the Mahayana tradition, we mean transcendence of ego. In the Tantric tradition we do not speak of going beyond ego at all: it is too dualistic an attitude." *Cutting Through Spiritual Materialism*, pp. 218–19.

14. Guenther quotes gNyis-med Avadhutipa (another commentator on Saraha) in implying the superiority of Tantra to both Hinayana and Mahayana: "A low-level yogi is concerned with freedom from the one-sidedness of Samsara, a medium-level yogi with freedom from mere Nirvana, but the high-level yogi's understanding consists in the fact that he neither rejects nor accepts (i.e., identi-

fies himself with) the fictions that stem from a mind immersed in Samsara; that he neither rejects nor accepts a state of quiescence, which is a mind that has passed into Nirvana. Since Samsara is not an entity in itself, he is not afraid of it, and since Nirvana is not found as an entity in itself, either, he does not hope for it. This is the way of the yogis, and so Saraha concludes: 'Is freed from Samsara and Nirvana.' " *The Tantric View of Life,* p. 129.

15. The two passages are from Chap. 1 of "Six Chapters Concerning Aesthetic Analysis," an early manuscript version of *Aesthetic Analysis* (1936). We find this passage in the published version: "The feeling is strictly aesthetic, however, only if it is directed exclusively upon the object, so that it is properly the feeling of that object, not an irrelevance suggested by some incidental aspect of it, but a content determinately given as actually present to active contemplation. Such contemplation, in fact, removes irrelevant feeling just by being fully directed discriminating attention. Contemplation that does not attend and discriminate is either not aesthetic contemplation at all, or it is the aesthetic contemplation of something else, bodily states instead of the presented object, or remembered or imagined content not unambiguously determinate in the object. What is given to full, unwandering, vital response, without penetration through and beyond the qualitative felt presence defined by the object, is exactly the aesthetic aspect of the world at the moment. What penetrates and goes beyond is non-aesthetic." Apollo edition (1967), pp. 19–20.

16. Tilopa preached to Naropa that it was not sense gratification or intellection that was to be condemned: "It is not the manifestations that have bound you in *Sangsara,* / It is the clinging that has tied you down." In Garma C. C. Chang, *The Practice of Zen.* p. 160.

17. The Emperor Wu of Liang asked the new arrival what was the holiest principle of Buddhism. Bodhidharma answered, "Vast emptiness," and there was nothing holy in that. Nor was there anything holy in building temples or supporting monks and nuns. The Emperor did not understand, and Bodhidharma went off "to look at the wall" in solitude, until Hui-k'o came to be his disciple.

18. "Recent Progress in Buddhist Studies," in *Thirty Years of Buddhist Studies,* p. 29. Alan Watts also reminds us to consider Zen in its historical contexts: "Zen is a medicine for the ill effects of this conditioning, for the mental paralysis and anxiety which come from excessive self-consciousness. It must be seen against the background of societies regulated by the principles of Confucianism, with their heavy stress on propriety and punctilious ritual. In Japan, too, it must be seen in relation to the rigid schooling required in the training of the *samurai* caste . . . it does not seek to overthrow the conventions themselves, but, on the contrary, takes them for granted. . . . Therefore Zen might be a very dangerous medicine in a social context where convention is weak, or . . . where there is a spirit of open revolt against convention ready to exploit Zen for destructive purposes." *The Way of Zen,* p. 141.

19. *Zen Buddhism: Selected Writings of D. T. Suzuki,* ed. William Barrett, pp. 60–61.
20. Cf. Alex Wayman, "The Mirror-like Knowledge in Mahayana Buddhist Literature," *Études asiatiques,* 25, 1971.
21. The classical Zen statement on the efficacy of meditation was Huai-jang's reply to his student Ma-tsu's statement that he was meditating because he wished to become a Buddha. The master picked up a tile and began to rub it on a stone, "to make a mirror." Ma-tsu wondered, "How can you make a mirror by rubbing a tile?" "How can one become a Buddha by sitting in meditation?" In Heinrich Dumoulin, S.J., *A History of Zen Buddhism,* p. 98.
22. Quoted in Chang, p. 182. Thomas Merton verbalizes the immediacy of Zen in these terms: "But the chief characteristic of Zen is that it rejects all these systematic elaborations in order to get back, as far as possible, to the pure unarticulated and unexplained ground of direct experience. . . . The whole aim of Zen is not to make foolproof statements about experience, but to come to direct grips with reality without the mediation of logical verbalizing. . . . The Zen experience is a direct grasp of the *unity* of the invisible and the visible, the noumenal and the phenomenal. . . ." *Zen and the Birds of Appetite,* pp. 36–37.
23. Kenneth Ch'en, "Economic Background of the Hui-ch'ang Suppression of Buddhism," *Harvard Journal of Asiatic Studies,* 19 (1956), 80: "The famous Ch'an monk Shen-hui, although he was over ninety at the time, participated actively in this campaign to sell certificates (to anyone who wished to become a cleric, 756, to get cash for the government in the An Lu-shan rebellion) at Lo-yang; the subsequent triumph of the Southern Ch'an school of Hui-neng over the northern school of Shen-hsiu was believed to have resulted in large measure from Shen-hui's activities."
24. Philip Kapleau's *The Three Pillars of Zen* has two sections that have special interest in this regard: interviews of ten Westerners with Yasutani-roshi, and the enlightenment experiences of eight contemporary Japanese and Westerners.
25. Although Dogen was a trained literary and religious scholar and did not, like other monks, "discard the sutras of the Buddha," learning was not his first requirement of new students. He suspected concern for literary quality and preferred simple, direct devotion. "Nothing can be gained by extensive study and wide reading." "Students of the Way should neither read the scriptures of other Buddhist teachings nor study non-Buddhist texts. If you do read, examine the writings of Zen. . . . Even if you cannot compose verse, just write what is in your heart." *A Primer of Soto Zen,* a translation of Dogen's *Shobogenzo Zuimonki* by Reiho Masunaga, pp. 8, 33.
26. *Zen and Japanese Culture,* p. 182. In another culture, Parson Weems reports that outfielders Joe DiMaggio and Babe Ruth would start running at the crack of the bat, intuitively plotting trajectory from first sight and sound.
27. Hakuin (1685–1768) seems to have used the term "Great Doubt" to describe the zero-experience, as a preliminary to satori. "Once the Great Doubt

arises, out of a hundred who practice, one hundred will achieve breakthrough." In his own experience: "Without there is bright coolness and white purity. As if devoid of all sense one forgets to rise when he is sitting, and forgets to sit down when he is standing. In his heart there remains no trace of passion or concept, only the word 'nothingness,' as if he stood in the wide dome of heaven. He has neither fear nor knowledge." The transition from the Great Doubt to the Great Enlightenment Hakuin calls the Great Dying. "If you wish to attain the true Nonego you must release your hold over the abyss. . . . This is termed seeing into one's own nature." It is a moment of unbelievable joy. (In Dumoulin, pp. 258–59.) Po Shan, who made *i chin,* the doubt sensation, an important part of his teaching, also anticipates Hakuin's distinction between dhyana and satori. A person may meditate "until he reaches a state as limpid as water, as lucent as a pearl, as clear as the wind, and as bright as the moon. At this time he feels his body and mind, the earth and the heavens, fuse into one pellucid whole—pure, alert, and wide-awake." But this state is not enlightenment. "As a matter of fact, his body reeks with sicknesses. He has not yet gained Zen." (Chang, p. 108.) At this point one must seek out a master, if not before.

28. The term "Zen sickness" is applied loosely to states ranging from Fa Kuang's chronic condition down to the temporary state of unpleasant visions one opens up in the process of free meditation. Dumoulin, commenting on Hakuin's state of anxiety due to over-exertion in Zen practice despite tuberculosis, says, "The thousand phenomena which Hakuin beheld night and day point to the state of visions and hallucinations, a state of psychic overstimulation which is well known in Zen and of which the Zen masters warn, calling it the 'domain of the devil' *(makyo)*" (p. 261).

29. For example, the "space therapy" formulated by Trungpa Rinpoche's group, in which the various Buddhas of Tibetan tradition are related to forms of neurosis, and new techniques derived from Vajrayana are used to achieve insight that reduces ego-stress.

Chapter 8: What Is Nirvana?

1.The same author says elsewhere: "The main idea of this [popular] mysticism consisted in the belief that through practice of concentrated meditation a condition of trance could be attained which conferred upon the mediator extraordinary powers and converted him into a superman. Buddhism adapted this teaching to its ontology. Transic meditation became the ultimate member of the Path towards quiescence, the special means through which, first of all, wrong views and evil inclinations could be eradicated, and then the highest mystic worlds could be reached. The superman, the Yogi, became the Saint. . . ." *Buddhist Logic,* I, 6.

2. Edward Conze, *Buddhist Thought in India,* p. 253. "There is here no duality of subject and object. The cognition is not different from that which is cognized, but completely identical with it."

3. "Even in this life" the nirvana-ed man is "withdrawn, given nirvana, feeling happiness in himself, and he spends his time with his soul identified with Brahma" (Anguttara Nikaya II, 206). The distinction is made between jivanmukti, freedom while alive, and videhamukti, freedom on release from the body, or moksa, which "implies dissolution or merger of the disembodied individual self (Jivatman) in the Supreme Self." H. K. De Chaudhuri, "Samadhi: A Psychological Study," *Bulletin of the Ramakrishna Mission Institute of Culture* (Calcutta), December 1969, p. 352.

4. Quoted in W. T. Stace, *Mysticism and Philosophy,* p. 309, from *Meister Eckhart,* translated by R. B. Blakney, sermon 12, p. 153.

5. James, in note 5 of the chapter, says: "Professor Tyndall, in a letter, recalls Tennyson saying of this condition: 'By God Almighty! there is no delusion in the matter! It is no nebulous ecstasy, but a state of translucent wonder, associated with absolute clearness of mind.' "

6. H. K. De Chaudhuri cites James and disagrees: "True mysticism is alive and practical, not passive and theoretical. . . . The mystic is on the quest for the Transcendent One. . . . Living union within this One is a definite state or form of enhanced, higher life which implies a definite psychological experience." (Pp. 340–41)

He says elsewhere: "Generally speaking, two distinct and mutually opposed types of mysticism are traceable in the Indian religion, viz. monistic and theistic . . . ; or intellectual (jnanin) and voluntary or emotional (bhakta). The Christian mystical tradition is, on the whole, opposed to monism." *God in Indian Religion,* p. 5.

7. In Foreword to Sisirkumar Ghose, *Mystics and Society,* p. ix.

8. Edition of Susil Gupta (1961), p. 42; first ed. by Royal Asiatic Society (London, 1923).

9. Ananda, the closest disciple, was not arhant until the night before he was to recite the sutras at the First Council, because he was slow in achieving trance. On the need for the transforming yogic experience. Eliade quotes Nagarjuna: "In Ananda the sthavira, who has heard, remembered, recited, and meditated all kinds of sutras, wisdom (*prajna*) is vast, whereas the concentration of thought (*citta samgraha*) is mediocre. But both these qualities must exist together if one is to be able to attain to . . . the destruction of impurities." *Mahaprajnaparamitacastra,* translated by Lamotte, I, 223, quoted in *Patanjali and Yoga,* p. 171.

10. See his edition of *The Jewel Ornament of Liberation* by sGam.po.pa, Chap. 17, "The Perfection of Awareness," pp. 202, 225n.

11. *Ibid.*, p. 219; see note 9 above.

12. Sikshasamuccaya 212, in *BT,* p. 180.

13. Quoted in Frederick J. Streng, *Emptiness: A Study in Religious Meaning*, p. 60.
14. The arguments are well presented in Guy Richard Wellbon, *The Buddhist Nirvana and Its Western Interpreters*, especially Chap. 8.
15. See Conze's discussion of Asanga in *Buddhist Thought in India*, p. 253.
16. *The Messianic Idea in Judaism and Other Essays on Jewish Spirituality*, pp. 213–14.
17. Rumi, the great Persian poet-mystic, denies that *Ana 'l-Haqq* is a presumptuous claim. "The man who says *Ana 'l-'abd* 'I am the slave of God' affirms two existences, his own and God's, but he that says *Ana 'l-Haqq* 'I am God' has made himself non-existent and has given himself up. . . . This is the extreme of humility and self-abasement." *Rumi*, edited by R. A. Nicholson, p. 184.

Some Muslim philosophers, questioning the Sufi mystic's claim to union with Allah, rely on the intellect rather than on ecstasy as the earnest of Allah's gift. Discussing Allah's creation of Adam after his own likeness, al-Ghazzali said, "For it [the intellect] is a pattern or sample of the attributes of Allah. Now the sample must be commensurate with the original, even though it does not rise to the degree of equality with it." Quoted in Alexander Altman, *Studies in Religious Philosophy and Mysticism*, p. 10. Ibn Bajja comes close to the Sufis: "In the appetitive soul there arises at this stage a condition similar to fear, and resembling a certain state when something tremendous and beautiful is perceived by the senses. This condition is called stupefaction. The Sufis have given exaggerated descriptions of this state." But his ultimate stage, Altman points out, is identical with the "acquired intellect," where intellect and intelligible are one.

18. Sermon 63, quoted in G. Feuerstein and J. Miller, *Yoga and Beyond*, p. 157.
19. *Modern Man in Search of a Soul*, quoted in Ghose, p. 75. The "passionate interest" is shown by scientists too. "Already hard-core scientists are intimating the possibility that the entire range of so-called super-normal or psychic powers may be brought within the scope of objectifying techniques, and in that sense absorbed as part of the body of traditional scientific knowledge." "Is a Science of Man Possible?" *Manas* (Jan. 26, 1972). But the anonymous author questions such turning of the subjective into the objective: "there is a sense in which it amounts to the reduction of the normal 'I-Thou' relationships between human beings to an 'I-It' relationship."
20. Stace, p. 99; James quotes the passage from H. F. Brown's biography of Symonds.
21. Curiously, the ganzfeld has an antecedent in the Buddhist theory and practice of meditation. In Guenther's edition of sGam.po.pa (see note 10 above), we find these passages: "Not to stay with anything is the practice of this awareness. Not to think and not to conceptualize is the practice of this perfection." (From the Saptasatikaprajnaparamita.) "Not to practice anything" and

"attentive contemplation of the sky." (From the Astasaharika.) "How can we fix our attention on the sky? The answer is given in the same work: 'The sky is beyond the reach of discursive thinking as is the perfection of this awareness.' " (Pp. 217–18) That this is not mere imagery becomes clear in Guenther's note: " 'Attentive contemplation of the sky' is a technical term which refers to an experience in which the object has lost its external reference and which we are wont to call 'pure sensation.' The sky as a vast expanse of blue is particularly suited to produce this experience as its uniformity does not distract us." (P. 230)

22. Deikmann, p. 32; quoted from Werner, *Comparative Psychology of Mental Development*, p. 152.

23. Ronald Fischer, "A Cartography of the Ecstatic and Meditative States," *Science*, 174, No. 4012 (November 26, 1971), 897–904.

24. They are (1) *delta*, frequency 0.2 to 4 Hertz (cycles per second), associated with deep, non-REM (rapid-eye-movement) sleep; (2) *theta*, 4 to 8 Hz, uncertainty, problem-solving, anticipation, reverie; (3) *alpha*, 8 to 13 Hz, tranquillity, relaxed awareness; (4) *beta*, 13 to 28 Hz, attention, anger, fear, surprise (the normal waking state). Some put the divisions at 3.5 and 7.5 Hz. One should not conclude from the "pleasantness" of alpha that it is preferable to other states. All operate to keep the organism in equilibrium and thriving.

25. The first tests were conducted in Chicago, the second at the Langley Porter Neuropsychiatric Institute in San Francisco. The report is in Tart, *Altered States of Consciousness*, Joe Kamiya, "Operant Control of EEG Alpha Rhythm," pp. 507–17: "I set up an electronic device which would turn on a sine-wave tone in the S's room whenever the alpha rhythm was present. The tone would disappear as soon as the alpha rhythm would disappear." (P. 510)

26. "My engineer devised a cycle period analyser and thus had a system whereby each EEG alpha wave cycle was compared against a standard duration: if the wave was *longer* in duration than the standard, the S hears a *high*-pitched click, while if the wave was *shorter* . . . he heard a *low*-pitched click. . . . I now told the S to try to increase the predominance of one kind of click over the other. . . . I can say that for some Ss the shift is as large as two cycles per second." (*Ibid.*, pp. 516–17.) "I do not know, and nobody really knows for sure what the significance of a change of alpha frequency is" (p. 517). See next note and note 54.

27. Simplistic interpretation of EEG data can be misleading. Ornstein warns, "A major research problem is that the EEG is a somewhat poor instrument for studying the most complex organ in the world.

"At first it was thought sufficient to monitor alpha from an arbitrarily selected area on the scalp. . . . many subjects seemed to report a common experience during alpha control. They described the 'high alpha' state as 'relaxed,' 'dark,' 'back of the head,' especially when alpha from the occipital area was being trained. But these communalities are no longer overwhelmingly impressive. A much more precise and complex configuration of electroencephalographic activity must be specified in order to study the relation of brain events to subjective events. . . . The appearance of a certain brain rhythm indicates a different mode of information-processing, *depending on the area from which it is recorded.* To speak, for instance, of a "high alpha" state without describing both where it is recorded from and the concurrent activity throughout the brain is an incomplete and almost useless statement." *The Psychology of Consciousness,* p. 199.

Similarly, Thomas B. Mulholland summarizes his "Occipital Alpha Revisited," *Psychological Bulletin* 79 (September 1972), thus: "All 'alpha' events are not functionally equivalent, nor are all 'no-alpha' events. Their position in the time series must be taken into account." (P. 176) He wants alpha to be defined in terms of "(a) location of the recording electrodes (b) frequency (c) amplitude and (d) the duration of the rhythms having the proper frequency and amplitude" (p. 177). In analyzing the classic "attention" hypothesis that all alpha events are equivalent and that alpha rhythms are blocked or attenuated by visual attention, he points out that the stage at which alpha occurs, and the brain region are important.

28. B. K. Anand, G. S. Chhina, and Baldev Singh, "Some Aspects of Electroencephalographic Studies in Yogis," in Tart, *Altered States of Consciousness.* The article refers to prior work by Bagchi and Wenger indicating similar results.

29. "In five 15-minute brainwave feedback sessions he was able to tie together in his mind the relationship between the tones produced by activation in the various brain wave bands and the states of consciousness he had learned in a Himalayan cave. Then he produced 70% alpha waves over a five-minute period of time by thinking of an empty blue sky 'with a small white cloud' sometimes coming by." From "Biofeedback for Mind–Body Self Regulation: Healing and Creativity," reprinted in *Biofeedback and Self-control 1972,* p. 163.

30. "Experiments in India on 'Voluntary' Control of the Heart and Pulse," *Circulation* (1961), 1319–25. Dr. Anand had studied four hundred yogins by the time he visited Dr. Neal E. Miller at the Rockefeller University in June 1972.

31. K. K. Datey, et al. " 'Shavasan': A Yogic Exercise in the Management of Hypertension," *Angiology* (1969), 325–33; quoted in Edward B. Blanchard and Larry D. Young, "Self Control of Cardiac Functioning: A Promise as Yet Unfulfilled," *Psychological Bulletin* (March 1973), 161.

32. Robert Keith Wallace and Herbert Benson, "The Physiology of Meditation," *Scientific American* (February 1972), 85–90.

33. Akira Kasamatsu and Tomio Hirai, "An Electroencephalographic Study on the Zen Meditation (Zazen)," in Tart, *Altered States of Consciousness,* pp. 489–501. The study was made in the ordinary Zen training hall, but the stimulation experiments with the same subjects were performed in a sound-free shield room of the laboratory. The subjects were 24 to 72 years old and had varied experience of Zen (20 disciples 1 to 5 years; 12 disciples 5 to 20; 16 priests over

20). As control subjects with no Zen experience there were 18 research fellows 23 to 33 years old, and 4 "elderly" men 54 to 60.

34. At the start, the alpha waves are 40–50 μV, 11–12 cycles per second. "After 8 minutes and 20 seconds, the amplitude . . . reaches to 60–70 μV predominantly in the frontal and the central regions. . . . After 27 minutes and 10 seconds, rhythmical waves of 7–8/sec. appear for 1 or 2 seconds. And 20 seconds later rhythmical theta trains (6–7/sec., 70–100 μV) begin to appear. However, it does not always occur." (P. 492)

35. The rhythmical theta train of one Zen Master was blocked by click stimulation and reappeared spontaneously several seconds later, but the alpha arousal reaction, often caused by stimulation in the drowsy state, was not observed. And in the hypnagogic state, large alpha waves were often seen, similar to those of Zen meditation. "But the large alpha waves seem in stage II or III of Zen meditation persist much longer than the pre-sleep pattern" (p. 495). In actual sleep, "alpha waves recede, spindles burst and slow waves appear, and consciousness is lost. Such a series of electrographic changes does not occur in Zen meditation and consciousness is not lost, since in Zen meditation there is no lack of awareness of things going on externally and internally." (P. 498)

Wallace reported, "The EEG patterns during meditation clearly distinguish this state from the sleeping state. There are no slow (delta) waves or sleep spindles, but alpha-wave activity predominates." "Physiological Effects of Transcendental Meditation," *Science* (1970), 1753.

36. With ordinary subjects, one would expect progressively shorter blocking time with repeated stimuli, as habituation sets in; and this happened to the control subjects with closed eyes (with open eyes, no alpha). With other masters and control subjects, results were similar to those in the primary test. Wallace's transcendental-meditation subjects were like the Zen subjects: "In almost all subjects, alpha blocking caused by repeated sound or light stimuli showed no habituation." *Ibid.*, p. 1752.

37. Similarly, Sariputra's appearance after his first meeting with the Buddha is remarked by Maudgalyayana: "Your countenance is pure and clear, and your senses serene. Have you found the immortal and the Way that leads to the immortal?" Conze, *Buddhist Thought in India*, p. 73, from *Mahavastu*, translated by Jones, iii, 63. And the Buddha, newly enlightened, met a mendicant, who said, "You appear to be refreshed by the sweet savour of a wisdom newly tasted. Your features shine with intellectual power." Conze, *Buddhist Scriptures*, p. 53, from *Buddhacarita*.

38. Gardner Murphy, the eminent psychologist, in the article "Are There Any Solid Facts in Psychical Research," *Journal of the American Society for Psychical Research*, 64 (January 1970), 3, listed as "solidly established facts":

"First, telepathy, or the transmission, as Myers defined it, 'of impressions of any kind from one mind to another, independently of the recognized channels of sense.'

"Second, clairvoyance, or the direct perception of an object or objective event, again without the utilization of the senses.

"Third, precognition, or the perception of an idea or an event which is in a future time. . . .

"Fourth, retrocognition, symmetrical to precognition, or a perception in present time of an object or event which is located in past time. . . .

"Fifth, psychokinesis, or the voluntary movement of objects as a result of agencies not known to belong to those of the physically recognized energies; and closely related to this, the phenomena of lights, sounds, odors, etc., which are apparently produced by a dynamic which transcends our present knowledge of physics.

"Closely parallel to all these are phenomena appearing to indicate that the subject is acting upon physical reality in some indirect way, perhaps producing a phantasm or apparition of himself which manifests itself at a distance, or a physical effect which can ultimately be recorded by physical instruments, but not at present a part of the known physical system of energies."

39. See the last paragraph of the preceding note.

40. For example, in attempting to explain the feats of probably the most thoroughly scrutinized and authenticated psychokinesist of modern times, Mme. Kulagina, the eminent Professor G. A. Sergeyev suggests that she is capable of producing radiation in the ultraviolet spectrum. At a wavelength of 2500 angstroms the ultraviolet would be bactericidal, and would explain her demonstrations of quick healing. He thinks it would also explain a recent experiment set up by Benson Herbert, English physicist and director of the Paraphysical Laboratory in Wiltshire, and editor of the *Journal of Paraphysics*, for Mme. Kulagina on April 15, 1973, in Leningrad: "a hydrometer floating upright in saturated saline solution, protected by an earthed screen and monitored by an electrostatic probe . . . to eliminate electrostatic forces." Blowing hard at the hydrometer merely made it bob; shaking the table did less; the subject's electrostatic field force was about three-fourths that of other individuals present, and they were as close to vessel (three feet) as she was. Even if strings could have been attached somehow despite the scrutiny of the respectable scholars present, they could not have made the hydrometer move as smoothly as she did, *back and forth*:

"Kulagina slowly moved her arms, raising them so that the palms of her hands faced toward the instrument. Shortly after, the hydrometer began to move away from her in a straight line across the full diameter of the vessel, a distance of two and one-half inches, and came to rest at the opposite side, the transit occupying some 90 seconds. She then lowered her arms and remained quite still. The hydrometer remained stationary for two minutes, then commenced to move again, at the same speed as before, retracing its path until it stopped by the edge of the glass nearest to her." Sergeyev suggested that the motion was caused by ionization of the solution. A bit later that day Kulagina caused a compass case to turn 45° counterclockwise, then to slide across the table toward her, in irregular zig-zag jerks, 2 to 2.5 cm each. Also by touching Herbert's arm she inflicted a burn; she held a camera edgewise against his colleague's arm; the camera remained cool, the arm was burned. The compass-moving cost her much more energy than the burning. Herbert, "Spring in Leningrad: Kulagina Revisited," *Parapsychological Review,* July–August 1973.

One point of relevance of psychokinesis to the mystical experience and to Buddhism is this: if physical energies already known are involved in pk (see note 63 below) and other psi activity, including telepathy and clairvoyance, then by the law of parsimony we need not proceed to such hypotheses as Stace's "Universal Mind" supervening on man's activity and informing the mystical experience; we can rest with such explanations as Deikman's deautomatization hypothesis, supported by EEG study. Or if the energies are new and of a different order (see next note), we may be on our way to the "mystical" concept of mankind growing toward spiritual unity through easier, more controllable thought transfer, as the new energies become better understood. Then the "Overmind" hypotheses of the mystics Teilhard de Chardin and Sri Aurobindo become more than inspirational figures of speech. Or if we follow Arthur Koestler's advice and suspend trying to make scientific sense of psi, just as those who know best, the theoretical physicists, have given up trying to make sense of nuclear physics, then we can believe pretty much what we wish, within the bounds of aesthetic intellectual decorum and reasonably authenticated evidence (as this author accepts reports of telepathy and is irritated by commercial astrology).

In another report on Kulagina, Sergeyev is quoted as reporting that during an experiment the EEG showed recorded waves from the back of the skull (the visual projection area) of an amplitude that was approximately fifty times the strength recorded during the relaxed state immediately preceding the movement of the objects. EEG readings taken simultaneously from other points on the head showed no change in brain activity. In one experiment film wrapped in paper was placed under the object to be moved; the track of the object was left as if the film had been exposed to light. This suggests a radiation impulse. See J. G. Pratt and H. H. J. Keil, "First Hand Observations of Nina S. Kulagina Suggestive of PK Upon Static Objects," *JASPR,* 67, No. 4 (October 1973), 381 ff. The type of waves is not mentioned. We learn, in a discussion of another Russian psychokinesist: "While PK effects were being observed in Mikhailovna, she was operating almost exclusively on a strong, self-induced theta rhythm. Her blood sugar and endocrine measurements showed that she was in a state of controlled rage. . . . In contrast, telepathy appears to be connected with alpha waves that, instead of occurring in a state of rage, are produced by mental and physical relaxation. Muscle tone is decreased, respiration is depressed, carbon dioxide pressure is increased, the oxygen tension is lowered." Review by Carroll B. Nash of Lyall Watson's *Supernature,* in *Parapsychology Review,* 4 (September–October 1973), 12.

41. Murphy (see note 38 above) proposes "a reality in between mind and body, . . . an interaction between our bodies and some unknown reality outside time and space," similar to Myers' "metetheric" (*Human Personality*, I, xix: "that which appears to lie after or beyond the ether, the metetherial environment denotes the spiritual or transcendental world in which the soul exists"). This "reality" is of a different order from the extremely subtle but still "physical" substance of the citta in early Samkhya thought.

42. Margenau, "ESP in the Framework of Modern Science," *JASPR*, 60 (July 1966), 215.

43. Haakon Forwald suggests that the psychokinetic deflection of cubes in one of his experiments is related to gravitation, because of negative results in electrostatic, magnetic, and radioactive investigations. His hypothesis is dictated by parsimony. "In parapsychology it should not be necessary to introduce some hypothetical 'psi field,' since a structural gravitational field seems in principle to exhibit elements which are required for bringing parapsychological experiences within the framework of a recognized system. And the use of a 'field' which is already known in physics should be of great advantage when the problem is to try to fit parapsychological phenomena into the general scientific picture." *Mind, Matter and Gravitation: A Theoretical and Experimental Study*, Parapsychological Monograph No. 11 (1969), p. 66. The source of energy? "The energy necessary for cube displacement appears to be produced by the cube material through the transformation of a tiny part of the cube mass to energy, according to Einstein's formula $E = mc^2$. . . . The study suggests that the mind is a non-energetical quality, but that it can interact with matter and energy on the microphysical (structural) level." (P. 1) The theory coincides with recent explanations of poltergeists: the impulse for the things that go bump comes from a psi-sensitive individual, but the energy comes from the objects or their environment.

Scientists in eastern Europe have broken through the semantic bind of such terms as "psychic" and "parapsychology." "It should be noted that the Russians and Czechs themselves do not claim that there is anything psychic about their results. They are approaching psi as a biological effect that can be studied within a discipline they call 'bioenergetics.'" David Ellis, "The Chemistry of Psi," *Parapsychology Review*, 4 (September–October 1973). And at the First International Congress of Parapsychology and Psychotronics in Prague in June 1973, the new term "psychotronics" was favored and the old "parapsychology" was called a blind alley by the eminent Czech Zdenek Rejdak.

44. Koestler also elaborates on the contradictions of modern physics and concludes: "the unthinkable propositions of quantum physics make the unthinkable propositions of parapsychology a little less preposterous." Address on "The Perversity of Physics," given at the Parapsychological Foundation Conference on "Parapsychology and the Sciences," in Amsterdam (August 1972); printed in *Parapsychological Review* (May–June 1973). He also points out that action at a distance, in Newtonian physics, is an offense against common sense,

as are electromagnetic fields existing in a vacuum, the dematerialization of matter a half century ago by Einstein, De Broglie, and Schrodinger, and more recently Feynmann's positrons traveling back into the past. He also reminds his audience of the positive function of the human mind in all quantum physical measurements, and avers that "you cannot eliminate the observer from any quantum occasion, not because of the observer's fallibility, but because the observer no longer manipulates his models like the clockwork universe of the nineteenth century. Instead, the observer now operates with probability theory models that are mental constructs and our predictions refer no longer to a model but to a mental construct." (Pp. 2–3; see also Koestler's *The Roots of Coincidence,* 1972.)

45. Banesh Hoffman, *Albert Einstein, Creator and Rebel,* p. 234.

46. *ESP: A Personal Memoir,* p. 201. "Experient" is Heywood's term for the ESP-sensitive or recipient of ESP information or impressions.

47. Karlis Osis and Edwin Bokert, "Changed States of Consciousness and ESP," paper delivered at the 12th Convention of the Parapsychology Association, New York (September 1969). In this context we should mention the "sheep and goats" hypothesis proposed by Gertrude R. Schmeidler: subjects positively disposed to ESP (the sheep) are likely to achieve better scores than those who "don't believe in ESP" (the goats). Goats introduce a teasing problem: if their scores are consistently and notably *below* statistical probability, does this *prove* ESP? See J. B. Rhine and J. G. Pratt, *Parapsychology, Frontier Science of the Mind,* pp. 89–98, on psi-missing.

48. C. Honorton, R. Davidson, and D. Bindler, "Feedback Augmented EEG Alpha, Shifts in Subjective State, and ESP Card-guessing Performance," *JASPR* (July 1971), 308. A number of studies at the Dream Laboratory of Maimonides Hospital in Brooklyn have gone into ESP sensitivity in sleep, and the relation of ESP and meditation. See Montague Ullman and Stanley Krippner, *Dream Studies and Telepathy: An Experimental Approach,* Parapsychological Monograph No. 12 (1970). Also, Ullman, Krippner, with Alan Vaughan, *Dream Telepathy* (1973): "Our main surmise is that the psyche of man possesses a latent ESP capacity that is most likely to be deployed during sleep, in the dreaming phase. Psi is no longer the exclusive gift of rare beings known as 'psychic sensitives,' but is a normal part of human existence, capable of being experienced by nearly everyone under the right conditions." (P. 227)

49. Osis and Bokert, "ESP and Changed States of Consciousness Induced by Meditation," *JASPR* (January 1971), 23. Similarly, Ramana Maharshi, next to Ramakrishna probably the most revered Indian mystic within the last century, "transferred his own peak experiences to his disciples by using silent concentration; . . . psychic invasion" (p. 18).

50. Einstein is the paradigm of creative intuition. Hoffman, discussing the gravitational-field equations that govern the space–time curvature, says, "there is something about them that is intensely beautiful and almost miraculous. . . . How did Einstein manage to find the equations? . . . We begin—but only

begin—to see here the true stature of Einstein's intuition. What were the seeds that gave rise to this wonderfully unique structure?" Of all the background materials—Newton, Minkowski, Mach—"By what magic clairvoyance did Einstein choose just these two principles [equivalence and general covariance] to be his guide long before he knew where they would lead him?" (Pp. 22–24) Hoffman, a collaborator with Einstein, describes the man facing a problem: "There was a dreamy, far-away, yet inward look on his face. No sign of stress. No outward indication of intense concentration. No lingering trace of the previous excited discussion. Only a placid inner communion–Einstein working at his highest pitch. Minutes would go by. Then, quite suddenly, he would return to the world, a smile on his face, and an answer to the problem on his lips, but not so much as a hint of the reasoning—if such it was—that had led him to the solution." (P. 231)

In this discussion of creative intuition we are constrained to a sobering reminder: Hitler, scorning rationality, exalted his "intuition" and the common unconscious of the unified German folk.

51. Article in *Biofeedback and Self-control 1972*, pp. 164–65 (see note 29 above). The importance of the general reverie state rather than specific direction, and the fact that non-action is more efficacious than striving was impressed upon Dr. Green in an early feedback experiment. He sought complete relaxation, an absence of muscle-firing, as preparation for raising the temperature of one hand. Specific attempts by the student subjects to send directions to the hand brought the temperature *down*. But they succeeded when they "told the body" and relaxed; passive volition let the body find its own way to get the job done.

52. Lawrence LeShan, *Toward a General Theory of the Paranormal*, Parapsychological Monograph No. 9 (1969), p. 31, quoting from Garrett, *Telepathy: In Search of a Lost Faculty*, and Heywood, *ESP: A Personal Memoir*.

53. These similarities are derived from Bertrand Russell's four basic characteristics of the mystic's description of his experience. The fourth, that all evil is mere appearance, does not enter the comparison, although in the sensitized state preparatory to ESP perception, the ESP-sensitive's reports of benevolent feeling state are quite similar to the mystic's.

54. Rex G. Stanford and CaroleAnn Lovin, "EEG Alpha Activity and ESP Performance," *JASPR* (October 1970), 381, and "EEG Alpha Activity and ESP Performance: A Replicative Study," *JASPR* (April 1971). Also confirmed was the strongest finding of the first tests, the positive, linear relationship between pretest-test directional alpha frequency shift and precognition scoring; that is, the greater the increase in alpha from rest to test, the better the ESP performance. Thus a high alpha baseline, usually found in successful meditation subjects, is not necessary for ESP subjects.

55. "ESP and Changed States of Consciousness Induced by Meditation," *JASPR* (January 1971), 55. Honorton and Carbone indicated running into the same difficulty: "Several of the Ss [subjects] spontaneously offered comments

suggesting that they felt distracted by the tone during the Feedback condition and that they found it difficult to concentrate on the ESP task while attempting to generate alpha." *JASPR* (January 1971), 72.

56. "The Mystical and the Paranormal," *Parapsychological Review* (January–February 1973). The feeling of *unity* gives way in the need to impart specific information; the *nontemporal* cognition of God and nature cannot be sustained in the stress situation of the telepathist transferring information or the clairvoyant seeking objective knowledge; *objectivity* is less important to the mystic than to the psychic, who seeks to convince others and to account for his experience, if possible; *blessedness* and *holiness* are terms used by some mystics, but irrelevant to psychic activity; *paradoxicality*, accepted by the mystic, is alien to the psychic's desire for clarity; and the *ineffable* is directly contrary to the psychic's transfer of specific information through verbalization, perceptions, and images.

57. As one would expect, ESP is most likely to occur between people in continual interchange, such as parent–child, teacher–pupil, twins. See Dr. Berthold Eric Schwarz, *Parent–Child Telepathy: A Study of the Telepathy of Everyday Life* (1972), a record of the author's experiences with his children.

58. Kenneth Gaarder, "Control of States of Consciousness," *Archives of General Psychiatry* (November 1971), 433. Gaarder sees feedback helping in "the treatment of hypertension by feedback control of blood pressure, of vasoconstrictive peripheral vascular disease by the feedback learning of vasodilation, of anxiety by learning deep-muscle relaxation through feedback EMG, of epilepsy by feedback EEG teaching the suppression of spike activity." (P. 440) Budzynski and Stoyva have contributed deep-relaxation methods with feedback for the desensitization treatment of phobias, and have also applied feedback-induced muscle relaxation to the treatment of tension headache. *Journal of Behavior Therapy and Experimental Psychiatry* (January 1970).

59. For example, Green believes that the ability to remember is correlated with the percentage of alpha, and that alpha training can help students overcome mental blocks. And the ability of young therapists to listen to their patients and actually hear what was being said, was shown to improve after group Zazen thirty minutes a day for four weeks. Before the program, they often appeared so affected by statements patients made, or by their own concerns about how they should respond, or where they should go next, that they often failed to hear what the patient was actually saying. T. U. Lesh, "Zen Meditation and a Development of Empathy in Counselors," *Journal of Humanistic Psychology, 10* (January 1970), in *Biofeedback and Self-Control 1970.*

60. William James quotes Vivekananda in the "Mysticism" chapter in *Varieties of Religious Experience.*

61. Mulholland has used alpha feedback for group therapy and consciousness-raising sessions. See Jodi Lawrence, *Alpha Brain Waves*, p. 169.

Chapter 9: Toward the Unified World

1. It took a rapidly deteriorating environment and contrived "energy" shortages (which accelerated the deterioration) to impress on most what some have long known, that the world as corporate entity has been committing the unforgiveable sin of capitalistic enterprise: living off capital. E. F. Schumacher, in a seminal book, *Small Is Beautiful* (1973), makes the point clearly: "the modern industrial system, with all its intellectual sophistication, consumes the very basis on which it has been erected. To use the language of the economist, it lives on irreplaceable capital which it cheerfully treats as income. I specified three categories of such capital: fossil fuels, the tolerance margins of nature, and the human substance." (P. 19) His chapter on "Buddhist Economics" ("the systematic study of how to gain given ends with the minimum means") shows the way to the necessary new life style designed for permanence. This would reverse the prevalent irrational approach "that a man who consumes more is 'better off' than a man who consumes less" (p. 54), and propose a new aim: "to obtain the maximum of well-being with the minimum of consumption."

2. The phrase is taken from Benjamin Nelson's *The Idea of Usury: From Tribal Brotherhood to Universal Otherhood* (1949; 2nd ed., 1969). The evidence for and against primitive man's cooperativeness is discussed in Chap. 8 of Erich Fromm's *The Anatomy of Human Destructiveness* (1973).

3. "It's a dog-eat-dog world, and if anyone tries to get me I'll get them first. It's the American way of survival of the fittest. There is always someone trying to cut you down. As long as you're green you're growing, and as soon as you ripen you start to rot." This is the "philosophy" of Ray Kroc, "71-year-old apostle of persistence and builder of the [McDonald] hamburger chain which now has 2450 units across the country and 197 in Canada and abroad." *The New York Times* (Dec. 30, 1974), Section 3, p. 3.

4. V. R. Dhiravamsa (formerly Chao Khun Sobhana Dhammasudhi), *A New Approach to Buddhism*, p. 56. Krishnamurti, who disapproves of "special cross-legged meditation," agrees: "We think that by getting rid of a few people, by pushing aside the establishment, we are going to solve the whole problem. Every physical revolution has been based on this, the French, the Communist and so on and they have ended up in bureaucracy or tyranny." He calls for "total action . . . so there will be a new social structure, not the throwing out of one establishment and the creating of another." *The Impossible Question*, pp. 14–15.

Ronald Sampson, a Gandhian pacifist, puts it this way: "My general conclusion is that the belief in the possibility of advancing human welfare through working to secure political power is itself the most important single illusion which stands in the way of advancing that welfare. It provides the individual with the most plausible and widely offered of all excuses to justify his own failure to make the necessary changes to eliminate the contradictions within his own life." *The Psychology of Power*, p. 16. Gandhi, who had mastered himself and presumably had eliminated the contradictions within his own life, sought and secured political power to advance human welfare in India.

Some mystics and religious leaders have modified this distrust of social action, even though their vision tends to focus only briefly on contemporary distress and then leap toward global resolution. Ruysbroeck cited the mystic's "urgency to active righteousness." Bonhoeffer and Teilhard opposed Christian isolation; the latter declared that the apparent life is the arena of growth in "realizing God."

5. "Christian Hope and Social Evolution: *Thien Hsia Ta Thung* and *Regnum Dei*," a lecture given for the Faculty of Divinity, Cambridge University, November 8, 1972.

6. Anglo-Chinese Educational Institute (March 1973). Selections from the pamphlet appeared in the *Cambridge Review*, 94, March 2, 1973. Dr. Robinson visited China six times between 1953 and May–June 1972.

7. "Promise her anything but give her a drill press" is the headline of an advertisement for *Fortune* magazine in *The New York Times* (Aug. 1, 1972). The text reads: "How do you figure a country where the girls care more about their work than about their clothes and faces? Where factory managers spend a day a week at manual labor . . . where wages aren't as big an incentive as the common good . . . where workers take part in major business decisions?" The article, by Louis Kraar, states: "The dedication and discipline required for all this exertion are fostered by a relentless process of indoctrination, which stresses psychic rather than material rewards for individuals. . . . The do-it-yourself approach is part of a conscious effort to encourage wider participation of workers in decisions that used to be left to managers and technicians." "I Have Seen China—And They Work," *Fortune*, August 1972, pp. 111, 112.

8. In Arthur Waley, *Three Ways of Thought in Ancient China*, p. 121. The immediately preceding passage is: "It was commonly believed that in the old days eight families had worked together, and Mencius wanted to revive this system of collaboration, at any rate in remoter country districts (where perhaps it had not fallen altogether into abeyance), and to encourage the general spirit of cooperation that went with it."

9. The "paradox of the revolutionary" is discussed in an essay, "Buddhism and Revolution," by R. Puligandla and K. Puhakka, in *Philosophy East & West*, 20 (October 1970). "But after a successful revolution he himself becomes the defender of the status quo; the revolutionary movement loses its revolutionary character and degenerates into a conservative regime. . . . According to Buddhism, . . . history and society are the modes of actualization and perpetuation of man's karmaic energies; therefore, all attempts to realize freedom through socio-historical processes are doomed to failure" (p. 353). Because the Buddhist "finds the realization of freedom in the ultimate renunciation of social and political institutions of every kind" (p. 352), a direct clash of Marxian and Buddhist notions of freedom simply cannot occur without a prior debate on basic metaphysical doctrine. Chinese Marxists will settle for comparative free-

dom from starvation and peonage and trust that their masses will continue achieving greater mastery over their conditions of life and themselves, and perhaps even free themselves from the state itself. Then will be time enough to think of the absolute freedom proposed in Buddhism. A more immediate question is the freedom of individuals in a Marxian revolutionary state to follow the Buddhist way, according to which "meditation and deep and excruciating introspective analyses provide the only means by which man can free himself from the prison of the causal matrix" (p. 350).

10. Spiritual India suffered communal rather than revolutionary violence. Having chosen a mixed economy of socialism and private enterprise, she finds the private sector growing in power, especially in ownership of the most important means of production, the land. So the Green Revolution, like agribusiness in the United States, favors the large-scale producer controlling capital and machines and drives the small farmer off the land into urban misery. In China new agricultural techniques are applicable to already instituted cooperative land procedures without causing social disruption.

11. "Tachai was one brigade of a commune in a rocky and eroded part of Shansi Province, that with a spirit of self-reliance, and without aid from the state, transformed its hills and gullies into fertile fields by cutting stone, laying up walls, and carrying in earth. This transformation was carried out through collective effort after protracted political education and in the course of constant struggle against individualism and private-profit mentality. The result was a gradually rising standard of living for all members of the brigade, expanding sales of surplus grain to the state instead of demands for relief, the accumulation of reserves against bad years, the reconstruction of most of the housing in the village, and the establishment of many community projects to serve the people and community industries to supplement agricultural income." William Hinton, *Turning Point in China: An Essay on the Cultural Revolution*, p. 42.

12. As for karuna, those acts that generally come under the head of formal "charity" are now provided by a social-security system that is changing from familial to social (with encouraging effects on population control) and by increasingly effective distribution of medical care. See *Serve the People: Observations on Medicine in the People's Republic of China*, by Victor W. and Ruth Sidel (1973).

13. The passage in the poem by Chen Tzu-ang (656-698 A.D.) is in Robert Payne's *The White Pony:* "Why do they [men of affairs] not learn from the Master of Dark Truth,/Who saw the whole world in a little jade bottle?/Whose bright soul was free of Earth and Heaven,/For riding on Change he entered into Freedom."

14. Mao Tse-tung, "A Report on the Peasant Movement in Hunan," made in March 1927, in *The Road to Communism*, edited by Dun J. Li, p. 82. The source of the other information in the paragraph is Holmes Welch, *Buddhism Under Mao*, a painstaking gathering of data derived from wide reading and many interviews. He doubts the possibility of any practical convergence of

Communism and Buddhism. His translation of Mao's Hunan report is taken from a revised version in the *Selected Works* (Peking, 1961–65).

15. John and Sarah Strong, "A Post-Cultural Revolution Look at Buddhism," *The China Quarterly*, 54 (April–June 1973). Arthur F. Wright points to "the limited and shrinking area of belief and action" allowed religious individuals by state and party, which "reserve the right to control all education, communication, and public and private morality." Secularization of Buddhist property and clergy, begun under the Kuomintang and warlord governments, has continued. "Buddhist temples and shrines numbered 268,000 in 1930, declined to about 130,000 in 1947, and were sharply reduced to less than 100 in 1954. The clergy may well have numbered 500,000 in 1931. By 1954 the number had been reduced to about 2,500. Temple lands were completely taken over by the state. The clergy who remained in the few operating temples had to find the means to sustain themselves. . . . The state decreed that some of the ancient shrines were national monuments, 'testimony to the creativity of the Chinese people despite their feudal oppressors.' The cave temples of Tunhuang, Yunkang, Lungmen, and Mai-chi-shan as well as many old shrines in the cities were restored as cultural monuments." Wright anticipates continuing secularization of life in eastern Asia, and concludes, "Perhaps the most that can be hoped is that the gentle compassion and respect for others that came from Buddhism will linger as a kind of ethical substratum underlying the secular philosophies, the national cults, the state socialisms of the future." "Buddhism in Modern and Contemporary China," in *Religion and Change in Contemporary Asia*, edited by Robert F. Spencer, pp. 22, 26.

16. Rosalind Heywood quotes Leibnitz on the theory of gravity: "That one body should attract another with no intermediary is not so much a miracle as a sheer contradiction, for 'tis to suppose a body can act in a place where it is not." *ESP*, p. 33. Arthur Koestler regularly expresses scorn of scientists who reject the phenomena of parapsychology; they reverse the proper order of science in demanding explanations which they should be seeking. "Another psychologist wrote in the American journal *Science* that 'not a thousand experiments with ten million trials and by a hundred separate investigators' could make him accept extra-sensory perception." *The Roots of Coincidence*, p. 19. The book discusses the difficulties encountered in attempting to put parapsychology on a scientific basis. Polanyi wrote: "The method of disbelieving every proposition which cannot be verified by definitely prescribed operations would destroy all belief in natural science. And it would destroy, in fact, belief in truth and in the love of truth itself which is the condition of all free thought." *Op. cit.*

17. Aurobindo, the revolutionary who turned to yoga as the way to a more thorough-going revolution in the hearts of men, did not speak simply of improved communication; he spoke of "the change from the mental and vital to the spiritual order of life" which must first be accomplished in a great many individuals "before it can lay any effective hold upon the community." "Conditions for the Coming of a Spiritual Age," in *The Essential Aurobindo*, p. 187. He

also wrote: "Discoveries will be made that thin the walls between soul and matter; attempts there will be to extend exact knowledge into the psychological and psychic realms . . ." (pp. 189-190).

18. In 1929 J. H. Woodyer wrote of "qualitatively different laws, holding good at each level," in *Biological Principles*, a pioneering work according to Professor Needham, in a comment (*Science*, June 8, 1945) on an article by A. B. Novikoff. This article states: "The concept of integrative levels of organization is a general description of the revolution of matter through successive and higher orders of complexity and integration . . . continuous because never-ending and discontinuous because it passes through a series of different levels of organization—physical, chemical, biological and social. . . . new levels of complexity are superimposed on the individual units by the organization and integration of these units into a single system. What were whole on one level become parts in a higher one . . . the unique properties of phenomena at the higher level cannot be predicted, a priori, from the laws of the lower level." ("The Concept of Integrative Levels and Biology," *Science*, 101, No. 2618 [March 2, 1945], 209.) The article rejects vitalism and teleology, which are the essence of the Teilhard–Aurobindo approach.

19. "The Human Rebound of Evolution," September 1947, in *The Future of Man*, p. 211.

20. A group of U.S. computer scientists, invited to China in July 1972, reported that western literature is carefully collected and thoroughly processed. "Don't tell us what you have already published, tell us only what has not been published," they were told. "At Tsinghua, China's most important technically oriented institution of higher learning, we saw a pair of small computers that had been built entirely—including the transistors themselves, we were told—by students as part of their educational program." T. E. Cheatham, Jr., et al., "Computers in China: A Travel Report—Computer Technology Advances Rapidly in China with No External Aid," *Science*, 182 (October 12, 1973), 134.

21. Especially since the Russians are already there. At the 1973 Prague Conference on Parapsychology and Psychotronics (see above, Chapter 8, end of note 43), Professor Gennady A. Samolov of the USSR said, "Psychotronics must deal with the knowledge of communication between man and man, and between man and his environment."

22. Luis O. Gomez, "Emptiness and Moral Perfection," *Philosophy East and West*, 23 (July 1973), 371.

23. *Ibid.*, p. 373.

Bibliography

A. Buddhist Texts

Two indispensable collections of Buddhist materials in English are Henry Clarke Warren's *Buddhism in Translations*, mainly from Pali (Harvard University Press, 1896; Atheneum paperback, 1963), and *Buddhist Texts Through the Ages*, edited by Edward Conze in collaboration with I. B. Horner, D. L. Snellgrove, and Arthur Waley, all newly translated and covering Pali, Mahayana, Tantric, and Chinese and Japanese sources (Harper Torchbook, 1964; Cassirer, 1954).

Other collections are *Buddhist Scriptures*, selected and translated by Conze (Penguin, 1959); *A Buddhist Bible*, edited by Dwight Goddard (Beacon paperback, 1970; E. P. Dutton, 1938); and *The Buddhist Tradition*, edited by William T. de Bary (Modern Library, 1969).

The Pali Text Society (PTS) has published both editions and translations; its early translations have appeared in both the Sacred Books of the East (SBE) and the Sacred Books of the Buddhists (SBB) Series:

Digha Nikaya: *Dialogues of the Buddha*, tr. T. W. Rhys Davids and C. A. F. Rhys Davids, 1899–1921, SBB, Vols. 2–4. *Some Sayings of the Buddha*, tr. F. L. Woodward.

Majjhima Nikaya: *The Middle Length Sayings*, tr. I. B. Horner, 1954; *Further Dialogues of the Buddha*, tr. Lord Chalmers, 1926–27, SBB, Vols. 5, 6.

Samyutta Nikaya: *The Book of Kindred Sayings*, tr. C. A. F. Rhys Davids and F. L. Woodward, 1918–30, PTS Translation Series 7, 10, etc.

Anguttara Nikaya: *The Book of Gradual Sayings*, tr. Woodward, PTS Translation Series 22, 24.

Khuddaka-patha: *The Minor Sayings*, tr. C. A. Rhys Davids, 1931, SBB, Vol. 7.

Dhammapada: *Verses on Dhamma*, ibid. The Dhammapada is available in many translations since its early translation by Max Muller in 1881, SBE. P. Lal's version (Noonday paperback) is free and readable; S. Radhakrishnan's is more literal.

Sutta Nipata: *Woven Cadences*, tr. Woodward, 1945; tr. Fausböll, 1898, SBE, Vol. 10.

Theragatha and Therigatha: tr. C. A.F. Rhys Davids; in a modern definitive edition by K. R. Norman (Cambridge University Press).

Jataka Tales, tr. Fausböll, 1877-1897, SBE.
Vinaya Pitaka: *The Book of the Discipline*, tr. Horner (London, 1951).
Mahavastu, tr. J. J. Jones (London 1952).
Buddhaghosa, *Visuddhimagga, The Path of Purification*, tr. Bhikkhu Nanamoli (Colombo, Ceylon, 1956); tr. P. M. Tin, *The Way of Purity*, PTS Translation Series 11,17,21.
Buddhist Mahayana Texts. 1894, 1927, SBE, Vol. 49, translations of Ashvaghosha *Buddha-carita;* Sukhavati-vyuha; Vajraecheddika; Hrdaya, etc.
Lankavatara, tr. D. T. Suzuki, 1932.
Saddharmapundarika (*Lotus of the Good Law*), tr. H. Kern, 1884, SBE, Vol. 21.
Astasahasrika Prajnaparamita, tr. Conze (Calcutta, 1959).
Vajracchedika Prajnaparamita, (*Diamond-Cutter*) tr. Conze, (Rome, 1957); *Buddhist Wisdom Books,* (London, 1958).
Hrdaya Prajmaparamita (*Heart*), ibid.

B. Books

Altman, Alexander, *Studies in Religious Philosophy and Mysticism* (Cornell University Press, 1969).
Aurobindo, Shri (Aurobindo Ghose), *The Essential Aurobindo,* ed. Robert A. McDermott (Schocken Books, 1973).
Basham, A. L., *History and Doctrine of the Ajivikas: A Vanished Indian Religion* (1951).
Berry, Thomas, *Religions of India: Hinduism, Yoga, Buddhism* (Bruce, 1971).
Beyer, Stephan V., *The Cult of Tara; Magic and Ritual in Tibet* (University Microfilms, 1970; University of Wisconsin dissertation, 1969).
Bharati, Agehananda, *The Ochre Robe* (Rider, 1965; Anchor paperback, 1970).
———, *The Tantric Tradition* (Rider, 1965; Anchor paperback, 1970).
Bhattacharya, Benoytosh, *An Introduction to Buddhist Esotericism* (Oxford University Press, 1932).
Blofeld, John, *Tantric Mysticism of Tibet: A Practical Guide* (E. P. Dutton, 1970).
Chakravarty, Chintarahan, *Tantras: Studies on Their Religion and Literature* (Calcutta, 1963).
Chang, Garma C. C., *The Practice of Zen* (Harper & Row, Perennial Library, 1970; first published, 1959).
Ch'en, Kenneth, *Buddhism in China* (Princeton University Press, 1972).
Conze, Edward, *Buddhism: Its Essence and Development* (Harper Torchbook, 1959; Cassirer, 1951).
———, *Buddhist Thought in India* (Ann Arbor paperback, 1967; Allen & Unwin, 1962).

———, *Thirty Years of Buddhist Studies: Selected Essays* (University of South Carolina Press, 1968).

De Chaudhuri, H. K., *God in Indian Religion* (Calcutta, 1969).

Deussen, Paul, *Philosophy of the Upanishads*, tr. A. S. Gueden (Dover, 1966; first published, 1906).

Dhiravamsa, V. R., *A New Approach to Buddhism: An Introduction to the Meditative Way of Life* (1972).

Dumoulin, Heinrich, *A History of Zen Buddhism*, tr. from German by Paul Peachey (Pantheon Books, 1963; A. Francke, 1959).

Dutt, M. N., *A Prose English Translation of Mahanirvana Tantram* (Calcutta, 1900).

Eckhart, Meister, *A Modern Translation*, by R. B. Blakney (Harper Brothers, 1941).

Eliade, Mircea, *Patanjali and Yoga*, tr. Charles Lam Markmann (Funk & Wagnalls, 1969; Editions du Seuil, 1962).

Feuerstein, Georg, and Miller, Jeanine, *Yoga and Beyond* (Schocken Books, 1972; *A Reappraisal of Yoga*, Rider, 1972).

Forwald, Haakon, *Mind, Matter, and Gravitation; A Theoretical and Experimental Study*, Parapsychological Monograph No. 11 (Parapsychology Foundation, Inc., 1969).

Foucher, Alfred, *La Vie du Bouddha* (1949; abr. and tr. by Simone Brangier Boas, *The Life of the Buddha*, Wesleyan University Press, 1963).

Frauwallner, Erich, *The Earliest Vinaya and the Beginnings of Buddhist Literature* (Serie Orientale Roma, 1956).

Fromm, Erich, *The Anatomy of Human Destructiveness* (Holt, Rinehart and Winston, 1973).

———, et al., *Zen Buddhism and Psychoanalysis* (Harper & Row, 1970).

Gernet, Jacques, *Les Aspects économiques du Bouddhisme dans la société chinoise du Ve au Xe siecle* (1956).

Ghose, Sisirkumar, *Mystics and Society* (Asia Publishing House, 1968).

Glasenapp, Helmut von, *Buddhism, a Non-Theistic Religion* (George Braziller, 1966).

Grimm, George, *The Doctrine of the Buddha, the Religion of Reason and Meditation*, translated by Bhikkhu Silacara, 1958.

———, "Christian Mysticism in the Light of the Buddha's Doctrine," in Bimala Churn Law, ed., *Buddhistic Studies* (Calcutta, 1931).

Guenther, Herbert V., *Buddhist Philosophy in Theory and Practice* (Pelican Books, 1972; Shambala, 1971).

———, *The Life and Teaching of Naropa*, translated from the original Tibetan with a philosophical commentary based on the oral transmission (Oxford University Press, 1963).

———, *The Tantric View of Life* (Shambala, 1972).

———, *Treasures on the Tibetan Middle Way* (Shambala, 1971; originally *Tibetan Buddhism Without Mystification*, E. J. Brill, The Netherlands, 1966).

———, *Yuganaddha: The Tantric View of Life*, Chowkhamba Sanskrit Series III, introduction by Swami Agehananda (Benares [now Varanasi], India, 1952).

Herrigel, Eugen, *Zen: Including Zen in the Art of Archery*, with introduction by D. T. Suzuki, and *The Method of Zen* (McGraw-Hill paperback, 1964).

Heywood, Rosalind, *ESP: A Personal Memoir* (E. P. Dutton, 1964).

Hinton, William, *Turning Point in China: An Essay on the Cultural Revolution* (Monthly Review Press, 1972).

Hoffman, Banesh, *Albert Einstein, Creator and Rebel* (Harper & Row, 1973).

Hume, David, *A Treatise of Human Understanding* (Pelican Books, 1970).

James, William, *Varieties of Religious Experience* (Mentor paperback, 1958).

Jayatilleke, K. N., *Early Buddhist Theory of Knowledge* (George Allen & Unwin, 1963).

Johansson, Rune E. A., *The Psychology of Nirvana* (Anchor paperback, 1970; George Allen & Unwin, 1969).

Johnston, William, *The Still Point: Reflections on Zen and Christian Mysticism* (Harper & Row, Perennial Library, 1971; Fordham University Press, 1970).

Joshi, L. M., et al., *Buddhism* (Punjabi University, Patiala, India, 1969).

Kapleau, Philip, *The Three Pillars of Zen: Teaching, Practice, and Enlightenment* (Beacon Press, 1967; John Weatherill, Tokyo, 1965).

Koestler, Arthur, *The Roots of Coincidence: An Excursion into Parapsychology* (Random House, 1972).

Kosambi, D. D., *Ancient India: A History of Its Culture and Civilisation* (Pantheon, 1965).

Krishnamurti, J., *The Impossible Question* (Harper & Row, 1971).

———, *The Only Revolution* (Harper & Row, 1970).

LeShan, Lawrence, *Toward a General Theory of the Paranormal*, Parapsychological Monograph No. 9 (Parapsychology Foundation, 1969).

Lannoy, Richard, *The Speaking Tree: A Study of Indian Culture and Society* (Oxford University Press, 1971).

Lawrence, Jodi, *Alpha Brain Waves* (Nash, 1972).

Mahasi Sayadaw (The Venerable), *Practical Insight Meditation* (Unity Press, 1972).

Merton, Thomas, *Zen and the Birds of Appetite*, (New Directions, 1968).

Murti, T. R. V., *The Central Philosophy of Buddhism: A Study of the Madhyamika System* (George Allen & Unwin, 1955).

Narada, Thera, *A Manual of Buddhism*, Associated Newspapers of Ceylon (Colombo, 1953).

Nelson, Benjamin, *The Idea of Usury: From Tribal Brotherhood to Universal Otherhood* (2nd ed., enl., University of Chicago Press, 1969; first published, 1949).

Nikhilananda, Swami, *The Upanishads* (abr. edn., Harper Torchbook, 1963).

Nyanaponika, Thera, *The Heart of Buddhist Meditation* (Citadel Press, 1969; Rider, 1962).

Oldenberg, H., *Buddha, sein Leben, seine Lehre, seine Gemeinde* (1881; tr. 1882).

Ornstein, Robert E., *The Psychology of Consciousness* (Viking, 1972; W. H. Freeman paperback).

———, *The Nature of Human Consciousness: A Book of Readings* (Viking, 1973; W. H. Freeman paperback).

Pande, G. C., *Studies in the Origins of Buddhism* (University of Allahabad, India, 1957).

Pardue, Peter A., *Buddhism (Historical Introduction to Buddhist Values and the Social and Political Forms They Have Assumed in Asia)* (Macmillan, 1971; Crowell Collier and MacMillan, 1968).

Prall, David Wight, *Aesthetic Analysis* (Apollo paperback, 1967; Crowell, 1936).

Pratt, James Bissett, *The Pilgrimage of Buddhism and a Buddhist Pilgrimage* (Macmillan, 1928).

Rahula, Walpola, *What the Buddha Taught* (Evergreen paperback, 1962; first published, 1959).

Reymond, Lizelle, *My Life with a Brahmin Family* (Penguin; Flammarion, 1957).

Rhine, J. B., and Pratt, J. G., *Parapsychology, Frontier Science of the Mind* (Charles C. Thomas, 1957).

Rhys Davids, Catherine A. F., *Buddhism in England* (1940).

———, *Wayfarer's Words,* three volumes (Luzac, 1940–1942).

Robinson, Joan, *Economic Management, China 1972* (Anglo-Chinese Educational Institute, 1973).

Robinson, Richard H., *The Buddhist Religion: A Historical Introduction* (Dickenson, 1970).

Saddhatissa, H., *Buddhist Ethics* (George Braziller, 1970).

———, *The Buddha's Way* (George Braziller, 1971).

Sampson, Ronald, *The Psychology of Power* (Pantheon, 1966).

Sangharakshita, *The Three Jewels: An Introduction to Modern Buddhism* (Anchor paperback, 1970; Rider, 1967).

Saunders, Kenneth J., "The Quest for the Historic Sakya-muni," in Bimala Churn Law ed., *Buddhistic Studies* (Calcutta, 1931).

Scholem, Gershom, *The Messianic Idea in Judaism and Other Essays on Jewish Spirituality* (Schocken Books, 1971).

Schumacher, E. F., *Small Is Beautiful: Economics as if People Mattered* (Harper Torchbooks, 1973).

Schwarz, Berthold Eric, *Parent–Child Telepathy* (Garrett, 1972).

Shands, Harley C., *The War with Words: Structure and Transcendence* (Humanities, 1971).

Sidel, Victor W., and Sidel, Ruth, *Serve the People* (Josiah Macy, Jr. Foundation, 1973).

Snellgrove, D. L., *The Hevajra Tantra: A Critical Study,* London Oriental Series No. 6 (Oxford University Press, 1959).

Stace, Walter T., *Mysticism and Philosophy* (Lippincott, 1960).
Stcherbatsky, Theodore, *Buddhist Logic* (Leningrad, 1930; Dover paperback).
———, *The Central Conception of Buddhism and the Meaning of the Word "Dharma"* (Susil Gupta, Calcutta, 1956; Royal Asiatic Society 1923).
———, *The Conception of Buddhist Nirvana* (Leningrad, 1927).
Streng, Frederick J., *Emptiness—A Study in Religious Meaning* (Abingdon Press, 1967).
Suzuki, Daisetz Teitaro, *The Essentials of Zen Buddhism*, ed. with introduction by Bernard Phillips (E. P. Dutton, 1962).
———, *Manual of Zen Buddhism* (Evergreen paperback, 1960).
———, *On Indian Mahayana Buddhism*, ed. with introduction by Edward Conze (Harper Torchbook, 1968).
———, *Outlines of Mahayana Buddhism* (Schocken Books, 1963; Luzac, 1907).
———, *Zen and Japanese Culture*, Bollingen Series (Princeton, 1959).
———, *Zen Buddhism; Selected Writings of D. T. Suzuki*, ed. William Barrett (Anchor paperback, 1956).
Suzuki, D. T., Fromm, Erich, and De Martino, Richard, *Zen Buddhism and Psychoanalysis* (Harper & Row, 1970).
Swearer, Donald, *Buddhism in Transition* (Westminster Press, 1970).
———, *Secrets of the Lotus: An Introduction to Buddhist Meditation* (Macmillan, 1971).
Tart, Charles T., ed., *Altered States of Consciousness* (John Wiley, 1969).
Teilhard de Chardin, Pierre, *The Future of Man*, tr. Norman Denny (Harper & Row, 1964; Editions du Seuil, 1959).
———, *The Phenomenon of Man*, tr. Bernard Wall (Harper & Row, 1959).
Thittila, U, "The Fundamental Principles of Theravada Buddhism," in Kenneth W. Morgan, ed., *The Path of the Buddha. Buddhism Interpreted by Buddhists* (Ronald Press, 1956).
Thomas, Edward J., *The History of Buddhist Thought* (Routledge & Kegan Paul, 1933).
———, *The Life of the Buddha as Legend and History* (Routledge & Kegan Paul, 1927; 3rd ed., rev., 1949).
Trungpa, Chögyam, *Cutting Through Spiritual Materialism* (Shambala, 1973).
———, *Meditation in Action* (Shambala, 1969).
———, *Mudra* (Shambala, 1972).
Ullman, M., and Krippner, S., *Dream Studies and Telepathy: An Experimental Approach*, Parapsychology Monograph No. 12. (Parapsychology Foundation Inc., 1970).
Ullman and Krippner, with Vaughan, Alan, *Dream Telepathy* (Macmillan, 1973).
Underhill, Evelyn, *Mysticism* (E. P. Dutton).
de la Vallee Poussin, *The Path to Nirvana* (Cambridge University Press, 1917).
Waley, Arthur, *Three Ways of Thought in Ancient China* (Anchor paperback, 1956; first published, 1939).

Watson, Lyall, *Supernature* (Holt, Rinehart and Winston, 1973).
Watts, Alan, *The Way of Zen* (Mentor paperback, 1959; Pantheon, 1957).
Wayman, Alex, "Buddhism," in *Historia Religionum, Handbook for the History of Religions,* edited by C. J. Bleeker and G. Widengren, Vol. II, Religions of the Present, pp. 372–464 (E. J. Brill, Leiden, 1971).
Weber, Max, *The Religion of India: the Sociology of Hinduism and Buddhism,* tr. and ed. Hans L. Gerth and Don Martingale (Free Press, 1958).
Welbon, Guy R., *The Buddhist Nirvana and Its Western Interpreters* (University of Chicago Press, 1968).
Wright, Arthur F., "Buddhism in Modern and Contemporary China," in Robert F. Spencer, ed., *Religion and Change in Contemporary Asia* (University of Minnesota Press, 1971).
Yamaguchi, S., "Development of Mahayana Buddhist Beliefs," in Kenneth W. Morgan, ed., *The Path of the Buddha: Buddhism Interpreted by Buddhists* (Ronald Press, 1956).
Yampolsky, Philip, *The Platform Sutra of the Sixth Patriarch: A Text of the Tun Huang Manuscript,* with tr., intro. and notes (Columbia University Press, 1967).

C. Articles

Abbreviations:

ASC	*Altered States of Consciousness*
JAS	*Journal of Asian Studies*
JASPR	*Journal of the American Society for Psychic Research*
PEW	*Philosophy East & West*
PR	*Parapsychology Review*

Anand, B. K., Chhina, G. S., and Singh, B., "Some Aspects of Electroencephalographic Studies in Yogis," *Electroencephalography and Clinical Neurophysiology,* 13 (1961); in *ASC.*
Blanchard, Edward B., and Young, Larry D., "Self-Control of Cardiac Functioning: A Promise as Yet Unfulfilled," *Psychological Bulletin,* 79 (March 1973), 145–63.
Boyd, James W., "Symbols of Evil in Buddhism," *JAS,* 30 (November 1971).
Cheatham, T. E., et al., "Computers in China: A Travel Report," *Science,* 182 (October 12, 1973).
Ch'en, Kenneth, "The Economic Background of the Hui-ch'ang Suppression of Buddhism," *Harvard Journal of Asiatic Studies,* 15 (1956).
Datey, K. K., Deshmukh, S. N., Dalvi, C. P., and Vinekar, S. L., "'Shavasan': A Yogic Exercise in the Management of Hypertension," *Angiology,* 20 (1969), 325–33.

De Chaudhury, H. K., "Samadhi: A Psychological Study," *Bulletin of the Ramakrishna Mission Institute of Culture, Calcutta,* 20 (December 1969), 339–52.

Deikman, Arthur, "Deautomatization and the Mystic Experience," *Psychiatry,* 29 (1966), 324–38; in *ASC.*

Ellis, David, "The Chemistry of Psi," *PR,* 4 (September–October 1973).

Fischer, Ronald, "A Cartography of the Ecstatic and Meditative States," *Science,* 174 (November 26, 1971), 897–904.

Gaarder, Kenneth, "Control of States of Consciousness," *Archives of General Psychiatry,* 25 (November 1971), 429–41.

Gomez, Luis O., "Emptiness and Moral Perfection," *PEW,* 23 (July 1973), 362–73.

Green, Elmer, "Biofeedback for Mind–Body Self-Regulation: Healing and Creativity," in *Biofeedback and Self-Control 1972* (Aldine, 1973).

Herbert, Benson, "Spring in Leningrad: Kulagina Revisited," *PR,* 4 (July–August 1973).

Honorton, Charles, "Relation between EEG Alpha Activity and ESP Card-Guessing Performance," *JASPR,* 63 (October 1969).

———, and Carbone, Mildred, "A Preliminary Study of Feedback-Augmented EEG Alpha Activity and ESP Card-Guessing Performance," *JASPR,* 65 (January 1971).

———, Davidson, R., and Bindler, D., "Feedback-Augmented EEG Alpha, Shifts in Subjective State, and ESP Card-Guessing Performance," *JASPR,* 65 (July 1971).

Ingalls, David, review of Murti, *The Central Philosophy of Buddhism,* in *JAS,* 16 (November 1956).

Kamiya, Joe, "Operant Control of EEG Alpha Rhythm," in *ASC,* pp. 507–17.

Kasamatsu, Akira, and Hirai, Tomio, "An Electroencephalographic Study of the Zen Meditation (Zazen)," *Folio-Psychiatrica & Neurologica Japonica,* 20 (1966) 315–36; in *ASC,* pp. 489–501.

Koestler, Arthur, "The Perversity of Physics," *PR,* 4 (May–June 1973).

Lesh, T. U., "Zen Meditation and a Development of Empathy in Counselors," *Journal of Humanistic Psychology* (October 1970); in *Biofeedback and Self-Control 1970* (Aldine, 1971).

Margenau, Henry, "ESP in the Framework of Modern Science," *JASPR,* 60 (July 1966).

Mulholland, Thomas B., "Occipital Alpha Revisited," *Psychological Bulletin,* 78 (September 1972).

Murphy, Gardner, "Are There Any Solid Facts in Psychical Research," *JASPR,* 64 (January 1970).

Needham, Joseph, "A Note on Dr. Novikoff's Article," *Science,* 101 (June 8, 1945), 582.

Novikoff, Alex B., "The Concept of Integrative Levels and Biology," *Science,* 101 (March 2, 1945).

Osis, Karlis, and Bokert, Edwin, "ESP and Changed States of Consciousness Induced by Meditation," *JASPR,* 65 (January 1971).

Pratt, James G., and Keil, H. H. J., "First Hand Observations of Nina S. Kulagina Suggestive of PK Upon Static Objects," *JASPR,* 67 (October 1973).

Puligandla, R., and Puhakka, K., "Buddhism and Revolution," *PEW,* 20 (October 1970).

Robinson, Richard H. "Some Methodological Approaches to the Unexplained Points," *PEW,* 22 (July 1972).

Rogo, D. Scott, "The Mystical and The Paranormal," *PR,* 4 (January–February 1973).

Stamford, Rex, and Lovin, CaroleAnn, "EEG Alpha Activity and ESP Performance," *JASPR,* 64 (October 1970).

———, "EEG Alpha and ESP Performance: A Replicative Study," *JASPR,* 65 (April 1971).

Strong, John, and Strong, Sarah, "A Post-Cultural Revolution Look at Buddhism," *The China Quarterly,* 54 (April–June 1973).

Wallace, Robert, "Physiological Effects of Transcendental Meditation," *Science,* 167 (1970), 1751–54.

———, and Benson, Herbert, "The Physiology of Meditation," *Scientific American* (February 1972), 85–90.

Wayman, Alex, "The Mirror-like Knowledge in Mahayana Buddhist Literature," *Études Asiatiques, revue de la Société Suisse d'Études Asiatiques,* 25 (1971).

Wenger, M. A., Bagchi, B. K., and Anand, B. K., "Experiments in India on 'Voluntary' Control of the Heart and Pulse," *Circulation,* 24 (1961).

Index

Abhidharma Pitaka, 8, 33, 79, 86–87, 153, 200
abhinna (abhijna), 31, 41, 58, 175
Agamas, 13, 40
ahimsa, 63, 65, 69, 82
Ajanta, 103, 106
Ajita, 42, 58, 61, 73
Ajivikas, 62
Akshobya, 105, 214
alaya vijnana (store-consciousness), 100–101, 103–104, 154
alpha rhythm, 165, 166, 170–75, 180, 222, 224
Altman, A., 221
Amitabha (Amida), 21, 104, 105, 214
Amoghasiddhi, 105, 214
Anand et al., 172, 223
Ananda, 5, 11, 12, 15, 17, 20, 75, 91, 220
Anandamayi, 83, 90, 142
Annihilationists, 26, 39, 41, 48, 53, 61, 153
Arada Kalama (and Udraka Ramaputra), 3, 4, 7, 47, 200
arhant, 44, 45, 46, 72, 73, 74, 81, 85, 98, 107, 148, 164, 220
Asanga, 100, 103
Ashoka, 6, 10, 14, 15, 18, 37
asava (asrava), 13, 31, 75, 83, 94, 210
astrology, 81, 210
atman, 24, 43, 50, 52, 102
Aurobindo, 193, 194, 234
austerities (tapasya), 3, 7, 29, 34, 48, 206
Avalokitesvara (Avalokita), 95, 99, 105, 106
avyakrta (avakata), 39, 43, 61, 94
awareness, 32, 34, 134, 149, 163–64, 181

Barth, K., 155
Basham, A. L., 62, 69
Basho, 134, 135
Berry, T., 55, 58, 95
Bharati, A., 74, 83, 113, 115, 119, 121, 123, 208, 211, 215
bija, 122
biofeedback, 164, 169–70, 223
Blofeld, J., 113, 116
Bodhidharma, 126, 128, 217
bodhisattva, 45, 72, 92–93, 99, 105, 150, 153
Boehme, J., 159
Bohr, N., 177
Bokert, E., 175, 228
Brahma, 7, 52, 66–67, 68
Brahmajala, 11, 13, 40, 52, 59
Brahman, 34, 46, 47, 50, 52, 73
Brahmaviharas (Unlimiteds), 35, 147
brahmins, 23, 34, 51, 66
Brhadaranyaka Upanishad, 51, 53, 60
Bucke, R. M., 142
Buddhaghosa, 79, 82, 105

caste, 47, 65
Ceylon (Sri Lanka), 16, 21, 86
chakra, 122, 124
chakravartin, 1, 199
Chakravarty, C., 215
Ch'an, 127, 129, 133
Chandogya Upanishad, 51, 52

Chang, G. C. C., 128, 129, 131, 132, 136
Chinese Buddhist Association, 190
citta, 101, 154
Conze, E., 9, 10, 14, 18, 20, 28, 78, 79, 85, 92, 98, 102, 105, 116, 128, 148, 149, 151, 157, 202, 204, 209, 212, 213, 214, 220
Creator God, 68, 154
Cultural Revolution, 186, 189, 190

deautomatization, 143, 167, 174
DeChaudhuri, H. K., 146, 220
Deikman, A., 166, 167, 209
dependent origination (pratityasamutpada), 4, 13, 25, 26, 28–29, 32, 44–45, 97, 151, 205
depersonalization, 22, 32, 79, 204
Deussen, P., 60, 209
devekut, 155
dharma, 13, 45, 73, 96, 109, 143
Dharmakaya, 102, 103
Dhiravamsa, V. R., 182, 187, 231
dhyanas (jhanas), 4, 31, 41, 56, 95, 101, 149
Diamond-Cutter Sutra, 95
Dogen, 128, 134, 218
duality, 32, 38, 49, 60, 97, 100–101
duhkha (dukkha), 28, 45
Dumoulin, H., 129, 219
Dutt, M. N., 116, 117

INDEX

Eckhart, 32, 115, 141, 155, 156, 159, 160, 161
ecstasy, 22, 158, 168
Eightfold Path, 30, 55, 78
Einstein, A., 177, 228
Elders, 37, 80, 84–85
electroencephalograph (EEG), 164, 169, 170, 172, 180
Eliade, M., 141, 145, 147, 149, 150, 220
Enlightenment, 3, 4, 22, 111, 130–32, 165
enstasy, 22, 24, 41, 114, 119, 141, 149, 156, 158
Eternalism, 38, 44, 53
extra-sensory perception (ESP), 175–79, 196

Fire Sermon, 76
First Council, 11, 14, 15, 75
Fischer, R., 168, 169
Foucher, A., 50, 72, 199, 202, 205
Four Noble Truths, 29, 30
Four Omens, 1, 6
Frauwallner, E., 14, 15, 17, 210
Fromm, E., 131, 132, 138

Gaarder, K., 230
ganzfeld, 165, 221
Garrett, E. J., 178
Gernet, J., 213
Ghose, S., 156, 221
Godhead, 161
Godhika's suicide, 82, 202
Gomez, L., 196, 235
Green, E., 172, 177, 230
Guenther, H. V., 87, 110, 111, 112, 114, 115, 119, 123, 124, 125, 146, 204, 211, 212, 215, 216, 222
guru, 118, 119, 124

haiku, 135, 136
Hakuin, 137, 218
Han Shan, 136, 138
Heard, G., 156
Heart Sutra, 95, 99
Herbert, B., 225
Herrigel, E., 131
Heywood, R., 177, 178, 234
Hinayana, 28
Hinton, W., 233
Hoffman, B., 228
Hsuan Tsang, 106, 213
Hui-neng (Sixth Patriarch), 127–31
human nature, 183, 185
Hundred Flowers, 189
Huxley, A., 142, 156

Inge, W. R., 155
integrative levels, 193
intuition, 145, 154
Ishvara, 46, 58, 146

Jains, 63, 64
James, William, 142, 167, 208, 220
Jataka, 70, 199, 201
Jayatilleke, K. N., 52, 53, 57, 59–62, 65, 67, 209
jivanmukta, 140, 147, 154
jnana, 41, 57, 199, 207
Jones, J. J., 10
Joshi, L. M., 209
Jung, C., 157, 191

kaivalya, 64, 146
Kamiya, J., 170, 171, 222
Karle cave-temples, 91
karma, 23, 25, 54, 83, 94, 103
karuna (compassion), 33, 35, 89, 90, 109, 115, 233
Kasamatsu et al., 173, 174
Kassapa (Kasyapa), 5, 11, 71
Keith, A. B., 209
koan, 133, 165
Koestler, A., 158, 176, 226, 227, 234
Kondanya, 5, 75
Kosambi, D., 55, 62, 65, 69, 91, 200, 208, 209, 213
Krishna, avatar-lover, 104
Krishnamurti, J., 187, 207, 231
Kulagina, Mme., 225, 226
kundalini, 122

Ladder of Bliss, 74
Lannoy, R., 56, 68, 83, 175, 210
LeShan, L., 178
Lotus of the Good Law Sutra (Saddharmapundarika), 96, 105
Luk, C., 106, 214

Madhyamika, 42, 44, 98
Magadhi, 9, 12
Mahaparinirvana (-nibbana), 15, 17, 26
Mahasanghikas, 10, 15, 37, 80, 85, 88
Mahavira (Jain), 63–65, 74
Mahinda, 15, 86
maithuna, 116, 121
maitri (friendliness), 35, 80, 89, 186
Maitreya Buddha (Metteya) 36, 99, 106, 206
Makkhali Gosala, 62, 73

Malunkyaputta, 39, 43
manas, 100, 101
Manas, 192, 204, 221
mandala, 121, 165
Manjusri, 99, 102, 106, 107, 108
mantra, 50, 121–22, 165
Mao Tse-tung, 184, 187, 189–91, 233
Mara the Tempter, 3, 4, 12, 17, 67, 68, 82, 200, 202, 214
Margenau, H., 176
Materialists, 26, 53, 58, 61, 69
Maudgalyayana, 5, 57, 77
Maupin, E., 181
Maya, Queen, 1, 6, 199
meditation, 32, 171, 175, 179, 180, 181, 198
Mencius, 186, 187, 232
Merton, T., 218
Middle Way, 30, 44, 50
Milarepa, 45, 106, 111, 196
Miller, N., 179, 223
Mo Tzu, 89, 182, 184
moksha, 34
momentariness, 32, 33
mudita (sympathetic joy), 35, 80, 186
mudra, 119, 121, 216
mukti, 34
Mulholland, T., 223
Murphy, G., 176, 224, 227
Murti, T. R. V., 40, 41, 86, 87, 95, 110, 212
mystical experience, 22, 42, 73, 140–41, 168, 180–81, 196, 198

Nagarjuna, 20, 68, 87, 94, 97, 99, 106, 151–53
nairatmya, 50, 109, 119, 215
Needham, J., 184, 191, 193
Nikhilananda, 51, 54, 74
nirmana-kaya, 102
nirvana, 26, 27, 31, 36, 37, 48, 50, 64, 97, 140, 144, 154 passim
Nixon, R., 180
noosphere, 193
Novikoff, A., 235

Old Wisdom doctrine, 28, 86
Oldenberg, H., 42, 207
Oneness, 32, 73, 167–68
Ornstein, R., 164–66, 222
Osis, K., et al., 175, 228

Pakudha Kaccayana, 62
Pali, 10–12, 16, 18
Pali Text Society, 11

INDEX

Pande, G., 13, 22
Patanjali, 58, 142, 149
Patimokkha (Pratimoksha), 9, 11, 12, 14
Perfections, 93–98, 107
pluralism, 33
Plotinus, 32, 80, 155, 160
Polanyi, M., 192, 234
prajna (panna), 22, 28, 98, 114, 143, 146
Prajnaparamita, 95, 98, 105, 115, 153
Prall, D. W., 125, 217
Pratyekabuddhas, 84, 96
psychokinesis, 157, 225, 226
Puligandla, R., 232
Purana Kassapa, 61

Rahula (Gautama's son), 2, 5, 199
Rahula, W., 33, 83, 166, 203, 204
Ramakrishna, 90, 142
rebirth, 25, 26, 48, 52, 54
revolution, 232
Rhys Davids, C. 203, 206, 207
Rhys Davids, T. 17, 201, 205, 206
Rinzai Zen school (Lin-chi), 133
Robinson, J., 184–86
Robinson, R., 153, 205
Rogo, D. S., 179
Rumi, 221
Ruysbroeck, 32, 160

saddhu, 73, 81
St. John of the Cross, 158
St. Teresa, 32, 161
Sakyas, 5, 12, 200
samadhi, 4, 28, 57, 73–74, 103, 149
Samannaphal, 11, 13, 40
Samkhya, 58, 145, 147
sambhoga-kaya, 102
samsara, 24, 97
Sangha (Order), 7–9, 23, 32, 34, 73, 83, 91, 190
Sangharakshita, 100, 106, 203
Sanjaya Belatthiputta, 59
Saraha, 112, 117, 118, 124
Sariputra, 5, 19, 57, 77, 78, 224
Sarvastivada, 18, 28, 79, 87
satori, 130, 132
Saunders, K., 206
Scholem, G., 155

schools and sects, 14–16, 85–88
Schumacher, E. F., 186, 231
Second Council (Vaisali), 10, 12, 37, 85
Sénart, L., 46
Sergeyev, G., 226
setthi (sresthi), 69, 71, 75–76
sGam.po.pa, 88, 211, 213
Shakti, 115, 215
Shen-hsiu, 127, 129
Shen-hui, 130, 218
Shiva, 81, 115, 214
siddhi (iddhi), 31, 55, 56, 71, 76, 175
sila-samadhi-prajna, 28, 54, 73, 81, 93, 149, 150
skandha, 24, 29, 32, 95, 203
Skandhakas, 14–16, 19
skill-in-means (upaya), 19, 54, 90, 105, 109, 115
Snellgrove, D. L., 114, 119, 120, 216
Soto Zen school, 133
Stace, W. T., 157–59, 161, 162
Stcherbatsky, T., 37, 45, 86, 140, 143, 144, 153, 204
Streng, F., 151
Strong, J. and S., 234
"suchness" (tathata), 96–97
Suddhodana Gautama, 1, 6, 199, 212
Sufis, 156, 221
Sukhavati (Pure Land), 104
Sumedha Buddha, 36, 98
sunyata (Void, emptiness), 42, 44, 93, 95, 153
Suzuki, D. T., 100, 102, 103, 128–30, 134, 137, 162
Symonds, J. A., 142, 160

Tachai, 187, 191, 195
Tantra (Hindu and Buddhist), 110, 112, 113
Tao, 102, 126, 127, 178, 187, 188
Tara, 105, 106
Tathagata, 4, 6, 18, 19–20, 26, 27, 34, 36, 40, 66, 86, 92, 152, *passim*
Teilhard de Chardin, P., 183, 189, 193, 194, 197
Tennyson, A., 135, 142, 207, 220
tetralemma, 36, 43
Theravada (Sthavira), 18, 20, 38, 79, 87

Third Council, 15, 37
Thittila, U., 209
trade routes, 70, 91
trance (enstatic), 46, 49, 56, 93, 161, 165
triratna, 76
Trungpa, C., 162, 163, 211, 216

Upali, 11, 12
Upanishads, 6, 24, 49–53, 73
upasaka, 35, 106
upeksha (even-mindedness), 35, 80, 204

Vacchagotta, 38–40
Vaisali (Second Council), 10
vajra-and-lotus, 119
Vajrayana, 113, 154
varna, 17
Vasettha, 66
Vasubandhu, 87, 92, 100, 101, 103, 144
Vasumitra, 85, 88
vijja (vidya), 58
viharas, 5, 70
Vimalakirti, 97, 99, 106–9, 126
Vinaya Pitaka, 8, 33
vinnana (vijnana), 13, 204

Waldschmidt, 10
Waley, Arthur, 232
Watergate, 180, 183
Watts, A., 129, 217
Wayman, A., 214
Weber, M., 56, 57, 65
Weil, S., 156
Welbon, G., 207
Welch, H., 190, 191
Wenger et al., 173
Wienpahl, P., 131
work points, 185
Wright, A. F., 234
wu, 132

Yajnavalkya, 60, 80
Yasa, 7, 75, 85
yoga, 48, 55–57, 145, 171, 179
Yoga Sutras, 148
Yogacara, 100–102, 140

Zazen, 169, 174
Zen, 126–31, 139, 169, 174
Zen sickness, 138, 219